BETTER

and happier

TOGETHER

BETTER *and happier* TOGETHER

Stories of Epic Adventures During Our First Forty Years of Marriage

SHANNON A. JACKSON

In loving memory of my parents, Jack and Rosemary Knowles, Pug Jackson, and my dear friend Dorothea Ross who all enthusiastically read my work and encouraged me throughout their lives to keep writing what I always referred to as *Tales from the Trail*. Although they never saw the finished book, they reviewed forty years of letters and contributed to our story in ways that go far beyond words.

CONTENTS

INTRODUCTION

THE IDEA FOR THIS book was conceived during a discussion between me and my husband after watching the movie, *The Notebook* in 2005. Sitting on the couch, still teary-eyed and holding a handful of tissues, I made Don promise that if I were ever diagnosed with Alzheimer's disease, he would read my journals to me detailing the adventures we had throughout our marriage. My hope was that perhaps, just like Allie from the movie, I might gain periods of lucidity after hearing highlights of our life together. After agreeing to my request, Don suggested that I gather the stories into a single manual that would be easy for him to locate—in essence creating a book from my journal notes. Our conversation planted a seed that would lay dormant for twelve years until 2017 when we celebrated our thirty-fifth wedding anniversary. The present I gave my husband was a promise to write our story into a book within the next five years.

The fact that I planned to write a book without any formal training was typical of how we began so many of our adventures. Don always inspired me to learn new skills and encouraged me to become an author. I had written stories about our activities and shared them with my parents and Don's mother, Pug, my entire adult life. After my folks passed, my siblings and I cleaned out our family home and discovered a couple dozen of my letters that my mom and dad had saved in a drawer. Shortly thereafter, Pug was diagnosed with cancer. In her final days, she gave me a clear plastic storage bin containing all the letters and cards I had written to her from the day I married her son. These cherished letters, along with my journals, contributed to the narrative in each chapter of the book.

For more than four decades, my husband has provided me with a variety of topics for correspondence. Don is the dreamer in our relationship. He is responsible for our creation of a "Bucket List" early in our marriage and always made the initial effort to bring items on the list to fruition throughout the years. Along with an innate desire to try new things, Don possesses a great sense of humor, a high energy level, and a drive to challenge himself physically. He has taught me to laugh often and embrace living life to its fullest. It has been extremely gratifying to experience and document our journey together.

The chapters in the book are written in accordance with the passage of time and start with the unique circumstances of how we met. All the stories, however, stand on their own and can be read independently. At the heart of it all, *Better and Happier Together* is a forty-year love story.

RACQUETBALL...
WHERE IT ALL BEGAN

"I'LL GET IT," I called out to Jeri, my college roommate, when I heard the phone ring while studying for my nutrition and dietetics class. I was in a good mood after spending the afternoon at the local racquetball club playing a challenge ladder match. There had been an attractive guy watching from the court balcony that captivated my attention with a single smile. His direct stare jolted my entire system, leaving me distracted and struggling to concentrate on my opponent. After rushing through the final game, I quickly exited the court to search for the handsome man but found he had already left the building. Just the memory of his face and the possibility that I might run into him one day at the club made me happy. When I shared details of the afternoon and a description of my mystery man, Jeri started laughing.

"Oh my gosh, you're acting like you are in love with this guy and you don't even know his name!"

"He definitely made an impact," I said, smiling at her good-natured ribbing. "There's something special about this man that makes me really want to meet him but I'm also kind of worried he might be too young for me. The guy looks like he could be eighteen and a freshman at Tech." Grinning, I added, "Guess I'll just keep dreaming about him and hope that I find him one day."

Setting my lecture notes aside, I answered the phone with a quick *hello* and froze in place when the voice on the line asked, "Is this Shannon?"

"Yes," I answered and held my breath.

"Hi, my name is Don Jackson. I don't know if you remember seeing me, but I was watching your match this afternoon at the racquetball club."

As my heart started racing, I struggled to contain the excitement in my voice as I replied, "I remember you on the balcony."

Sounding relieved, Don went on to say, "You played a great match today. I heard your opponent call out your name and found your phone number on the challenge ladder board at the club. I called hoping you might want to play a few games with me next weekend and grab some dinner afterward?"

Oh my gosh, this wonderful man was asking me out on a date. I quickly confirmed my interest and continued the conversation with a series of questions about him. As diplomatically as possible, I resolved my age concern by asking Don if he was enrolled at Texas Tech. Surprising me, he replied, "No, I've already completed graduate school back in Missouri." Adding the educational years in my head, I had reached the conclusion that Don was quite a bit older than me when he stated, "I'm twenty-eight years old." Laughing, I told him he looked much younger than his age and admitted I thought he was only a freshman. Although finding my comment humorous, Don confessed to being routinely carded when he went out for dinner making my first impression accurate since Texas' legal drinking age in 1980 was eighteen years old. I, on the other hand, was an old soul in a young woman's body. At nineteen, I was already a junior in college living eight hundred miles from home and working to put myself through school. I was focused on completing my education and starting a career as a dietitian. My discovery that Don was older and established in a profession was welcome news. I was ready to share my life with someone and build a future based on common goals. The timing of our chance encounter was perfect. Our racquetball dinner date the following weekend was a thrilling success and confirmed our compatibility as a couple.

Don and I would play racquetball together for the next several months. Although we achieved success individually, we found even more enjoyment and strength playing as doubles partners. All the stars aligned for us when I graduated from college and was offered a dietetic internship at St. Louis University the same month Don was promoted and transferred back to

Monsanto's World Headquarters in St. Louis. After driving to Missouri together, we married at the county courthouse the following week on May 12, 1982. The judge only performed marriages on Wednesdays between noon and two o'clock, so we tied the knot during Don's lunch break and celebrated afterwards, at his office with his co-workers. Our wedding day may have been nontraditional, but it was filled with joy and love.

Throughout our marriage, Don and I would marvel over the odds of meeting one another. Was it fate or simply coincidence? I had an apartment in Lubbock, while Don lived about fifty miles away in Plainview, Texas. He was not a member of my racquetball club and had been playing there as a guest only because a friend asked him for coaching advice. If Don hadn't looked down into my court and allowed our eyes to connect, odds are, our paths would never have crossed for the rest of our lives. As cliché as it sounds, I believe we experienced love at first sight. The fortunate stroke of serendipity began what would become a fulfilling and rewarding lifelong relationship during which we have remained inseparable.

While pursuing our new career paths, we continued to compete in racquetball tournaments—now as "Team Jackson." As racquetball's popularity waned, Don's discovery of a new and more challenging sport changed the direction of our competitive efforts. By the end of our first year of marriage, we would be immersed in the world of triathlon.

MARRIAGE AND RACQUETBALL PHOTOS

1 Married during Don's lunch break and celebrated with co-workers—his boss gave him the rest of the day off!

2 Team Jackson's racquetball trophy collection.

THE DAWN OF TRIATHLON

ON FEBRUARY 18, 1978, the first-ever Hawaiian Ironman Triathlon was held on the island of Oahu, combining three existing events: the 2.4-mile Waikiki Roughwater Swim, 112-mile Round the Island Bike Race and 26.2-mile Honolulu Marathon. Fifteen competitors attempted this unprecedented test of human endurance but only twelve individuals were able to complete the race. Gordon Haller crossed the finish line in 11 hours, 46 minutes, and 58 seconds to become the first Ironman champion, igniting the phenomenon of triathlon racing around the globe. Within five years, the popularity and competitive field of the Ironman World Championship Race in Hawaii had exploded forcing organizers to cap the event at 2,000 participants. Race entry was limited to the winners of Ironman qualifying races held around the world. To provide a pathway for non-qualifying individuals to participate in the event, a lottery system was established to extend an additional one hundred invitations to athletes lucky enough to have their names drawn.

LAKE ST. LOUIS TRIATHLON

In 1981, John Howard won the Ironman race in Hawaii, creating a media wave of interest across his home state of Missouri. Following Howard's win, St. Louis organizers held the first Lake St. Louis Triathlon in July 1983. A mass marketing campaign was initiated six months prior to the event which included the posting of fliers at city racquetball clubs and athletic venues. When Don brought one of the brochures home after playing racquetball one evening, it completely changed the focus of our athletic efforts.

"Hey Shannon, take a look at this," Don said as he excitedly handed me a flier for a race to be held in July, nearly six months away. "This triathlon sounds fun and something we could do well. Let's compete this summer."

Studying the piece of paper, I noted the triathlon contained three types of racing efforts: a three-quarter mile swim followed by a twenty-five-mile bike leg and a 6.2-mile run. "I know we can run the distance and I suspect we could ride the twenty-five miles without any issue, but Don, I don't know how to swim," I laughingly told him while setting the flier on the counter. "I can dog paddle and maneuver myself in water to keep from drowning, but I know nothing about the strokes of a competitive swimmer." Staring at my husband with a slightly confused look on my face, I also added, "Honey, I don't even own a bike!"

"We talked about buying you a bike this summer so we could ride to-gether. We will just get one sooner, so we can start training in early spring when the weather warms up." Barely pausing to take a breath, Don added, "I can teach you how to swim and maybe even find a coach to give you a few lessons."

I quickly realized my husband was seriously considering competing in this unusual type of race and wanted me to join him in training for the new endeavor. As was often the case, Don's enthusiasm about trying something new overpowered any hesitancy I was feeling about the idea and after only a moment of hesitation, I found myself nodding my head in agreement as our discussion quickly transitioned to outlining a training plan for a three-event competition.

TRAINING PARTNERS

In January 1983, we were eight months into our marriage and living in an apartment outside St. Louis, Missouri. Don was working as a product man-ager for a large chemical company while I completed my education taking graduate school classes and providing free labor at the hospital to fulfill my dietetic internship requirements. Times were lean with only one of us employed. A local bike store had a good sale on Schwinn bikes, allowing us to pick one up at a reasonable price.

We also purchased a contraption called bicycle rollers which would allow us to cycle indoors during the long, icy St. Louis winter months. Bicycle rollers consist of three large cylinders attached to a frame which sits about six inches off the ground. The bike's front tire sits precariously on the front cylinder while the back tire is nestled between the two rear cylinders. Riding a bike on rotating cylinders requires a very smooth pedal cadence and good balance to stay upright. We became competent enough on the rollers that we could distract ourselves during training by watching television. MTV was first broadcast in August 1981, and I was one of millions who was immediately addicted to the new platform. I loved to cycle while watching music videos and pedaling to the beat of a song for entertainment. The hours we spent cycling indoors on the rollers allowed us to gain strength and prowess on our bikes before the spring cycling season began. By April, we felt fit and ready to begin a more strenuous training program on asphalt.

Swimming highlighted fundamental differences in our body types. My physique contained a high percentage of body fat allowing me to float like a log while Don was very lean and sank like a rock. Additionally, I possessed broad shoulders, a long torso and short legs that allowed me to ride high in the water. My body was made for swimming, and I quickly excelled at honing the necessary skills to become competitive. As promised, Don taught me the basic stroke, kick, and breathing pattern to freestyle swim. He also hired an Olympic coach for a couple lessons to ensure I was executing all movements correctly as I worked to increase power and speed in the pool. I had grown up shunning water sports; always dodging opportunities to swim in pools, lakes, and the ocean as a kid. Therefore, at twenty-two, I was quite surprised to discover I was a good swimmer with an innate ability to glide quickly through water. The positive results were certainly motivating, but I never truly enjoyed my time in the pool and had to force myself to jump in the cold water each morning to train before work.

Don's time in the water presented an almost comical result. Although he easily demonstrated a technically proficient stroke, his ankles lacked plantar flexion which made his leg's powerful scissor kick inefficient. The inability to point his toes, combined with a lack of body fat, forced Don to drag himself through the water with just his strong chest and arm muscles. Our pool had a glass viewing window below the water line which allowed me to witness Don swimming with a half-submerged body. The poor man was constantly fighting to keep himself afloat and moving forward. To improve his ankle flexibility, Don used swim fins while training. He kept cutting a few inches off the ends of the rubber flippers hoping his ankles would move in a more normal fashion over time. The result was two ridiculously short swim fins still ineffectively kicking on fused ankles. Fortunately, Don loved being in water which made his struggles tolerable.

Running was the event that Don did well—having competed in high school and college. When I watched Don during speed workouts, I marveled at how fast he sprinted across the tarmac, comparing his gait to the lightness of a gazelle. He was a beautiful runner, standing six feet tall with a lean small-boned frame comprised of fast twitch muscles which moved in a rapid, graceful stride. None of those attributes pertained to me which forced me to work hard to become competitive in the event. I was a tall, big-boned woman with a long torso and a short stride. Don bought me my first pair of running shoes just after we first met and patiently taught me how to pace myself to be able to run a full mile without stopping. With time and his continual coaching, I was able to improve my technique to become an efficient runner, but never faster than a seven-minute mile pace.

RACE DAY

"Oh my gosh, did you see the body on that guy?" I quietly asked Don while walking toward the starting area for the race. "He was ripped!" Swiveling my head from side to side, I continued to be impressed by the physiques of the athletes gathered on the sandy beach. "Wow, that woman is so muscular." I whispered. I had never seen so many beautiful bodies on display, as everyone stood in bathing suits waiting for the starting gun.

"Remember, you can never tell a book by its cover," Don quickly responded. "Don't psych yourself out thinking everyone is stronger. We've trained hard and we're both ready for today." He smiled at me before continuing. "Race your own pace and enjoy yourself. I'll see you at the finish."

After a quick grin and nod of my head, I turned my focus toward the lake and within a few seconds, a loud BOOM could be heard signaling the start of our first triathlon. Hundreds of people ran across the beach and dove into the shallow water to begin the three-quarter mile swim segment of the race. There was a large buoy moored in the lake at the halfway point that everyone had to swim around. I knew that spot was going to be extremely crowded, so I tried to swim hard from the start to get ahead of the mass of thrashing bodies. Slapped and kicked by flailing hands and feet, I continued to maneuver myself toward the front of the frothing water all the while thinking to myself, "This is nothing like swimming in a pool. What a wild, crazy mess!" The mass lake start was complete chaos and no place for the meek. It took every bit of my strength and sheer determination to keep breathing and advancing as I battled for position within the throng of competitors. As expected, the buoy was the most challenging area to navigate. I didn't want to be pinned against the metal, so I made the turn with two people between me and the anchored ball. Bodies were savagely shoved and slammed together as too many swimmers tried to pivot around the sharp angle. Gasping and fighting for a full breath of air, I powered forward to break free of the writhing group and head back toward the beach. I had no idea where Don was within the cluster of bodies surrounding me. I only hoped he made it safely around the dangerous turn and was swimming to shore as well. As it turned out, I gained a few minutes on Don during our swim, and ran across the sand with the first three dozen competitors out of the water.

Separate tents were set up for men and women to allow athletes some privacy during clothing changes. Don and I had each left a bag in our designated tent with bike shorts, jersey and cycling shoes for the second leg of the race. Shocked by the amount of time I lost struggling to slide dry clothes over my wet skin, I frustratingly thought, "Someone has to come up with a better idea for dressing more quickly." It was no surprise to see one-piece triathlete suits invented and on the market the following summer, elimi-nating the need for changing all together.

Our bikes were easy to locate; positioned in numerical order and held upright by their rear wheels in a wooden stand. I quickly hopped on mine and began the twenty-five-mile loop on the county roads surrounding Lake St. Louis. The cycling course was a hilly route through Missouri farmland separated by thick forests. The small amount of shade provided by the can-opy of overhanging trees was a welcome relief from the sun's intense heat. St. Louis was often stiflingly hot during the month of July, and this year was no exception. Our race day was turning out to be a real scorcher. There were volunteers standing on the side of the road with water hoses offering to spray riders to cool them down. I signaled my desire to be sprinkled and enjoyed the immediate cooling effect from the wind evaporating the wetness from my skin.

Cycling was my strongest event in the triathlon and as a result, I was making excellent time until I came upon a blind ninety-degree corner. A car heading toward me in the opposite lane was driving too fast and swerved across the centerline into my lane, forcing me off the road. Without a shoul-der and only gravel alongside the curve, my wheels slipped out from under me causing me to fall to the ground on my right side and chest. Stunned, but realizing no bones had been broken, I quickly got back on my bike and started pedaling down the road all the while thinking, "Keep moving. You're okay. You haven't lost too much time. Pedal, pedal, pedal!" Although I was angry that the man driving the vehicle hadn't even stopped after almost hitting me, I tried to use the adrenaline dump to my advantage and focus solely on the race. There were about forty bleeding cuts on the right side of my calf and thigh, but I figured the oozing blood would help clean out the dirt, so I ignored the pain and kept moving. With only five miles of the bike course remaining, my thoughts alternated between encouraging myself to cycle harder to wondering, "Where is Don? He's faster than me on a bike. Why hasn't he passed me yet?" His parents, who were watching us race, would later tell us he had been less than a minute behind me coming into the swim to bike transition area. As expected, Don had been gaining on me throughout the bike section and had closed the gap to a hundred yards.

After another quick trip to the tent to change into running shorts and shoes, I started the final 6.2-mile run. Don and I had practiced the transition from cycling to running dozens of times, but I still was not prepared for how heavy and horrible my legs felt during those first few jogging steps. My mind was giving me directives, "Pick your feet up, find your rhythm. Pace yourself!" My body, however, struggled to cooperate. After a quarter mile of jogging, my movements finally became more fluid, and I began to race in earnest. The 10K run was an out and back course ensuring I would pass Don at some point. I wasn't sure if he was still behind me or had changed into running clothes more quickly and was now in front. Either way, I was relieved that we would see each other soon.

The temperature had risen throughout the morning to an alarming ninety degrees with matching humidity. Don's parents had felt it necessary to leave the venue during our run when his mother became overheated standing in the hot sun and started to feel nauseated. There were even more volunteers with water hoses on this section of the course offering a cooling mist to runners as they ran past. Growing up in south Texas and having only been away for a year, I was still acclimated to the "Hell on Earth" conditions I had grown up in, allowing me to thrive in the stifling heat and suffocating mugginess the nearby Missouri and Mississippi Rivers produced.

Excitement coursed through my body when I recognized Don running toward me shortly after I had passed the halfway point. Drawing closer to one another, I finally understood why Don hadn't caught me in the race; the heat was claiming another victim. Don's face was beet red, and his gait was much slower than usual. I quickly yelled to him from across the road to pick up his pace and keep moving. Although I meant the words to be encouraging, Don would later ask me, "Why were you shouting at me? Don't you think I would have run faster if I could have?" Throughout our marriage, whenever a discussion about triathlons occurs, Don always retells the story of my yelling at him during our first race. Upsetting him had never been my intention, but his anger did provide a boost of energy, allowing him to run faster and catch me by the end of the race.

After crossing the finish line, I turned around to give Don a congratulatory hug when two men rushed over to see if I needed help getting to the medical tent. They were staring at the cuts on my right leg where blood still oozed from my wounds. Don also took notice of my mangled leg and asked, "What happened to you?"

A bit confused by everyone's level of concern, I explained to the medical personnel, "Guys, I'm fine. This happened on the bike course when I swerved to avoid being hit by a car and I fell off my bike in loose gravel."

Looking very surprised, one man asked, "You ran the racecourse with your leg like that?"

Glancing at the torn skin, I shrugged and said, "Yeah, I really wanted to finish the race."

Weighing in on the conversation, the other man interjected, "Some of those cuts look deep. Why don't you come on over to the medical tent so we can at least clean the scrapes before you head home?"

"Sounds like a good idea," Don said, ushering me toward the tent to get bandaged.

INSPIRED BY THE CHALLENGE

Although we left the race that day a bit battered and bruised, we were both excited to have achieved our goal of completing the triathlon course and additionally thrilled to learn my efforts had resulted in a first-place finish in my age category. Between the extreme heat and my fall, the day had been far from perfect for either of us. Yet, this strenuous athletic competition sparked a desire to push ourselves further and to keep participating in these types of events.

As we continued to hone our skills and grew more in sync with one another, Don became the perfect racing partner. His finishing times were usually on par with the first-place female. Keeping pace with Don during a competition almost always assured me a win in the women's race or at least a position on the podium. Using Don as my rabbit, I was able to finish in second place at an Ironman Triathlon Qualifier in Salt Lake City earning me an invitation to the World Championship in Hawaii. Utilizing the lottery system, we tried to get an invite for Don to join me at the race but were unsuccessful. Without my husband and partner racing by my side, the time commitment to train for a twelve-hour competition felt like a sacrifice instead of enjoyment. After four years of competing in triathlons, we decided to switch our focus to another activity we both loved: long distance cycling. We had previously tried to qualify for the 1983 Paris-Brest-Paris Bicycle Race but were unsuccessful. The famous race is held every four years, and the 1987 event was on the horizon. We set a new goal to be racing in France by September of the following year.

TRIATHLON PHOTOS

1. Watching MTV while training on bike rollers.

2. Don entering changing tent following swim segment of the St. Louis Triathlon, 1983.

3. Shannon finishing the bike course after crashing during the St. Louis Triathlon, 1983.

4. Don heading out on the bike course of the St. Louis Triathlon, 1983.

5. Shannon, bloodied and bruised, finishes the race—wins age category in the St. Louis Triathlon, 1983.

6. Shannon wearing the first triathlon suit on the market in 1984. Posing with her triathlon and long-distance racing bikes.

7. Finishing second place Women's Overall in the 1985 Salt Lake City Triathlon qualified Shannon to race in the Hawaii Ironman.

PARIS-BREST-PARIS
BICYCLE RACE

TOTALLY EXHAUSTED AND ALONE, I slowly pedaled my bike down the dark backcountry road between Bellême and Nogent-le-Roi during the early morning hours of August 27, 1987. The cold, wet stretch of pavement separating the two small French towns was less than fifty-three miles long, but it would take me five and a half hours to cover the short distance in the drizzling rain. After watching the sun rise three times during the last seventy hours and 667 miles of racing, I was emotionally at my lowest point on the 750-mile Paris-Brest-Paris (PBP) racecourse and trying hard to summon the mental fortitude to make myself continue the event. My mind was on a continuous loop screaming at me to "STOP" while alternating with a persistent shout of "DON'T YOU DARE GIVE UP!" Fortunately, while warring with myself at this critical juncture, the rain stopped, and the first rays of dawn started to streak across the sky. There was something magical about the sunrise; it provided a warm energy that gave me strength and brightened all my dark thoughts of doubt. Tears of happiness began to fall as I felt my willpower and tenacious spirit once more take hold. The finish line was only eighty-three miles away and Don would be there waiting for me. Today I would finally reach my goal and fulfill the dream we had set four years earlier; to complete the oldest and largest international randonneuring event known as the Paris-Brest-Paris Bicycle Race.

Why I was witnessing a fourth sunrise on my own is another crazy Don and Shannon story that started with a conversation during the first year of our marriage. After working a weekend shift at the local hospital, I came home to find Don excited to share an article he had read in the March 1983 issue of *Bicycling* magazine. It was about a long-distance bike race held in France once every four years and scheduled for August 24, 1983. Don provided a summary of the event. "The race is called Paris-Brest-Paris and it's 750 miles long. The course starts in Paris, heads west across the country to the coastal town of Brest and then back to Paris. It has a mass start and it's an all-out effort with no scheduled stops, just check points along the route. Each person must make it back to Paris within ninety hours or be eliminated. Americans can qualify for a starting position by completing a series of four brevets held here in the states. Only after successfully finishing the sanctioned 200-, 300-, 400- and 600-kilometer rides in a specified amount of time will a rider be allowed to participate in the grand randonneuring event in France." Following his summary, Don quickly added, "In 1975, only four Americans completed the race because it was so grueling. Thirty-four more Americans tried in 1979 and a man named Scott Dickson finished third. The article said they expected more than a hundred riders from the US to compete this August hoping not only to complete the course but to become the first American to win the race. What do you think? Is this something we should do?"

I was a little overwhelmed by the distances Don was describing but at the same time, the idea of a trip to Paris sounded really nice. "Maybe," I cautiously responded while quickly trying to restructure in my mind a strategy for participating in both the St. Louis Triathlon and the long-distance cycling event. "Are you thinking the brevets would be a part of our triathlon bike training?"

"Absolutely," Don answered. "We need some long-distance bike rides, and the brevets would be perfect for those miles. The first brevet is 200 kilometers which is just 124 miles. We could easily do that distance and then increase our mileage with each qualifier." We had already ridden a local century ride, so it seemed doable.

"I like the idea of riding the longer distances with a group. There is more safety in numbers. Let's give it a try." My mind immediately shifted gears to our training calendar and the need to add the PBP qualifiers to our weekend schedule. "When is the first brevet?"

"The article mentioned mid-April. I'll contact the organizing agency and find out the exact date and what we need to do to sign up for all the brevets. I think this will be fun!"

The seed for long-distance bike racing had been firmly planted. Don and I successfully completed three of the four brevets in April, May, and June 1983. Unfortunately, the July date for the 600-kilometer Midwest qualifier conflicted with our first triathlon. Undeterred, we contacted the US Randonneur Association and learned the last remaining 600-kilometer qualifying event in the US was being held in Syracuse, New York. Don and I drove across the country to participate in the brevet two weeks after our triathlon race. A heat wave hit New York the weekend of the event which caused more than half the field to not meet the cutoff time. The extreme heat triggered a migraine that forced me to stop riding just before midnight. With the two of us stranded in the middle of nowhere, Don also abandoned the qualifier to get me to the nearest hotel for the night. Recognizing that Mother Nature had doomed most of the participants, the sponsors organized another 600K brevet two weeks later, but Don and I were not able to take time off from work and once again, drive two thousand miles to participate. Although our 1983 attempt was unsuccessful, we vowed to take the knowledge we had gained from riding the brevets and use it to compete in the 1987 Paris-Brest-Paris race.

THE ROAD TO PARIS

In the four years between 1983 and 1987, Don's career path required us to move three times: from St. Louis, Missouri to Boise, Idaho; on to Indianapolis, Indiana; and then back to St. Louis. New jobs in new locations demanded more of our time but never stopped us from training and participating in triathlons, biathlons, running, and cycling events. We loved the time spent outdoors training together and enjoyed sharing common goals. In early 1987, we were once again living in St. Louis and ready to focus our efforts on the qualifying brevets and the PBP race in Europe.

The first two sanctioned brevets of 200 kilometers (124 miles) and 300 kilometers (186 miles) went smoothly. We had met dozens of people at the qualifiers back in 1983 and most of these individuals were once again pedaling alongside us hoping to fulfill the requirements to compete in France. To make the long qualifying rides more fun, everyone passed the time telling stories of their experience cycling previous brevets and other long-distance events. Don and I contributed to the laughter by sharing the lesson we learned while riding our first 200-kilometer brevet in 1983. The rules had stated that all cyclists had to be 100 percent self-sufficient. I explained I was married to a man who took that statement literally. "In an effort to be totally self-supported, we mounted large panniers on our bikes and filled Don's packs with every bicycle tool he could possibly need to fix a mechanical issue, including a full set of box wrenches. My bike panniers were stuffed with enough food and water to last the entire day. We knew the route would pass several convenience stores and restaurants, but we thought the rules meant we had to carry our own food. We must have had twenty pounds in our front panniers. You can't imagine how scary it was trying to steer with those heavy packs on the front of our bikes."

While people were laughing, fully understanding our situation, Don added, "Shannon and I almost fell multiple times when bumps in the road shifted the weight making steering uncontrollable. It took us much longer than we had planned to cover the 124 miles, but we did make the cutoff time, barely. We learned the hard way the real meaning of the phrase self-reliant and only brought absolute necessities with us on the rest of the rides."

After chuckling at our inexperience, others shared stories of naivete during their early years of long-distance racing. Caught up in the camaraderie of all the cyclists, the miles and the day passed quickly.

The 400-kilometer (248 miles) brevet brought our plans to a halt when Don's work schedule required him to travel outside the country over the same weekend as the sanctioned event. After much communication with the US Randonneur organization, we obtained permission for Don to self-qualify by riding the route the following weekend on his own. The two brevets he had already completed in 1987 combined with his 1983 riding history convinced the governing body to grant his request.

I completed the 400-kilometer tour riding with our friend, Bob Cox, an engineer and amateur bike frame builder, who was also a strong, long-distance cyclist. Don and I had met Bob in 1983 and had developed a friendship over the years riding together in various Midwest cycling events. I enjoyed Bob's company and knew he would help me if I got myself into any trouble on the course while Don was away. The 248-mile qualifier was held in Illinois on a route that was relatively flat. Drafting behind a large group of cyclists on the open agricultural roads, the brevet went smoothly for both me and Bob. Don would ride alone on these same roads a week later in excessive heat, high winds and on Father's Day when, surprisingly, most of the convenience stores were closed for business.

The plan was for Don to cycle on his own while I worked my shift at the hospital. After work, I would become his support vehicle carrying food, beverages and whatever else he might need to finish the ride. When I found Don beginning his eleventh hour of pedaling on the black tarmac, he was beet red, nauseated and extremely dehydrated from excessive sweating. Salt was all over his face, crusting on his helmet straps and creating ring marks on his clothing. He had battled horrible headwinds in dangerously hot temperatures which reduced his average speed throughout the day. Without the convenience stores being open, Don consumed a limited number of calories from the foods he was carrying and not enough water. Farmers had allowed him to fill his water bottles from their faucets but still he had not been able to drink enough fluid to meet his needs. With too many miles still to go and time running out, we had to face the reality that Don could not complete the required distance within the established time frame. Sadly shaking his head, Don put his bike in the back of our Volkswagen GTI and then climbed in the car for the ride home. Four years of hopes and dreams roiled around inside the vehicle while we both remained silent digesting the enormity of the moment. It wasn't until the next day that we discussed the situation and made a plan for the rest of the summer.

Don refused to give up on our dream to compete in the PBP bicycling event. Although I wanted the experience to be the two of us riding in France together, he convinced me to keep racing and assured me that he would participate by supporting me in my effort. Don felt we had already invested too much of our lives, training time, and money into the effort to totally abandon the goal again. With his help, I successfully completed the 600-kilometer (372 miles) brevet in July and then spent the remaining weeks before traveling to Europe continuing to improve my strength and endurance.

To duplicate the physical demands of riding the PBP racecourse distance, I developed a unique weekend training program. Arriving home from work on a Friday, I would eat a small dinner and then start my ride at 6:00 p.m. toward Lake of the Ozarks, about 175 miles from St. Louis. Don would drive our car while I pedaled my bike on Missouri's hilly, backcountry roads that provided challenging terrain with limited traffic. I rode throughout the night while Don followed me with his headlights illuminating the way and the flashers going to keep me safe from passing cars. Arriving in Branson/ Lake of the Ozarks around mid-morning on Saturday, Don and I would get a hotel room, sleep for four hours, and then duplicate the effort on our return trip to St. Louis. Whatever time we arrived back home on Sunday, we ate a quick meal, showered, and then went to bed for some much-needed rest and recovery before going to work the next day. In this manner, I forced my body to exercise for long stretches without sleep, became accustomed to riding in the dark and learned to accept the pain brought on by 350 continuous miles on a bike.

Our friend, Bob Cox, joined us on the second weekend training tour to the Lake of the Ozarks. We made pedaling the miles as fun as possible with lots of conversation. At one point, Don drove in front of us with our car's hatchback open and the radio blasting rock music through the rear speakers. Bob and I sang along to the songs and laughed at our off-key effort; just happy to be outdoors training for our big adventure. We both appreciated Don's support and knew his contributions to our cycling regimen increased our chances for success in France. When the departure date for Europe arrived, I felt ready to compete. I knew the actual racecourse was double my weekend effort, but my job and sixty-hour work week did not allow me to push myself any farther. That fact would come back to haunt me on the lonely roads in France.

PARLEZ-VOUS FRANÇAISE?

Upon arriving in Paris, our first order of business was getting my bike inspected by the PBP officials. With nearly three thousand cyclists from fourteen different countries participating in the 1987 event, the process was a lengthy ordeal. While maneuvering our way through the check-in pavilion, I could hear a variety of different languages being spoken around me. As expected, the most dominant was the melodic cadence of French.

"I'm glad I practiced my French all summer," I commented while waiting in line. "I think those language tapes are going to be helpful." Most of the officials we encountered spoke some English, but all of them seemed to become more friendly after we attempted to communicate with them in their language. They inspected my bike to ensure that my brakes and lights were in working order and the required reflectors, bell, and fenders were present. Once approved, I was issued a race number and corresponding plate to attach to my bike, an identifying leg band which was to be worn throughout the race and a booklet with photo identification to present to race officials for control stamps along the racecourse. There were no cell phones or internet in 1987. To keep track of a rider's progress and ensure their safety, there were fifteen checkpoints where competitors were required to stop and allow officials to time stamp and sign their race ID booklets. To keep everyone honest, there were also two secret checkpoints with special stamps and code names that had to be present in the booklet to qualify as an official PBP finisher at the end of the race.

A CENTURY OF RACING

Paris-Brest-Paris is described as the oldest, continuously run cycling event in existence. The first race was held in 1891 and was marketed as an incredible test of human endurance on a bicycle. Frame builders sponsored the race to promote cycling as a viable mode of transportation. The original challenge captured the public's interest so strongly, spectators gathered along France's country roads and city street corners day and night, cheering racers on with offerings of food, water, and encouragement. The first winner, Charles Terront, arrived back in Paris after three days of riding, to an exuberant crowd of over ten thousand people. The French adoration and devotion to cycling was evident then and continues today.

The racecourse for Paris-Brest-Paris continues to run through many of the same village locations that it did a hundred years ago. With the invention of cars, the route to reach each of these small towns has been slightly altered over the years to allow participants to ride on less dangerous country roads. The start in 1987 began deep in the heart of Paris and traveled across the country to Brest and then returned on many of the same roadways. The last one hundred miles, however, detoured on an entirely different course from Bellême to Nogent-le-Roi and ended with a lovely, forested finish in the rural Paris suburb of Rueil-Malmaison.

There have been many changes to the PBP race since 1891, but one tradition that has remained intact was the 4:00 a.m. start time. The tradition of thousands of cyclists exiting the city of Paris before sunrise was now important because it allowed racers to avoid rush hour traffic. With nearly 3,000 participants, competitors began lining up on a deserted city street near the Eiffel Tower a full hour before the event would begin. Bob and I stood straddling our bikes midway down the mass and along the outside edge of the throng so we could talk with Don until the actual race began. Nervous excitement permeated the air as adrenaline surged through the crowd. As four o'clock neared, I waved goodbye to Don, made sure my front and rear lights were illuminated, and then readied myself for the gun to go off. After hearing a loud bang, a writhing line of red taillights began moving forward. The 1987 Paris-Brest-Paris Race was underway.

The modern day PBP has two informal categories: the Race and the Ride. There is a small group of cyclists who solely focus on being the first to cross the finish line while thousands of other competitors participate in

PBP with the singular goal of completing the incredible distance within the ninety-hour time limit. Each of these individuals has their name placed in the revered PBP logbook alongside more than a century of other racers and receives a commemorative finisher's medal inscribed with their racing time. Although my PBP experience started as a Race with a goal to reach the podium, it quickly and unexpectedly transitioned into a Ride against the clock.

AN INAUSPICIOUS BEGINNING

"Good luck, Bob. Here we go!" I shouted as we made our first pedal strokes within the sardine packed road of cyclists. The first few miles of the PBP racecourse were led by a control car and had policeofficers blocking most intersections to ensure riders stayed safe as they made their way out of the city. I decided to follow behind Bob where I felt more protected within the crowded corridor of cyclists. He was good at finding narrow openings between bikes to safely maneuver past slower riders. Bob and I had hoped to ride together as much as possible allowing us to draft on windy sections and keep each other awake through the night. It was a good idea, but the plan failed early on when I unexpectedly got a flat tire and came to an abrupt halt only thirty minutes into the race. I quickly yelled, "Hey Bob, I've got a flat. I have to stop!" With racers still yelling to one another and the loud sounds of the city all around us, Bob never heard my shouts and continued to ride away, never realizing I was no longer on his rear wheel. There was nothing I could do but move to the side of the road, run to the corner streetlamp, and start fixing my flat tire under the light. I was heartbroken as I watched thousands of cyclists pass by while I worked on my bike. Don had provided multiple tutorial sessions on how to change a flat tire, so I was proficient at the process but not extremely fast. Within fifteen minutes, I was the only person standing on the dark street. In a field of almost 3,000 racers, I was now in last place.

In my heart and mind, I was still racing the PBP. Adrenaline was coursing through my body and urging me to move quickly as I started to pedal my bike. The problem was there was no one to follow and I didn't know the way. Cycling GPSes did not exist in 1987. I had to rely on reading a map and finding PBP stickers in the dark to remain on the racecourse. Relying on just the stickers worried me most because I knew it would be very easy to miss a turn and become lost. I forced myself to slow down at each intersection until I found a lime green PBP marker confirming I was still on track. Every time I saw the illumination of a cyclist's red taillight ahead, I would speed up to the person only to discover it was commuter on their way to work. I was constantly rolling through the up and down feelings of excitement and disappointment while remaining in last place. It wasn't until I was out of the city and moving with a good deal of speed on a county road that I made contact with the back of the field and started to pass other racers. Heading west, I felt the warm rays of my first sunrise wrap around me, blanketing my body in a calming embrace. Feelings of anxiety transitioned to determination with the dawning light allowing me to move even faster while focusing my thoughts on a singular mantra, "Reel them in one-by-one." Finally, I was racing the PBP.

BELLÊME TO BREST

Relief flooded my system when I saw Don standing at the first checkpoint station in Bellême. More than anything else, I needed his comforting hug. After taking a few seconds to hold him and collect myself, I explained what had happened and why I was so delayed. Bellême was only one hundred miles from the start, but it had taken me seven hours and forty minutes to cover the distance. My goal had been to reach the first control point in less than six hours. Between the flat tire, slowing down or stopping to verify racecourse directions and battling headwinds on my own, I had moved much slower than planned.

"Bob left about thirty minutes ago," Don said. "He was hoping you were right behind him. We kept waiting but then started to wonder if something serious had happened to you. He decided to just keep going in case you were out of the race."

I wasn't surprised they had both worried. My arrival time resulted in an average speed that was uncharacteristically slow for me, making the men think something bad had occurred. With Don's help, I quickly refueled while he refilled my water bottles and checked my tires. I needed to keep moving to make up lost time. With another quick hug, I said goodbye, again, and started pedaling down the road.

After leaving Don at that first checkpoint in Bellême, I rode hard, trying to improve my position within the field. The course was heavily windswept making me truly miss my buddy, Bob, and the ability to draft with him. I tucked in behind a few groups of cyclists but was not able to stay in the pace lines either because the sustained effort was more than I could handle, or the riders made certain I understood that I was not welcome. Some small pelotons did not want a stranger with unknown cycling skill riding in their group. Too often, I found myself in no man's land, trying to cruise along in a headwind. The magnificent mountains of the Tour de France so prominently displayed on television were nowhere to be found. Our route was described as a working-class course, not a tourist attraction. It was pretty at times but not stunning. Instead of high mountain passes, we cycled extremely hilly terrain that ultimately demanded each racer climb over 35,000 feet of elevation before crossing the finish line. The racecourse was 750 miles of relentless up and downs that challenged the body and the mind.

The first thirty-six hours of racing had become a blur by the time I pulled into the halfway point at Brest. Don was waiting for me at the control station with news on my current placement. "The women's race leader is an American from the Midwest—Kay Ryschon. She's still here but is about to start riding again. You've caught up to the front of the women's race. Great job!" I smiled in acknowledgment of what I had been able to accomplish during the last 375 miles of pedaling. I had seen the sunrise twice and had not been off my bike for more than fifteen minutes throughout the last day and a half. I was tired, but the exhaustion felt familiar because I had completed the same distance on my training rides to the Lake of the Ozarks. I knew the real challenge was ahead of me. I would need to push my body into unknown territory to endure another 375 miles to the finish line.

INTO THE UNKNOWN

When I saw Don at the control point in Loudeac, about 500 miles into the race, I had started to crumble. Don helped me off my bike, sat me on the ground and shoved a ham sandwich and a water bottle into my hands. He then began to share a new game plan. "It's time for you to get some sleep. You're running on fumes. There are cots next door to sleep on. We can have someone wake us in four hours so you can get back on the road. It's time to recharge and this is the place to do it." I knew I was no longer able to make a rational decision, so I relied on Don to do it for me. After eating a few bites of the sandwich and drinking a full bottle of water, I finally let my body relax and fall into a deep sleep. When the volunteer woke us up four hours later, my muscles were stiff, and my stomach was nauseated. I had slept but didn't feel rested. I just hoped my overall fatigue and light headedness would lessen after I started moving on my bike.

To distract myself from the developing aches and pains from too many hours cycling, I focused on positive thoughts by replaying in my mind the special moments I had experienced in the race. I had been delighted at seeing my first castle when I was coasting downhill into the town of Fougères. The building had a moat and was adorned in lights that illuminated its historical significance. I had been so struck by the image that I immediately thought of Dorothy's line from the *Wizard of Oz*, "We're not in Kansas anymore!" Finding Fougères's castle only 200 miles into the race had kept me wondering what other treasures I might discover while cycling the remaining 550 miles on the racecourse.

I remembered being shocked by a young French girl who requested my autograph in Brest. I explained to her that I was no one famous; just an American woman cycling the PBP. She had replied in broken English, "Please sign. You bike fast. Please?" Taking the pen from her hand, I quickly wrote "Thanks for the support" followed by my name. It was such a special moment, just thinking about it again made me smile as I pedaled along at four o'clock in the morning.

Next, my thoughts moved on to the teenagers who had stood on the street corners yelling "Allez, Allez" (Go, go!) as they waved racers through a turn to stay on course. I remembered the old ladies who had sat in wicker chairs on the side of the road cheering "Bonne course" (good race) or "Bonne route" (good trip) and clapping for every passing cyclist, regardless of age or nationality. Even the tiny towns made up of only ten houses still had at least seven people standing on the side of the road at dusk supporting all the competitors who passed by them. The French seemed to consider all racers to be heroes. While musing about all the encouragement I had witnessed, it happened again; a lone voice called out to me in the night "à droite" (to the right) as I approached a dark street corner. I knew that person had been sitting in darkness for hours to protect me and other cyclists from becoming lost. I quickly yelled back, "Merci, merci!" Truly, the most amazing part of PBP was the support and enthusiasm of the French people. They created a festive atmosphere all along the course that bolstered a rider's confidence and cadence even when fighting extreme fatigue.

THE FRIENDLY STRANGER

Rain and wind battered the cyclists in the dark early hours of the third day. Unbeknownst to me, the 1987 PBP would go down in history as the year with the worst recorded weather. While I pedaled toward my six-hundredth mile and was struggling in the elements, three hundred other competitors succumbed to the wrath of Mother Nature and abandoned the race before the light of dawn. The cold rain was zapping my energy and leaving me feeling miserable, but I focused all my thoughts on a string of encouraging words, "Keep moving, don't stop. You can do it. One more mile!"

I must have had a determined look on my face when a middle-aged French PBP racer pulled up beside me and said, "Bonjour!"

With a limited French vocabulary, I replied with the same word, "Bonjour." When the Frenchman laughed at my American accent, I asked if he spoke English, "Parlez-vous anglais?"

"No," he answered. "Parlez-vous français?"

I held up my hand indicating a tiny bit. The Frenchman started speaking with a string of sentences that I didn't understand but his meaning became clear when he went in front of me and waved for me to draft behind him. We were heading into a fierce headwind and following his rear wheel provided much-needed relief. There may have been only a 20 percent reduction in my effort but emotionally, I experienced a 100 percent improvement in my attitude. I quickly thanked him, "Merci, merci!" We made pretty good time for the next hour and a half on our way to Tinténiac.

At one point, the Frenchman heard me gasp and then moan which made him laugh before saying, "No, no, no!" The view of the road ahead appeared to show red taillights climbing a huge hill. In the dark, the television tower was not visible, but its red lights made me think I was about to climb up into the clouds. Chuckling, he told me we would turn right before the perceived climb. I only understood the word "à droite" (right), but that was all I needed to know to calm down and continue. The Frenchman knew the racecourse route which allowed me to relax and feel less stress no longer having to find my way in the dark. Prior to his arrival, I had been looking for the PBP stickers at every intersection which were now florescent pink in color for the return trip to Paris. My third sunrise was masked by a dark sky and gray clouds. Still, I rallied my strength with the dawn of a new day and even took a few pulls at the front of our little two-person peloton.

Don was waiting at Tinténiac when the Frenchman and I pulled into the control point. After getting our booklets stamped, he turned to me and waved goodbye, wishing me "Bon courage" (Good Luck). I waved in return as I thanked him for his help. Although I never got my new friend's name and would never see the Frenchman again, he will always be remembered for all his support and compassion when I needed it most.

SO NEAR AND YET SO FAR

My arrival in Bellême around 11:00 p.m. was the second time I had to get off my bike for a quick nap. It was pouring rain and the shelters were already full of soaked cyclists, so Don and I tried to rest crammed inside the tiny three-cylinder Peugeot he had rented. I fell asleep for two hours and then made myself get back on my bike in the cold, miserable weather. Bellême was only one hundred miles from the finish line, but my body seemed like it might fall apart before I could get there. My legs had swollen to an alarming size while resting in the car. I struggled to get my wool leg warmers over my thighs that were now almost twice as big as normal. I looked at Don in a bit of a panic. "What is going on with me? What is happening here?"

He shook his head. "I don't know. You've sat on a bike seat for more than sixty hours. Your body is majorly stressed and reacting to your extreme effort. Do your legs throb? Are you in severe pain?"

"Pain? My whole body hurts! But no, I'm not in severe pain. Just usual muscle fatigue so I guess I'm okay to keep riding."

The next surprise occurred when I went to use the bathroom. I had been riding in rain for hours and my skin was already chaffed from days of sitting on my bike saddle. Cycling in wet shorts had further broken down my skin to the state of being raw. Urinating on the tender areas produced a terrible stinging sensation that caused me to moan.

"Are you okay?" Don asked from inside the car after hearing my pain filled groan.

"I think the blisters on my crotch have turned into open wounds because going to the bathroom makes that whole area feel *on fire*!" I knew Don was feeling helpless and upset about what I was enduring. While getting ready to leave and in effort to cheer him up, I made the comment, "I only have a single century to go. I can do this!"

After giving me a long hug, Don responded, "I know you can. But how about eating a Kit-Kat to help you get started." Don knew I liked Kit-Kat candy bars and somewhere along the way he had found one for me. The surprise treat made me smile and provided some sugar to get me going. With a final wave, I disappeared into the darkness on the lonely road from Bellême to Nogent-le-Roi.

The rain continued to fall, as I slowly pedaled down the wet backcountry roadway. A lone car slowed down behind me for a moment and then gently passed by my slow-moving form. Although I did not recognize him, it was Don. He would later share how watching me ride my bike in such bleak, dismal conditions had produced an indelible image that haunted him and would be seared in his mind for the rest of his life. He went on to explain that witnessing the hardships I had already endured and seeing my continued willingness to suffer had filled him with an even greater amount of love, respect, and admiration for me. And last, Don verbalized how much he regretted not being there right by my side.

Don's journey during my time on the PBP racecourse was not without his own set of challenges. Support vehicles were not allowed to help a rider outside of the control point locations. If a cyclist received assistance along the racecourse, they were disqualified. Support vehicles were required to display a special placard in the front window and were forbidden to travel on the same roads as the racers. As Don explained after the race was over, he stayed lost most of the time and in two instances, barely made it to the control location ahead of me. He also went without sleep, staying awake to watch for my arrival at the control stations and to help supply me with food and make bike repairs as needed. Don would be just as exhausted as I was when the race was over, not from physical exertion but from lack of sleep and worry. The only time he ever risked traveling on the same road with me was near the end of the race when he became lost. It was then that he watched me for those few precious seconds pedal in the rain on my way to Nogent-le-Roi.

With only eighty-three miles to the finish line, I witnessed my fourth sunrise and once again, drew strength from the dawning of the new day. It took every ounce of stamina I had to fight the fatigue and doubt that clouded my mind like the dark gray skies hovering overhead as I pedaled in the early morning light. I mentally clung to a continuous loop of short, positive thoughts, "Keep moving, you're almost there, one more mile." I rode into the checkpoint of Nogent-le-Roi at 8:30 a.m. and decided to take a break from my bike for coffee and pastries. There were only forty-eight more miles to the end of the race, but I knew each mile was going to be brutal. Carbs and caffeine seemed like a great idea to get me going again. Don let me know Bob was also in Nogent-le-Roi and currently taking a nap in the school gymnasium. Laughing, I told Don, "It took me over 700 miles to catch up to Bob and now I am going to miss riding with him again because he's sleeping! Tell him I hope he catches up to me. I'd still like to ride the racecourse with him." Waving goodbye one last time, I rolled away from Don and began the short but arduous journey to complete the race.

THE FINISH

The Paris-Brest-Paris Bicycle Race ended with a surprise hilltop finish. Even though there was a sign that indicated there was only one kilometer remaining, the sight of ascending asphalt was emotionally devastating. My quadriceps and core stomach muscles had nothing left for the climb. When I started up the hill, I could barely hang onto the bike and move with enough momentum to stay upright. Although I was outwardly silent, my mind repeatedly yelled, "One more pedal stroke. Come on, one more pedal stroke." As each agonizing rotation of the crank slowly brought me closer to my goal, the 500-meter sign became visible. Climbing on a winding forested road with trees blocking the view of the finish line ahead, I heard the screams and bells before I saw the crowd. Rounding the final curve a few minutes later brought tears to my eyes when I saw hundreds of spectators lining the road cheering me on to the finish. Just like the racers of a hundred years earlier, the French people enthusiastically welcomed me to the end of this extraordinary randonneuring event. I crossed the finish line at 1:30 in the afternoon; a full eighty-one and a half hours after I had started the race nearly three and a half days earlier.

After providing the officials with my ID booklet verifying completion of the course, Don was there to help me off my bike and to give me a much-needed hug. "You did it! Congratulations! I'm so proud of you." I was speechless and just hugged him harder. The relief of completing the race left me drained. Don helped carry both me and my bike the short distance to the car. Once he had me stuffed in the vehicle, we drove back to Leo Lagrange; the dormitory where dozens of American racers were staying while in Paris.

When I arrived at our lodging, I quickly showered four days of grime and sweat from my body and then fell into bed and slept for more than twelve hours. It would be several days before I could truly process what I had accomplished and adequately describe the experience for Don. We both slowly adjusted to post-race vacation time by becoming tourists and visiting all the special highlights, including Versailles, Notre-Dame cathedral, the Eiffel Tower, the Louvre, and an enjoyable walk down the famous Champs-Élysées from the Arc de Triomphe to the Place de la Concorde.

RACE RESULTS

Americans left their mark on the 1987 PBP race by winning nearly every category: first-place male (44 hours), first-place female (62 hours) and first-place men's tandem (56 hours). There were 2,756 total racers with 230 Americans in the starting lineup. Only 2,117 participants (81 percent of the field) successfully completed the race within the 90-hour time limit. Americans had the highest attrition rate with 50 percent of cyclists abandoning the race. With time, the US Randonneuering Association would continue to grow in both size and strength and become even more competitive in future PBP events.

As far as personal standings, my 81.5-hour completion time secured third place US female and eleventh overall out of 127 participants in the women's race. I had started PBP hoping to reach the podium based on my qualifying 372-mile brevet time of twenty-seven hours back in the states. Given the early mishap of having a flat tire and having to battle the elements alone without the benefit of a massive peloton to block the wind and lead the way, I was satisfied with what I was able to accomplish.

The most important things I learned during those four days of riding in France went far beyond my ability to sit on a bicycle seat. Competing in Paris-Brest-Paris allowed me to tap into an unknown well of inner strength that would serve me many times throughout the rest of my life including critical moments while hiking the Continental Divide, climbing Denali, surviving a heart ablation, and enduring the passing of loved ones. In 1987, I was a young twenty-six-year-old woman still figuring out what things were important to me. PBP was the first big event that Don and I did not accomplish together, and I found the adventure to be less meaningful without him.

Our previous combined experiences had felt richer because we shared the same memories and could relive the laughter, joy, amazement, and intensity of those moments throughout our marriage. Following PBP, I never felt the desire to race, vacation, or travel without Don; not because I couldn't go it alone, but because I chose to experience life by his side. Simply stated, we both discovered we are *better and happier together*.

PARIS-BREST-PARIS PHOTOS

1 Official control station card with required stamps including two secret locations.

2 Documented finishing arrival time: 81 hours 33 minutes.

3 Leo Lagrange Dormitory where dozens of American racers stayed.

4 Honoring the 1891 traditional start time of 4:00 a.m.

5 Windy and cold during the 90 Hour Event— 1987 would go down as the worst weather in PBP Race history.

6 Enjoyed visiting many tourist attractions post race—the Eiffel Tower included.

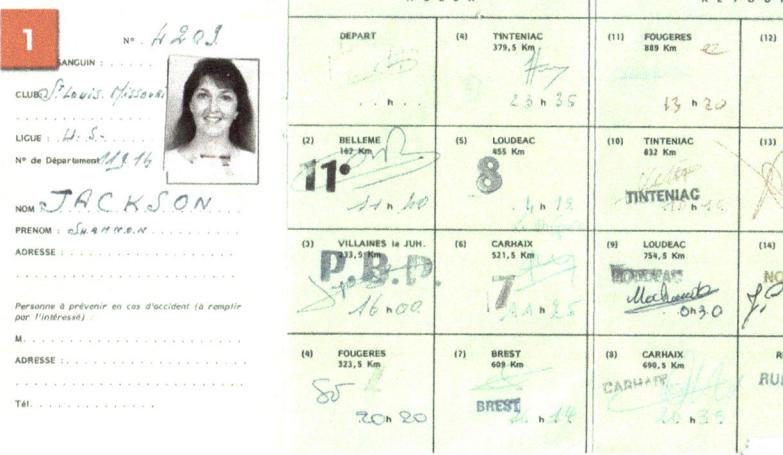

ALLER | **RETOUR**

DÉPART	(4) TINTENIAC 379,5 Km	(11) FOUGERES 889 Km	(12) VILLAINES la JUH. 980,5 Km
	2 h 35	13 h 20	VILLAINES 18 h 15
(2) BELLEME 167 Km	(5) LOUDEAC 455 Km	(10) TINTENIAC 832 Km	(13) BELLEME 1052 Km
11° · 14 h 00	8 · 4 h 15	TINTENIAC	BELLEME 03 h 00
(3) VILLAINES la JUH. 233,5 Km	(6) CARHAIX 521,5 Km	(9) LOUDEAC 754,5 Km	(14) NOGENT le ROI 1137,5 Km
P.B.P. 16 h 00	7 · 11 h 25	LOUDEAC 0 h 30	NOGENT-LE-ROI 8 h 30
(4) FOUGERES 323,5 Km	(7) BREST 609 Km	(8) CARHAIX 690,5 Km	RUEIL - MALMAISON 1215 Km
20 h 20	BREST h 15	CARHAIX 20 h 35	RUEIL 13 h 33

N° 4203

SANGUIN :
CLUB : St Louis Missouri
LIGUE : U.S.
N° de Département : 11916
NOM : JACKSON
PRENOM : SHANNON
ADRESSE :

Personne à prévenir en cas d'accident (à remplir par l'intéressé) :
M.
ADRESSE :
Tél.

CONTROLES SECRETS

ACP [3]

La sécurité des Participants la nuit est assurée par :
RUBAN SCOTCHLITE
BRASSARDS REFLECTORISES
Brevet 3M Minnesota de France
Fabrication CODUPAL à COMPIEGNE
LA CROIX ROUGE FRANCAISE
EST PRESENTE A TOUS LES CONTROLES
Partout et toujours MICHELIN Pneus Hi-Lite
Les Piles ALCALINES VARTA éclairent vos nuits
T.A. vous offre le Bidon Souvenir
du 11e PARIS BREST PARIS
PARIS BREST PARIS est assuré par le GAN

POINTAGE DE L'HEURE D'ARRIVEE
13 h 33
Sur Horodateur

SIMPLEX INTERNATIONAL EQUIPMENT

SIGNATURE DU PARTICIPANT A L'ARRIVEE
Shannon Jackson

HOMOLOGATION

Le Brevet a été accompli en
81 heures 33 minutes

Le Président de l'A.C.P.
J.C. MASSE

La Présidente
de la
Commission des Randonneurs
S. LEPERTEL

N° 4203

RANDONNEURS EUROPEENS

11e
PARIS BREST PARIS
24 au 27 Août 1987

Brevet International Randonneur
1.200 km

organisé
par

L'AUDAX CLUB PARISIEN
(Challenge National Georges NAVET)

Sous le patronage de
Monsieur le Secrétaire d'Etat
auprès du Premier Ministre
chargé de la Jeunesse et des Sports

avec le concours
de la Ville de Rueil Malmaison
de l'Abeille de Rueil
et des Sociétés amies de Normandie
et de Bretagne

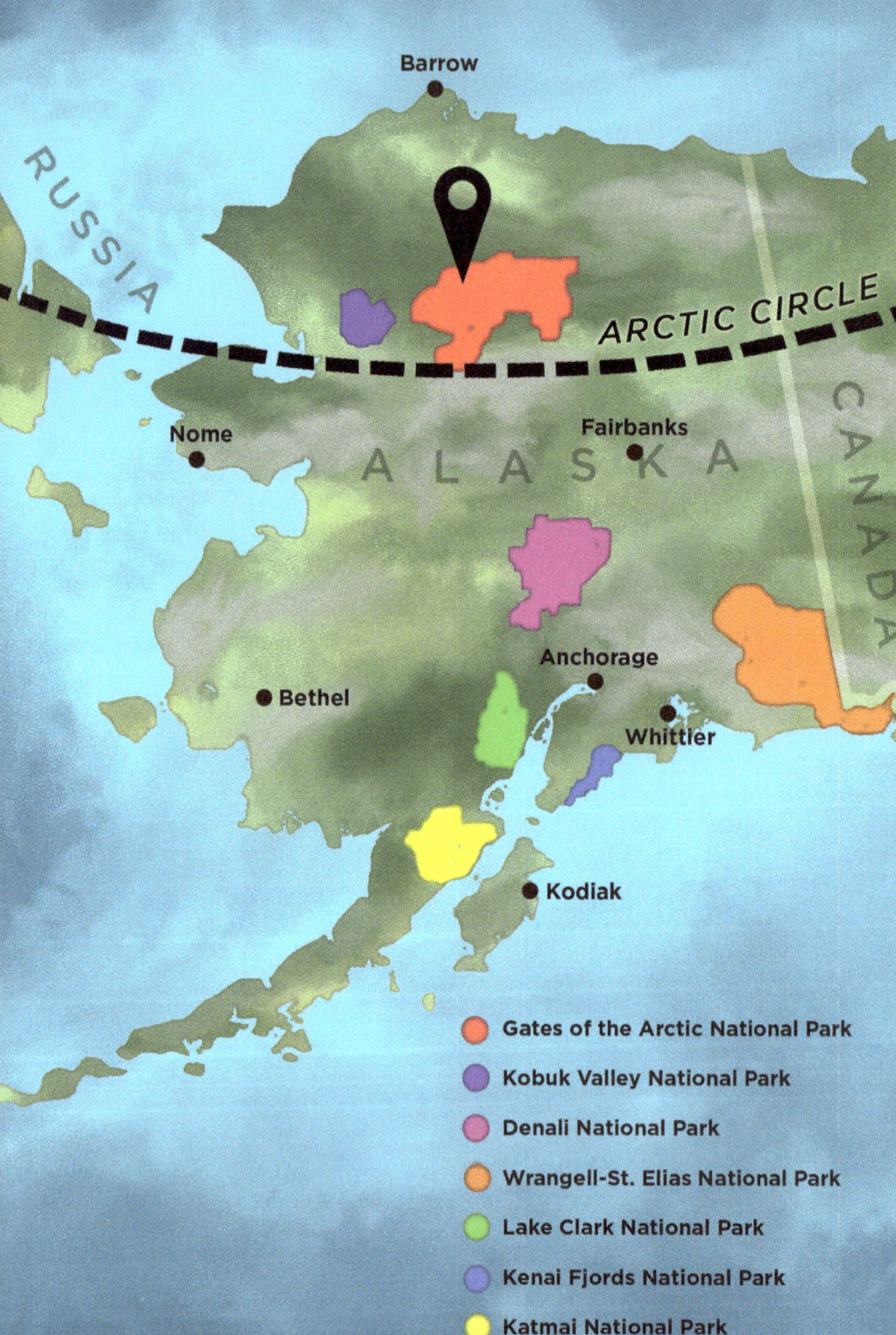

RUSSIA

Barrow

ARCTIC CIRCLE

CANADA

Nome

Fairbanks

A L A S K A

Anchorage

Bethel

Whittler

Kodiak

● Gates of the Arctic National Park

● Kobuk Valley National Park

● Denali National Park

● Wrangell-St. Elias National Park

● Lake Clark National Park

● Kenai Fjords National Park

● Katmai National Park

GATES OF THE ARCTIC
NATIONAL PARK

THE ARCTIC CIRCLE, BROOKS RANGE, ALASKA

"Where the hell is Anaktuvuk?" the pilot yelled, staring at the huge map of Alaska pinned to the wall of the trailer. Frustration emanated from him as he urgently surveyed the land contours surrounding the small Inuit town near Alaska's North Slope. Gleaning the few pieces of information needed to chart a new course, he ran back out to his airplane, mounted the steps, and took off in a second attempt to deliver his passengers to the tiny village in the Arctic Circle. Cheryl, the receptionist at the front desk of the airport, seemed oblivious to the pilot's outburst as she continued her work behind the counter.

When silence returned following the plane's takeoff, I called out to her from our seats on the other side of the room, "Does this happen often? Do pilots frequently have trouble finding the towns they are flying to?"

Cheryl looked over at me and smiled before answering, "Not usually but there's an active brush fire up north and between the smoke and the cloud cover, visually locating the village and the runway can be difficult."

The Frontier Flying Service twin engine airplane was not equipped with instrumentation for landing which forced the pilot to land the aircraft by sight. Although Cheryl's answer made sense, I had been feeling uneasy since Don and I had landed in Bettles Field, Alaska a couple hours earlier.

Witnessing the pilot's uncertainty and multiple efforts to find a well-known destination was not making me feel any better about our future itinerary.

Don and I had just begun our big adventure in northern Alaska. My husband had always been fascinated with the wildness of the Brooks Range and loved the idea of exploring an area that only a handful of people visit in any given year. He had convinced me that backpacking along the Alatna River in the Gates of the Arctic National Park would be a wonderful vacation and an opportunity for great wildlife viewing. We started our trip on August 16, 1990, with an early morning flight out of St. Louis, Missouri and traveled for thirty-six hours on three different airplanes to finally reach Fairbanks, Alaska. The Dalton Highway, from Fairbanks to the northern coastal town of Prudhoe Bay, was built in 1974 for the Trans Alaska Pipeline but was closed to the public until 1994. In 1990, flying was the only way to visit Gates of the Arctic National Park and remains the primary option as the Dalton Highway only skirts close to the eastern perimeter of the park and no roads were ever built within its boundary. From Fairbanks, Frontier Flying Service flew small passenger planes to Bettles Field, a small community located thirty-five miles into the Arctic Circle. From there, Sourdough Air Service managed a bush pilot operation which transported hikers and hunters in and out of the Brooks Range and the National Park.

My state of nervousness was a mixture of excitement about starting our journey, combined with the stark realization that all semblance of normalcy had been left behind the moment I stepped off the Frontier Airlines plane in the tiny town of Bettles Field. My senses were bombarded by the harshness of living and surviving in the Arctic Circle. Rusty equipment and peeling paint was the standard in a place where functionality was the only requirement for continued use. The airport runway was an open field where dirt and gravel had been leveled to allow small aircraft to land and takeoff. A couple pieces of firewood were used as chocks to stabilize a plane's tires between flights. A plywood structure served as the airport terminal with a handful of mismatched chairs for seating passengers waiting on routinely delayed flights. Handprinted signage added to the decor and completed the visual presentation of the daily challenges faced by the hardy individuals who worked and lived at this latitude. There was nothing nearby that was clean, shiny, or new. Every item, whether it was furniture, construction materials, mechanical equipment, electronic devices, or general supplies, bore the outrageous expense of having to be flown in from hundreds of miles away. As a result, everything in the town was well used and dilapidated. As I absorbed my surroundings, I realized Bettles Field was just our first step in moving away from civilization. By the end of the day, Don and I would be fully immersed in what was considered one of the most uninhabited and inhospitable places in the world.

Interrupting my musings, Cheryl let us know our bush pilot would be delayed another hour but confirmed we would be flying out later in the day. We had been shocked when told earlier that we might need to find accommodations for the night. An interesting thing about life in the Arctic Circle, flight schedules were all tentative. The weather dictated when a plane ride happened. As was our case, poor weather delayed a client pickup in the Brooks Range which had the domino effect of delaying our being delivered to the Gates of the Arctic National Park. Flight delays of a few hours were routine this far north and postponements of a few days were not uncommon. I was relieved to hear we would not lose a full vacation day and our trip would start roughly as planned.

A short time later, Cheryl called out from across the room, "Your pilot, Jim, is pulling up in his truck. You two can grab your gear and head outside to load up. Jim will drive you over to the lake for takeoff."

Walking down the wooden terminal steps, Don hesitated and then looked at me with a concerned look in his eyes. "Would you go back in and make sure Cheryl has our correct pickup date? I've got a gut feeling something isn't right."

While Don greeted Jim and started loading our packs, I rushed inside to confirm our return flight. "Cheryl, we thought we should check one more time to make sure you had the right pickup date for us. What day do you have us scheduled for?" All Sourdough Air Service bush pilot flights were handwritten in a calendar style ledger. As Cheryl repeatedly flipped back and forth through the pages of the book, my heart rate increased.

Sheepishly, Cheryl looked up at me and said, "I can't find your pickup date on the schedule. It must be on a note somewhere and not entered in the book yet. What day do you want us to come get you?"

Stunned by her answer and frozen in place, a few seconds passed before I could respond with the date and location. I watched as Cheryl wrote the information in the flight ledger. As she looked up to say goodbye, a look of relief passed between us. Not having our retrieval date documented was a serious mistake that might have threatened our lives. Don and I were being flown two hundred miles into the interior of the Brooks Range away from all civilization. A hike back to Bettles Field would have meant surviving more than a month of subsistence living while enduring a difficult trek across the tundra. Don's intuition had saved us from danger before taking a single step in the park. As the trip unfolded, we would rely on his instincts a few more times to keep us safe.

Our pilot, Jim, was a strong, robust man that looked to be in his late thirties. His manner of dress, along with the state of his truck, blended perfectly into the landscape of Bettles Field. Both were tidy but old and well-worn. The conversation during the short drive to his float plane started out pleasant but quickly turned serious when Jim asked about the type of firearm we were carrying. He was clearly disappointed when we answered that we brought a 44-magnum handgun. Jim went on to explain he much preferred his clients be armed with a large caliber rifle or a shotgun. Reluctantly, he was still willing to deliver us to our desired destination.

Don and I were flown to Gaedeke Lake, the headwaters of the Alatna River in the center of the Gates of the Arctic National Park. The iconic Alaskan river snaked along the valley floor of the northernmost region of the Continental Divide. I had never ridden in a float plane and was curious about landing on water. I was pleasantly surprised by how much smoother the touchdown felt on the surface of the lake compared to tires on asphalt. Jim maneuvered the plane across the lake to reach a grassy section of shoreline. After wading to shore, he used a rope to pull the plane as close as he could to firm land. When my first step off the plane's float submerged my boot in water, I quickly understood why Jim wore knee-length rubber boots. The land looked solid but was saturated with water. I would need to become much more astute at recognizing the invisible puddles if my feet were going to stay dry throughout our week of hiking. After unloading our packs from the plane, we said our goodbyes to Jim and reconfirmed we would be waiting for him at the same location the following Saturday.

Standing on the bank of the still lake, we watched Jim smoothly takeoff and ascend over the mountain ridge until he was out of sight. The views from our floatplane had showcased enormous mountains with braided rivers flowing through expansive valleys. The land was massive and remote. As a feeling of extreme solitude descended upon me, I looked up to find Don staring out at the landscape with a smile on his face. He broke the silence by saying, "This place is amazing. Let's find a dry area to set up camp and go exploring." Our Arctic Circle backpack adventure had officially begun.

ARCTIC SURPRISES

After hiking a short distance from Gaedeke Lake, I asked Don to take a photo of me to capture our first few moments in the park. Aside from capturing the vast openness of the landscape, the picture is a reminder of all the new experiences we encountered during the first hour of hiking across the tundra. In a matter of minutes, my cotton khaki pants were damp up to midcalf from brushing against wet vegetation. Cotton clothing had been a terrible choice for the Arctic and ended up buried in the bottom of my pack for the duration of the trip. Fortunately, I brought a pair of synthetic long johns and Gortex outer pants that would become my uniform for the trip only to be alternated with shorts on the warmest of days. Gortex was recently introduced on the market and was touted as the most waterproof product available at the time. Alaska proved to be a great testing ground for the brand. The pants were a success and are still functional thirty years later.

I literally stumbled over my introduction to tussocks, the basketball size bundles of grasses that covered the tundra. From our plane, the Arctic terrain looked smooth and easy to navigate. What we discovered was a minefield of unstable cotton grass clumps, growing as tall as a foot in height and nearly impossible to avoid. My biggest fear was to accidentally step on one while carrying a full backpack, fall off the wobbly mound and sprain or break an ankle. Thankfully, I wore high-cut hiking boots which made me feel a little better about my odds of hurting myself.

Another unique characteristic of the Arctic tundra is the existence of a thick subsurface layer of permanently frozen ground called permafrost. Across the Brooks Range, permafrost can be found one to three feet below the ground. This icy layer of earth is completely nonporous; roots and water cannot penetrate its surface. Only the top layer, called active soil, thaws each summer, and provides a shallow root zone for the bushes and plants to thrive during the short growing season. Spring snow melt and summer rains percolate through the dirt, saturating the active soil until the water, with nowhere else to go, forms standing pools across the terrain. In addition to tussocks, the mosaic of puddles and squishy ground cover added to the challenges of staying upright while walking.

During our plane ride into the park, Jim had told us a story about a hunting party he delivered to the Brooks Range. One of the men in the group had died of a heart attack early in their trip. Without any means of communicating the need for a faster retrieval, the remaining men scraped away the top layer of active soil and laid their friend on the permafrost to preserve his body until their pickup at the end of the following week. The hunting party's handling of their deceased friend was a shocking tale to hear. I wondered if Jim shared the information as a means of ensuring Don and I knew what to do if something happened to one of us. We were being flown into an extremely remote location without any way to call for help. Don and I had talked about the risks of being 100 percent self-reliant during our trip. We understood the many dangers we might encounter during our Arctic adventure but at thirty-eight and twenty-nine years of age, we felt strong, healthy, and ready to tackle any situation that came our way.

Climbing up on the edge of the foothills surrounding Gaedeke Lake, we were able to find a dry, level spot to set up camp. With our tent perched high enough to overlook the Alatna River Valley below us, I marveled at the panorama and the realization that there was not a single tree anywhere in sight. Permafrost inhibited the growth of tree roots. Small alder and willow bushes were in abundance along the riverbanks, but an actual tree was nowhere to be found. My mind started to review the items we had in our packs to resolve our food storage predicament. The traditional method of hanging food high off the ground to keep it safe was not going to work in the Arctic. While Don was setting up our sleeping gear inside the tent, I asked him, "Without trees for hanging the food bags, have you given any thought to how we might keep our food safe from animals?"

"The complete lack of trees surprised me. We should have brought bear canisters. Luckily, most of our food is freeze dried or in air-tight packaging. If something does get into our supplies, the land is covered in berries and there is an abundance of fish and game. We could survive a week living off the land. Any ideas?"

I shared my initial thought of using our pots and lids as a critter alarm system by placing them on the food bags overnight. Building on this concept, Don and I developed a strategy for guarding our supplies. We wrapped our food bags in a small spare tarp and tied it with cord to create a secure bundle which we set a hundred yards from our tent but in direct line of sight from the doorway. Our two pots and lids were strategically balanced to create noise if disturbed which would alert us that our food needed protection from scavengers. August in the Arctic provided almost twenty-four hours of daylight. We experienced a few hours of twilight in the early morning but never a completely dark sky allowing us to verify the animal scavenging our cache was harmless and to run them off. Luckily, we encountered very few intrusions during our entire trip. Bears and wolves in the park experience little or no contact with humans and generally, do not associate people with food. It seemed the larger predators found our human scent to be frightening and they avoided us and our provisions entirely.

Sitting on a rock some distance from our tent, eating my freeze-dried meal, I brought up a topic that had puzzled me all evening, "Where are all the mosquitoes? I haven't seen one since we got here. Have you?"

Don shook his head. "No mosquitoes or biting flies. It is the end of the season, so I was hoping to have fewer insects to deal with, but I sure didn't expect there to be zero bugs on our trip."

"You know how I attract mosquitoes; if there is even one nearby, it will find me."

"Don't jinx us. Just enjoy your dinner and the fact we can eat without having to deal with head nets."

Don's comment reminded me of just how bad our situation could have been and that our being able to sit calmly without the need to swat at pesky insects was a real treat. Grinning widely, I said, "You're right. I'm going to enjoy this moment and hope it lasts the rest of our trip." Our best Arctic surprise was being gifted a week of backpacking in the Brooks Range without mosquitoes. We would celebrate this rare occurrence in an unusual way a few days later.

MIGRATION CELEBRATIONS

We woke up the next morning full of energy and ready to go for a long hike. Our goal for the day was to move our camp ten miles downriver to an area on the map that showed a narrowing of the mountain corridor creating a canyon of sorts. We thought the terrain might naturally funnel animals through the constricted section of land allowing us to see more wildlife. Our first waypoint on the map was the inlet of the Weyahok River, one of many tributaries to the Alatna River. The Weyahok was only five miles from Gaede-ke Lake, and we expected to reach the confluence within a couple hours. Don and I were able to maintain a three to four miles per hour pace back home on our training walks. After falling off a few tussocks, I slowed my stride to safely step over and around the uneven countryside. The day provided a reality check for me regarding my hiking prowess on tundra. The fastest pace I could achieve was a little over a mile an hour. During our lunch break, I shared my frustrations. "I can't believe how slow I am walking. These wiggly tussocks are such a pain but they're still easier to deal with than walking at an angle on the hillsides. It's going to take all day to reach that canyon."

Seemingly unaffected by the terrain, Don replied, "Don't worry about how fast you are going. We have nowhere we have to be, so take your time and don't hurt yourself. We can camp anywhere."

"Do you realize how lucky we are that we changed our drop-off and retrieval to Gaedeke Lake? Can you imagine how hard this trip would have been if we had kept our original itinerary of backpacking to another lake? I thought we could easily cover the distance we originally planned but it would have killed us to walk those miles."

Don thought about my comment for a few seconds and then responded, "We would have covered the ten to fifteen miles each day because we would not have had a choice. Hiking on tundra would have made for some long days, but you and me together? No doubt we would have reached the lake."

Don always believed that we were stronger together and that with each other's support we could meet the challenges life threw our way. His confidence in our abilities made me feel better but, in my mind, we had avoided another disastrous event when we decided to return to Gaedeke Lake for our plane ride back to civilization.

We steadily continued our journey down the river valley for another five hours and reached the narrowed canyon by late evening. Once again, we set up camp on a flat expanse at the base of a foothill, but the natural topography allowed us to be much closer to the water. I could hear the faint trickling of the river in the early morning stillness as I laid in my sleeping bag. When I detected a strange grunting sound in the far distance, I rolled over to find Don grinning as he climbed out of his bag and started to get dressed. Peeking out the tent door, we could see across the valley floor to where a large herd of caribou was feeding on the hillside. I excitedly whispered, "Oh my gosh! There must be a couple hundred out there."

Don said, "I'm guessing they are part of the Porcupine Herd. They migrate down the Alatna from the North Slope to their southern winter-feeding areas. Let's go check them out."

Slowly and as quietly as possible, we fully unzipped the tent door and crawled outside. I grabbed my camera on the way out. There were indeed a few hundred caribou grazing on the lichen and grasses growing on the foothill across from our campsite. I took a few pictures while the morning sun illuminated their bodies against the red, brown, and yellow colors of the autumn ground cover. Looking up and down the river valley, we could see animals in both directions all moving in a southernly flow.

As luck would have it, we had timed our Arctic vacation perfectly with the migration of the famous Porcupine Caribou Herd. The Gates of the Arctic National Park is home to four caribou herds: the Western Arctic, Central Arctic, Teshepuk, and the Porcupine. These herds total over half a million animals with the Porcupine contributing 110,000 ungulates to the count. Unbeknownst to us, we had started our hike down the river valley just ahead of the migrating herd which caught up to us overnight and now surrounded our campsite. Our vacation became a migration celebration as thousands of caribou leisurely walked downriver alongside us for the duration of our trip.

Over the next couple days, we moved farther into the narrow canyon, hiking with the herd. The mountain walls funneled the caribou into tighter groupings across the constricted valley floor. Additional water runoff from the mountainsides nourished the alder and willow bushes resulting in taller, thicker vegetation along the riverbanks. Using the plants for cover, Don and I were able to get quite close to the animals to watch their behavior. The caribou constantly grunted and snorted, producing sounds similar to deep belly belches. Mixed in with the vocal communications was another unique noise created by their ligaments slipping over bones in their feet. At first, I thought the clickety-clack I was hearing was caused by hooves on rocks but then I realized the rhythmic sound was produced on all types of terrain. A group of caribou walking together sounded very much like a crowd of people playing castanets. There was a soothing musicality to the herd with the tinkling of their hooves and their burping notes of communication. I found myself smiling at the pleasing presence they imbued on the tundra.

By midweek, we found the caribou had accepted us as part of the landscape allowing us to walk the canyon corridor alongside them. Our closest encounter occurred one afternoon when I decided to wash my hair, enlisting Don's help with pouring rinse water over my head while I squatted on the rocky riverbank. I was not paying attention to anything but the icy cold water giving me an ice cream headache and the tightening of my hair follicles to the point I thought my hair might break off at the root. While I was wringing out my hair, I heard the familiar grunting and clicking sounds of a caribou. Waving at Don to get his attention, I pointed at the thick willow beside me and silently mouthed the word, "caribou." When we stood up to look over the tall growing vegetation, the tips of enormous antlers came into view. A large bull sporting a rack that spanned six feet in length was nibbling on lichen a few feet away from us. He slowly raised his head to look our way, acknowledged our presence, then moved calmly toward the open tundra. I quickly grabbed my camera, but by the time I focused on the bull, he was several yards away. Although I was not able to get the close-up photo I wanted, the picture I took will always remind me of our extraordinary hike alongside the caribou in the park.

THE BARE "BEAR" NECESSITIES

We started our return hike to Gaedeke Lake the following morning. Caribou passed by as we moved upstream against their southerly flow. The tundra seemed easier to navigate now that my pack was lighter with half my food consumed. I had also developed a good feel for how to walk safely on roly-poly tussocks allowing me to move at a faster speed. When Don and I reached the confluence of the Weyohuk and Alatna Rivers, we decided to make camp for the night. Throughout our trek, we had marveled at how we could hike all day and still see our starting location miles away. The land was so open and expansive, we could easily detect the shimmering of Gaedeke Lake five miles upstream. Enjoying our dinner while watching a few straggling caribou meandering down the valley, we noticed a strange change in the weather. The temperature had grown very warm, and now with the stillness of the evening, the air was not cooling. I woke the next morning to find Don dressed in shorts, out gathering blueberries for our breakfast cereal. Wild blueberry bushes grew across the tundra. In the harshness of the arctic climate, the low growing shrubs were small but produced the sweetest of berries. Apparently, the bears were also enjoying the fruit. We frequently hiked past piles of their blue tinted scat.

I emerged from the tent and noticed the early morning air felt exceptionally warm against my bare legs and arms. I mimicked Don by dressing in shorts and a T-shirt to enjoy the summer heatwave that seemed to be moving through northern Alaska. During breakfast, Don started a discussion about the Arctic and early humans. "Throughout our whole trip, I have been thinking about how little this land has probably changed over thousands of years. So few people visit this part of the world that it seems untouched by human hands. Can you picture a wooly mammoth crossing the tundra being chased by a Neanderthal man wielding a spear? I want to celebrate our trip with an *Early Man Day*."

"What does that mean exactly?"

"We have a really unique situation here. We are in the Arctic where no other people are going to show up or surprise us, there are no mosquitoes, and the weather is weirdly warm. Let's pretend we are early humans and walk around naked today!"

Nearly choking on my granola, I said, "Seriously? No clothes?"

Don smiled and wiggled his eyebrows. "It could be fun. Let's get naked!"

Chuckling as I undressed, I threw my clothes back in the tent and grabbed my camera. This was one of our crazier ideas of fun and I wanted to take a picture to document the day. My favorite photo of the trip shows Don, standing on a large rock, wearing only his boots, and staring out at the landscape. No one could have predicted what happened next. While I was setting my camera back in the tent, Don and I heard a commotion in the alder bushes along the river. Seconds later, a deer broke through the vegetation and came charging up the hill heading straight for our camp. To my utter shock and disbelief, the deer was being chased by a huge grizzly bear focused solely on capturing a meal of venison. As the deer ran through our camp, I lunged for the bear spray just outside the tent while Don picked up the handgun and started waving his arms and yelling at the bear. Luck was with us as our antics not only caught the bear's attention but surprised the animal enough that the grizzly made a ninety-degree turn and ran straight up a steep mountainside away from our campsite. Frozen in place from the shock of the encounter, I watched this magnificent animal easily climb the vertical terrain; muscles rippling as the early morning sun reflected off its fur. Far too many seconds passed before I recovered enough to grab my camera and take a photo. Although the bear can only be seen as a small image on the pictures I took, the vision of his powerful body looms large in my memory. Don's version of our encounter has been recounted throughout the years with his own unique description. "There I was, standing naked on a rock facing down a huge charging grizzly bear who took one look at my enormous dangly parts and with great fear, ran off in the other direction!" Regardless of what action or startling sight caused the bear to flee, Don and I were grateful that our unbelievably absurd grizzly encounter would always be a story with a happy ending.

THE ARCTIC—UNIQUELY WILD

We spent our last day in the Arctic hiking near our retrieval point, searching the land for hidden treasures. Don found a set of caribou antlers attached to a skull which made us think our grizzly bear had hunted successfully on at least one occasion in this location. All the streams in the area seemed to have an abundance of arctic grayling that could be seen darting through the rock beds when we approached the water's edge. In the late afternoon, Don and I decided to try our hand at fishing. Although we hadn't packed a rod and reel, we brought some monofilament line and a spinner hook that we tied to the end of my hiking pole. With a little effort and a few quick flicks of my wrist, the grayling kept us entertained as they repeatedly hit my line. With our grizzly bear experience still fresh in our minds, our angling day was limited to catch and release. Neither of us wanted to attract another bear into our camp with the aroma of fresh fish in the air. We made sure we washed the grayling smell off our hands at the end of the day before making camp far from our fishing hole.

Our trip to the Arctic offered a uniquely wild backpacking experience. The caribou migration was amazing to see and had attracted bears and wolves. Eagles, hawks, and foxes lived in the tundra and fed on the abundance of smaller game such as arctic hares, ground squirrels and the streams full of fish. During dinner on our last night, Don commented, "There are so many animals here. The whole area feels alive!"

"It's also strangely quiet," I replied. We were both awed by the silence that had surrounded us throughout our vacation. There were no people, cars or airplanes making noise—only the wind blowing, the rivers gurgling and the animals calling to one another.

After pausing for a moment to look around at the beautiful landscape and mountains standing guard over the valley, Don said, "I'm glad we came. I really enjoyed being here." I felt the same way. We had visited one of the most remote places in the world and witnessed the natural wonders of a land untouched by civilization.

ARCTIC CIRCLE PHOTOS

1 Flown into the Arctic Circle to the tiny frontier town of Bettles Field.

2 Plywood structure for airport terminal—everything was well worn at this latitude.

3 Flown to Gaedeke Lake—our starting location for our hike in the Brooks Range, Alaska.

4 First few minutes after landing on Gaedeke lake—khaki cotton pants were wet and a terrible choice for the Arctic, introduced to tussocks and the vastness of the land.

5 Washing my hair in the icy waters of the Alatna River.

6 Bull caribou surprised us by the river.

7 Don's *Early-Human Day*!

8 Catch and release fishing for grayling using my hiking pole.

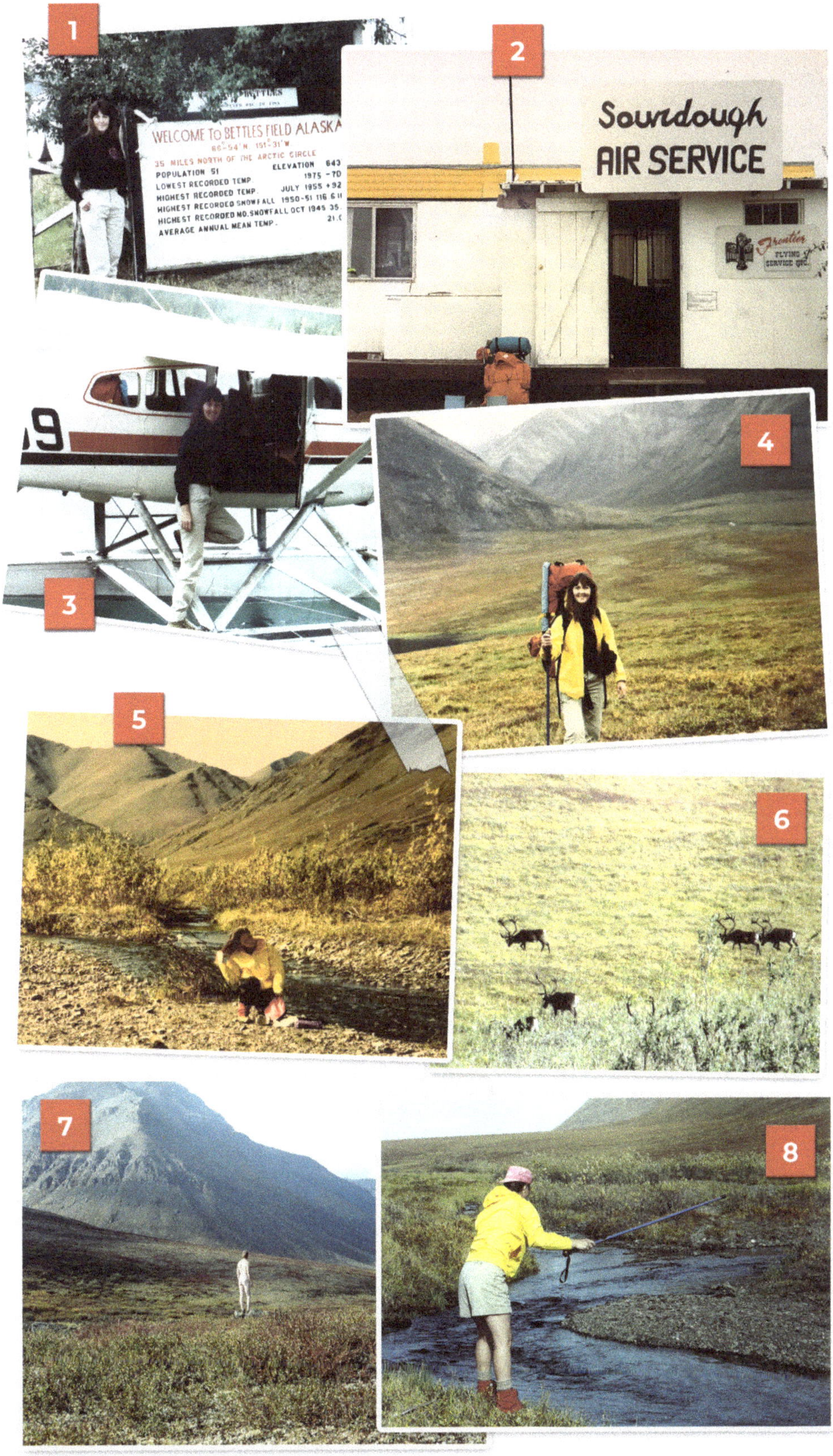
1
WELCOME TO BETTLES FIELD ALASKA
35 MILES NORTH OF THE ARCTIC CIRCLE
ELEVATION 643
POPULATION 51
1975 -70
LOWEST RECORDED TEMP.
JULY 1955 +92
HIGHEST RECORDED TEMP.
HIGHEST RECORDED SNOWFALL 1950-51
HIGHEST RECORDED MO. SNOWFALL OCT 1945
AVERAGE ANNUAL MEAN TEMP.
2
Sourdough
AIR SERVICE
Frontier
FLYING SERVICE INC.
3
4
5
6
7
8

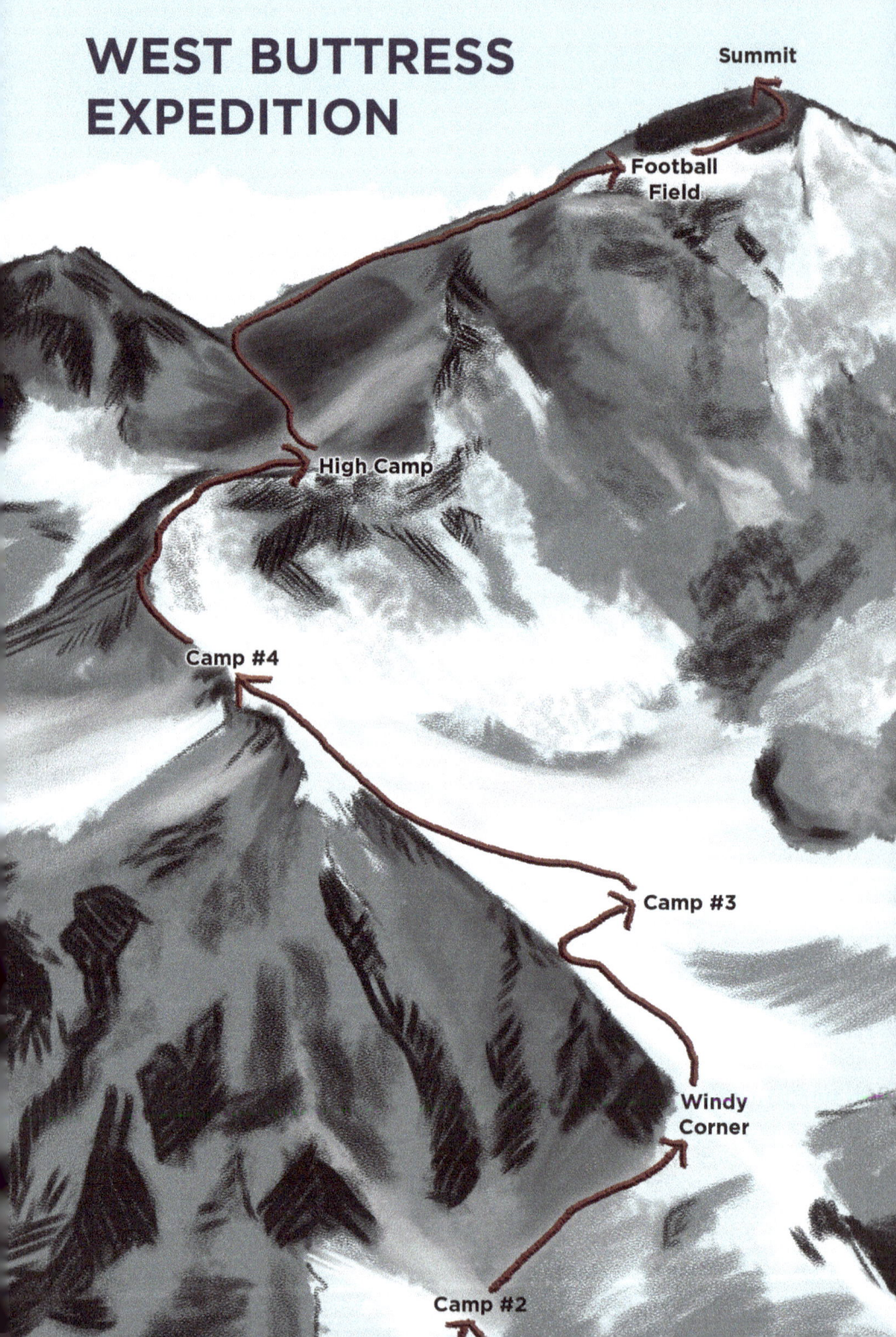

DENALI
WEST BUTTRESS EXPEDITION

Summit

Football Field

High Camp

Camp #4

Camp #3

Windy Corner

Camp #2

DENALI

AS THE PLANE TOUCHED down on the tarmac in Anchorage, Alaska, I found myself feeling appropriately tired and stiff from ten hours of traveling but also strangely nervous. With an elevated heart rate and a stomach full of butterflies, I excitedly thought to myself, "I'm here. This is really happening!" Don and I were going to climb Denali, the tallest mountain in North America.

Spring of 1993 would be the start of a new life for me and Don. We were quitting our jobs working for Fortune 100 companies and moving across the country to a small mountain town in Idaho. We chose to start our journey by tackling Alaska's highest peak.

Don and I arrived at the Anchorage airport in early afternoon on April 30th after a long day's travel starting in Philadelphia, Pennsylvania. After retrieving four large duffel bags from the luggage conveyor belt, we started scouting the airport in search of the rest of our climbing team. It was not hard to locate the Rainier Mountaineering Incorporated (RMI) group. We found two men in a seating area by the door; each surrounded by two large duffel bags. "Are you guys with RMI?" I asked. They smiled and nodded yes. After shaking hands and exchanging names, the conversation shifted to mountaineering and easily continued for the next hour and a half as teammates arrived from all over the lower forty-eight states. There were three RMI guides and nine clients in our group. Once everyone arrived at the airport, we loaded our gear into an old school bus for the three-hour drive to Talkeetna. Reserving the front six rows for seating, the rest of the bus was filled from floor to ceiling with expedition gear.

April 30th was a gorgeously sunny day with very few clouds which set the scene for the most unforgettable bus ride north. There was a buzzing of conversation with everyone getting to know each other for the first two-and-a-half hours of travel until we topped a large hill about twenty miles from Talkeetna. All conversation came to an abrupt halt and was followed by silence as Denali became visible on the horizon. The beautiful day afforded us the luxury of seeing the mountain in all its glory without any clouds to obstruct our view. The guides were as impressed as the clients and asked the bus driver to pull over so we could all get out and take a few pictures.

The photo Don took was not able to capture the enormity of the mountain. Denali is a part of the Alaska Range and is surrounded by numerous mountains with peaks ranging from 12,000 to 17,000 feet of elevation. The view before us was shocking because it showed this magnificent giant at 20,310 feet towering over them all. Smiles broke out on everyone's faces. After taking a few photographs, we boarded the bus for the remaining miles to Talkeetna. There was little discussion for the duration of the bus ride. The atmosphere was filled with anxiety and nervous anticipation of the adventure ahead. A group dinner and an early bedtime ended the day, a perfect beginning to our trip.

SAFETY IS NO ACCIDENT

Our first full day together was a busy one. After an eight o'clock breakfast at the Roadhouse restaurant, we met at the Hudson Air Service hanger. The focus of our gathering was to ensure all the team gear was in working order, to inventory food supplies and for the guides to review our personal gear. RMI had sent a personal packing list to each client; they knew from experience that everyone would regard the list as a place to start and add unnecessary luxury items. Little did we realize just how heavy our packs were going to be once we split up the team gear and added it to our personal stash. It was the guides' job to convince us that we did not need items such as one client's collection of books which included *War and Peace*. Humorously, the biggest point of contention involved the subject of toilet paper. The guides encouraged us to take only one roll each for twenty-one days. As a woman, that logic did NOT compute. One of our guides was a woman named Emily. She encouraged the ladies to use a handful of snow for wiping, conserving toilet paper for when it was truly needed. After careful consideration, I took two rolls for myself. There were hardships I could endure but running out of toilet paper was not one of them.

The team gear included tents, cook stoves, pots with lids, food, fuel, climbing ropes and bamboo wands for flagging safe routes around crevasses. Each tent was erected and inspected for any tears in the fabric or faulty zippers and to ensure all poles, stakes and tie-downs were present and functioning. The same care was taken to ensure camp stoves were operating efficiently and that our climbing ropes were in excellent condition. Once on the mountain, we had to be completely self-sufficient.

Once all the items were reviewed and approved, we packed our gear and supplies back into duffle bags to be transported to base camp. The weather looked promising for flying out the next day. But before we could receive clearance, we had one more important step to complete at the ranger station. Each climber was required to pay a climbing fee, sign a waiver, and watch a presentation on the rules for climbing Denali. There was no new information shared in the video, but it was a good reminder of the dangers and responsibilities we faced as mountaineers.

More than one thousand people attempt to climb the mountain each year but only half of them make it to the summit. The route is over twenty miles long with 13,000 feet of elevation gain to the top. With a summit elevation of 20,310 feet and subarctic location, Denali is one of the coldest mountains on earth, rivaling Everest with severity of weather. A handful of people die every year on the mountain while attempting to reach its peak. The year before our climb was the deadliest with eleven fatalities. The park ranger ended the presentation by reminding us to work as a team and take care of each other. With this requirement completed, we headed over to a local Mexican food restaurant for a group dinner and then retired early to bed. Tomorrow we would finally face the mountain.

BASE CAMP

The group met a little after eight in the morning at the Hudson Air Service hangar. Don and I were on the second flight to base camp at 7,200 feet on the Kahiltna Glacier. Tree line ended at approximately 2,000 feet and all the mountain above this elevation was encased in snow and ice year around. The plane had hard rubber tires for taxiing on asphalt and was also equipped with skis for landing on the snow. As the forecast predicted, it was another lovely clear day and perfect for the forty-five-minute flight to the base of the mountain. With one plane making multiple ninety-minute trips, it took all morning to get the team and our large volume of gear to base camp. Once we arrived, we immediately started leveling areas on the hard packed snow for our tents. We then constructed a snow ledge for the cooking area and unpacked our gear for our first night on Denali. Most of us had come from cities close to sea level so the effects of an altitude of 7,200 feet were noticeable. I found all the tasks made me a little winded. Spending the night at base camp would give the team a chance to acclimate.

Every climber was expected to haul a portion of the enormous amount of team gear up the mountain. We were each given a small plastic sled that we attached to the hip belt of our packs using a short length of rope. Distribution of food supplies and equipment was based on percent body weight. I weighed one hundred forty-five pounds. Fully loaded, I had fifty-five pounds of personal items on my back and would be pulling another fifty-five pounds of team gear on the sled. The stronger, heavier men carried several more pounds of team gear. And the guides carried even more.

Our three guides consisted of two men, Brent and Mark, and one incredibly strong woman named Emily. After watching Emily wrestle her backpack into place, I asked her about the unconventional method she used for loading up. "My pack weighs a huge percentage of my weight. I don't want to throw my back out trying to lift it and swing it around my body, so I came up with an alternative system," she explained. Emily would lay her pack on the ground, lay down on top of it and tighten all the straps across her chest and hips. She would then roll over with the pack on her back like a turtle shell. From there, she would use core muscles and arm strength to pull her knees under her and stand. Emily's system seemed to work for her, however, I was content to use the more standard style of hefting the weight onto my knee and having Don help me lift the pack onto my back. Fortunately, the higher we climbed, our packs and sled would continue to get lighter and more manageable with the consumption of food and fuel over the next three weeks. The load was heavy but tolerable.

Once our little tent city was erected, we roped up into three, four-person teams, and practiced the rest step method of walking and crevasse-rescue. Walking around on the flat, safe snow at base camp allowed us to review and sharpen our rope handling skills while getting to know our teammates. Don and I knew only one person in our group, Cyndi, whom we met during a winter RMI climbing course on Mt. Rainier. Karen, who was from the east coast, made a third of our team female. In 1993, not many women were climbing big mountains. I was excited to have all the women on the expedition with us. Little did I know that half would not complete the trek. The rest of the team consisted of Joe, Greg, Charles, Pat, and Dick. Pat was a friend of Cyndi's. She told us that Pat was an incredibly strong and experienced climber. Those characteristics would become apparent as our journey unfolded and I would be forever grateful that Pat was a member of our team.

RMI required everyone on a Denali expedition to complete one or more RMI climbing courses on Mt. Rainier in Washington state. Only the individuals who were able to show proficiency handling an ice axe, managing a rope, and hiking at elevation were approved to become clients on Denali. Don and I had taken two of these courses during the last nine months. Because of this required training, we were comfortable being roped up with strangers and relying on them for our safety.

Don took several pictures in base camp. The scenery was stunning. The views were unlike anything I had ever seen, a landscape of snow with towering granite peaks in every direction. Standing in front of my tent, I could see Mt. Hunter rising in front of me at 14,573 feet and to my right, Mt. Foraker at 17,400 feet. There were no browns, greens, or vegetation of any kind to be found, just a pristine white blanket adorned with colorful dots of tents and climbers working to ready themselves for the adventure ahead.

There were a couple of independent climbers ahead of us, but our RMI guided group would be the first team to ascend the mountain in 1993. Our guides would have the responsibility of establishing fixed ropes in the areas that needed them. They would also carry many extra wands to flag crevasses on the route. Don and I chose to climb in the early season because we thought it would be safer. In early season the snow bridges, covering hidden crevasses, are more likely to be frozen and can be walked over without collapsing. Also, we wanted fewer people on the mountain and a less crowded climbing experience, so we chose the first available team date. At this moment looking at all the glorious, untracked snow surrounding me, I was happy with our decision.

CAMP ONE: 9,500 FEET

Our first day of hiking started out with lots of sunshine. I was so worried about being cold on the trip and here I was dying of heat. The temperature on the lower mountain rose to fifty degrees in the middle of the day. The reflection of the sun off the snow, however, felt much warmer and was blinding. I was happy to be wearing my glacier glasses with dark lenses and frame protection that blocked the sun's reflective glare. Our expedition began with an easy walk on what has been coined by climbers as Heartbreak Hill. The route loses elevation for a few miles before it finally starts to climb. It took us six hours of climbing to regain the elevation lost during the first two hours of walking in the morning.

The weather can change rapidly on the mountain, and our first day was proof of that. The sunshine and warmth quickly disappeared as clouds rolled up the glacier and engulfed us in snow. We set up our first camp at 9,500 feet elevation in a whiteout. Don was feeling a bit nauseated when we reached camp; we suspected he was dehydrated from the heat. He was not very hungry at dinner. Of course, I was ravenous and had no trouble finishing my portion of food. I went to bed a little wet and weary, but content. Nighttime on the mountain was never dark. There were a few hours of twilight but never a totally dark sky. I wondered if the light would impair my ability to sleep but found I was tired enough each evening that an illuminated tent did not keep me awake.

CAMP TWO: 11,000 FEET

We awoke to a sunny day. Don's stomach was still feeling a little weak, so having to face instant oatmeal for breakfast was hard for him. He did his best to choke down a packet and ate a granola bar to round out the meal. RMI provided our breakfast and dinner meals. Clients were required to bring lunch and snack items to eat throughout the day. Our routine was to stop every couple of hours for about fifteen minutes. We had been trained to follow the same regimen at each break. We began by removing our packs and immediately putting on a warm coat. We would then retrieve our food bag and sit on our packs to get weight off our feet. After eating a snack and drinking water, we applied another layer of sunscreen and urinated just before the rest time ended. There is no such thing as privacy on a rope team. No one was allowed to unclip from the rope at any time. Therefore, taking a pee meant announcing you needed to go and then dropping your drawers. Privacy only occurred when the other members of the team turned their heads.

The first order of business when setting up camp was to locate a snow drift or prominent feature in the snow and dig out an area for a latrine. By excavating a space, the size of a recliner, we created a three-sided shelter in which "to do our business." A contractor bag placed in the center and supported by crisscrossed bamboo wands, acted as our toilet. The rule for disposing of solid waste on the mountain was to carry the garbage bag until we passed a large crevasse and then pitch the bag into the chasm. One of the hardest things our head guide asked us ladies to do was to urinate outside of the bag. Brent wanted to avoid carrying frozen urine. I understood why he did not want the extra weight, but trying to control my body was a truly difficult task. It was much easier for the boys to comply with the request. I will say that no one lingered while squatting over the makeshift commode in the morning. The cold wind blowing across tender skin made everyone quick and efficient. Later, hiking behind Brent, I watched him throw the bag into the first crevasse we crossed. I wondered what the bottom of that fissure must look like with thousands of bags of poop.

I recently read that waste management rules have completely changed over the years on Denali. Now all climbers are issued a Clean Mountain Can (CMC) by the Park Service. They resemble plastic paint cans and to use them, the owner unscrews the top, squats over the opening, and then puts the lid back on. Mountaineering teams must return the same number of used CMC's that are checked out to them at the start of their expedition. Climbers are required to haul their waste up and down the mountain. I guess my concern for our method was warranted after all.

Once again, our sunny morning turned into a snowstorm late in the afternoon. We arrived at 11,000 feet in a whiteout after many hours of hiking. Once there, the team started the routine of setting up camp. We even cut blocks of snow to build a wall around our tent city. That night I got an intense migraine. I drank extra water and did pressure breathing exercises hoping it would go away. Pressure breathing is a technique taught to all climbers by RMI. It is performed by pursing your lips tight and blowing hard which forces air across the membranes of the lungs delivering more oxygen into the blood. At high elevations, it can significantly help with altitude sickness symptoms such as a headache. I suffered intense pain from midnight to five o'clock in the morning. The extreme migraine pain caused severe nausea but fortunately, no vomiting. Nighttime temperatures were dropping to five degrees and the thought of being sick outside in the cold was not a welcome idea. At breakfast the next morning, I was now the one staring at my oatmeal and wondering how I was going to get it down. I knew today was going to be a long hard effort, so I forced myself to eat my cereal.

The agenda for the day required climbing up to 13,200 feet to an area called Windy Corner to cache a load of gear. We would then hike back down to our camp at 11,000 feet. RMI's philosophy was that climbers acclimate better to altitude by making high carries and then sleeping at a lower elevation. The 2,200 feet of climbing was riddled with crevasses and vertical enough to require that we wear crampons. Even with the spikes on our feet, the mountain side was too steep to walk straight up so we traversed in switchbacks from side to side. That made the hiking easier, but with a sled full of gear, gravity was constantly tipping our sleds over or making them slide downhill and pulling us with them.

With the route sharply tipped to the sun, we also encountered our first rotten snow which caused a few snow bridges to collapse under our weight. Don was in line behind Brent and on three occasions, Brent walked right over a snow bridge only to have it cave in when Don set foot on it. Two of his falls were stopped knee deep but one fall buried his body up to his shoulders. Don said, "It is the strangest feeling to be standing one minute and the next hanging by your arm pits with your feet dangling in a crevasse." Anytime a climber goes down, anyone who experiences or sees the fall yells "FALLING" and everyone on the rope team immediately assumes a self-arrest position. This position requires they drop to their bellies, dig their toes and the pick end of their ice axe into the snow to save their teammate from a deadly fall. In addition to Don, Karen dropped into two crevasses as well. No one was hurt, but we all spent a lot of time laying on the snow keeping each other safe. At the end of the day, I was exhausted from the combination of climbing a very steep route, wallowing around on the snow arresting falls and managing the adrenaline dump that came with each shout of FALLING. I was glad to get back to 11,000 feet and already have camp set up.

It was our guide Emily's, 30th birthday. After showing such strength and leadership during our trip, Emily ended the day with a visit to the latrine where she slipped on a patch of frozen urine and fell on her shoulder. She fell hard enough and at the perfect angle to break her collarbone. Her birthday would be her last day with us. Luckily, Emily was able to head down the next morning with a few members of the medical station staff who were descending from 14,200 feet to basecamp for supplies. No one was allowed to hike on the glacier alone.

REST DAY

On May 7th, our fifth day on the mountain, Brent decided we could all use a rest day. We woke to a sunny morning which made part of me restless to keep going because of the great weather but the other part of me was worn out and happy to take a break. With the day off from climbing, I capitalized on the opportunity to hang all my clothing, shoe liners and sleeping bag in the sunshine to thoroughly dry. Normally, I acted as a human clothes dryer at night while sleeping. At the end of each day, I changed into my bedtime clothing of dry socks, underwear and base layer top and bottoms. My wet hiking clothes were stuffed in my sleeping bag with me so that my body heat would dry them overnight. The bag became crowded with my boot liners, water bottle and pee bottle crammed in with me as well. In fact, anything that I didn't want to freeze such as sunscreen, ChapStick and lotion, had to be included in the bag.

Overnight temperatures were around five degrees and would only get colder the higher we climbed. I had not been concerned about the cold nights because of a special down sleeping bag Don purchased for me. The bag was rated to fifty degrees below zero and was filled with so many feathers the loft fluffed up a full thirteen inches off the ground. Most sleeping bags lay flat and unassuming; mine commanded attention through height and form. When ordering the bag, Don called the manufacturer and talked to one of the company representatives. At first, the salesman discouraged him from buying this bag for a climb on Denali because the model was designed for even colder conditions like the extremes of Antarctica. Don finally said to the man, "I don't think you fully understand my concern. If my wife gets cold on this trip, I will never be able to go on another one and I will never hear the end of it."

The salesman paused for a few seconds and then politely responded, "Mr. Jackson, I will be happy to send our bag to you. It will be perfect for your wife." It proved to be an ideal choice for the expedition and our marriage, as I slept warm and comfortable every night.

Our rest day was also Pat's birthday. Brent broke out a special treat for breakfast; he served Cheerios. You would have thought it was an actual cake given the way all of us reacted. After several days of instant oatmeal, Cheerios made the meal feel like a celebration. Dinner that night was a delicious meal of lasagna. All our evening meals consisted of three courses. They started with a hot cup of soup, then a boil in the bag entrée, and some type of starch side dish or dessert to add calories. Menu entrées included turkey casserole, Bar-B-Q pork, and beef stew. They all seemed to taste good to me. Perhaps being extremely tired and exhausted at the end of each day improved the flavor of the food being served. We enjoyed all the meals and went to bed satisfied and content each evening.

CAMP THREE: 14,200 FEET

Everyone woke up well rested and ready for the big day ahead. We were climbing 3,200 feet to the 14,200-foot elevation camping area known as Genet Basin which also housed a small ranger station and medical tent. The day went smoothly with crevasses marked by wands from our previous carry to Windy Corner. No one took a fall, and the sun kept the temperature comfortable throughout the early afternoon. Once again, snow clouds rolled up the glacier at the end of the day and engulfed us for the last seven hundred feet of climbing. The team set up camp in a snowstorm at negative five degrees Fahrenheit. As Don and I were securing the last tie down rope, Brent came by our tent to talk to us. "It's been a really long day and I know you are tired. Get your gear unpacked and get into your warm, dry clothes and bag. Set your food dish out in the vestibule. I will fill it up and deliver your dinner, so you are not standing out in the snowstorm to eat. Drink all your water while you wait and leave your empty bottle for Mark to refill before you go to sleep tonight." I was so relieved not having to stay outside in the elements while our dinner was being prepared.

In addition to my dry set of clothes for sleeping, I also put on a wool sweater we were told to bring. Sitting in my bag with my upper body exposed, I wore my Marmot 8,000-meter parka. Half the team had purchased the jacket for their Denali trip. There was so much down in the coat that when we stood together during our meals, we all looked like the Michelin Man in the tire commercial with big, round, puffy upper bodies. The coats were amazingly warm, and I was glad to have it with me, especially this evening. The overnight temperature dropped to minus fifteen degrees. I thought that was pretty darn cold. I had no idea what was in store for me in just a couple days.

We stayed in our sleeping bags until the sun kissed our tent the next morning. I awoke to a very frosty tent interior. Even with the door and rear window unzipped just a crack to let the water vapor from our breath escape, the inside of the tent was heavily frosted. The best piece of equipment I had was not my $750 sleeping bag but my seventy-five-cent sponge. That sponge was invaluable in mopping up all the water that dripped from melting frost or the snow that fell off our coats when we entered the tent. Being able to wipe down the walls and the tent floor helped us manage our moisture issues daily. I swore I would never go camping again without one.

Our goal for the day was to hike back down to 13,200 feet and pick up our cache at Windy Corner. We walked right by it on the previous day's ascent because we already had full sleds and packs and did not want to try to handle the extra weight on such a long climb. It was an easy descent with empty packs. We retrieved the cached items and hiked back up to camp three. To assist in further acclimation, Brent had us work on building an igloo for the cooking area and cutting blocks of snow to create a wall around our tents. I would have much rather lazed around in my tent all afternoon, but Brent kept telling us that we would feel better if we forced our bodies to work at each new level of altitude. I had already experienced two nights struggling with nausea and headaches. Since I suffer from migraines, I figured the discomfort was just my head causing me grief, but now I also questioned if maybe I had a touch of altitude sickness as well.

The original client paperwork sent from RMI discussed the prevalence of altitude sickness during mountaineering expeditions. Knowing that each of us was likely to encounter nausea, they requested that each client bring their favorite food item for a snack on the climb. They wanted us to have on hand a food that would be appealing even when we felt ill. For me, that was white chocolate covered Oreo cookies. In 1993, these cookies were only on the store shelves during the Christmas holiday. I loved them. I bought several boxes and stuck them in the freezer so I could take them on our expedition. Walking around all day at an altitude of 14,200 feet with a slightly soured stomach, I started to understand why RMI had made the request. I had not broken out my special treats yet but at this point I was thinking today just might be the day.

The other problem I was facing was—my face. Even though I applied sunscreen repeatedly throughout the climb, the intense reflection of the sun's rays off the snow fried my skin. I now had large, quarter size blisters on my face and my lips were swollen and blistered as well. Unbeknownst to me, Brent had spoken to all the other clients and encouraged them to say they did not have a mirror if I asked for one. I must have looked hideous because he was afraid if I saw myself, I would demand to be taken off the mountain. Don and I did not bring a mirror, so all I could do was ask him how my face looked. He purposely remained calm while describing my condition. "You have four large blisters on your cheeks and lower jawline. They are crusting over and should be healed in a couple days." He ended with a quick, "You'll be fine." Don suggested we tie a bandanna across my face to protect it from additional sun. As it turned out, ignorance is bliss. Not knowing how bad my face looked, I never considered giving up on our goal.

Karen, however, admitted defeat and demanded to be taken down and flown off the mountain. The explanation she gave Brent was that she was cold, tired, and didn't want to go any farther. Her quitting was devastating news that impacted the entire team. RMI Mountaineering guidelines for Denali included two important rules: no individual can ever climb alone, and clients can never be left without a guide. We had already lost Emily on the lower part of the mountain when she broke her clavicle which left only two guides, Mark, and Brent, to lead our expedition. If Mark guided Karen off the mountain, Brent had to stay with the rest of the team. But Mark would not be allowed to climb back to Camp Three by himself after sending Karen home and his presence was required to get the team safely to the summit. Karen created a situation that nearly ended everyone's dream of reaching the top of Denali. To our amazement and relief, our fellow climber, Pat, offered to join Mark in taking Karen to base camp. I will be forever grateful to Pat for his willingness to make that round trip effort, pushing himself to an extreme level of exhaustion and providing the opportunity for the team to continue the expedition.

With a new plan in place, the three of them left early the next morning and descended the entire 6,200 feet to base camp. Mark planned to get Karen on a plane to Talkeetna and then he and Pat would start back the next day. The men anticipated it would take them two days to make the return to 14,200 feet elevation. That was the plan, but of course things never quite go according to plan.

CAMP THREE: ON HOLD

May 10th dawned with clear, sunny skies at twenty-five degrees below zero. Even though I slept with my boot liners, when I took them out of my bag to put them on in the morning, the damp laces began to freeze and stiffen. The feel of the warm sun was a welcome relief while standing outside eating breakfast. Today was the second rest day for the group while Pat, Mark and Karen made their way downhill. Brent served us all a treat for breakfast when he offered a variety of Pop-Tarts! I even found my favorite flavor, brown sugar cinnamon, in the stash. Who would have thought that cold Pop-Tarts could taste so good. We all started smiling and laughing when he pulled the familiar packets out of the food bag. These little surprises were great morale boosters for the group and became highlights of the expedition.

Mid-morning, Brent led the team to the eastern edge of Genet Basin to an area appropriately called "The Edge of the World." There were too many clouds to fully appreciate the view, but Brent told us that on a clear day, we would be able to see where our first camp was located almost 5,000 feet below us. When we got back to our tents, Brent served another RMI lunch favorite of peanut butter and jam on pilot bread. Pilot bread is an almost indestructible, thick cracker that allows you to generously spread on the toppings. The unusual PB&J sandwich was a crunchy, tasty treat that I really enjoyed.

That afternoon, I needed to take a trip to the bathroom. Our current camp had the luxury of two wooden toilets, sitting side by side. The structures had a wooden seat and were made of plywood with a back and sides to block the wind. In addition to being the most comfortable bathroom accommodations on the trip, they also had the most incredible view. I was able to sit on the throne and gaze at a magnificent landscape with the peak of Mt. Hunter directly in front of me and Mt. Foraker just to my right. There were dozens of smaller mountains in view as well. The scenery at this altitude was spectacular.

The forecast warned of an approaching winter storm, causing everyone to become a little on edge. We were all concerned for Pat and Mark's safety during their return climb back to camp and still feeling frustrated with Karen's abrupt departure. Charles's hands had gotten really cold earlier on the climb and now they were feeling numb. He was worried he might have frostbite and was apprehensive about going higher and exposing himself to even colder temperatures. The team could not afford to lose another climber, so everyone was anxious regarding this new development. After dinner, my head started to pound. I drank over a quart and a half of water, pressure breathed for a couple of hours and then crashed.

Don was no longer in the tent with me. When Mark, Pat and Karen needed a tent for their downhill hike to Base Camp, a change in sleeping arrangements occurred. Cyndi and Karen had been tent mates but the women's tent was now being used for the downhill trek. Cyndi moved in with me while Don moved into the guide tent with Brent. Since my head was aching, I went to bed early while Cyndi read a book until late in the night. Meanwhile, over in the guide tent, Don had a fun time swapping stories with Brent and sipping whiskey. It never occurred to us to bring alcohol. But the guides were experienced and thought a nip in the evening helped with sleeping. Brent also had a transistor radio with ear buds that he shared. Amazingly, at this altitude, broadcasts from Anchorage, were clear. Don said between the booze and the music, he felt really relaxed and fell right to sleep.

The team would be forced to remain at Camp Three for the next four days. A winter storm blew in overnight, bringing high winds that reduced visibility to less than ten yards. Temperatures plummeted to fifty degrees below zero; the coldest conditions I had ever experienced. I was thankful for my big sleeping bag which allowed me to sleep warm and comfortable on such a dangerously cold night. Don had the strangest experience during the night when his pee bottle was full, and he had to go outside to urinate. At fifty below zero, his warm urine stream immediately froze and floated to the ground as ice crystals. He said it was the oddest-looking thing to pee a fan of ice. Even with the storm howling, Brent had the team suit up and work around the camp to keep us moving and acclimating. We dug out our tents, reinforced our cooking igloo, and built another row of snow blocks on the wall around our little nylon city. Clearing snow from our tents to keep them from collapsing was a continuous battle throughout the storm.

After dinner, Don hung out with me and Cyndi in our tent for the evening. Cyndi invited Greg, another teammate, to join us. There seemed to be a spark between the two of them and since Don and I were celebrating our eleventh wedding anniversary, the two new lovebirds decided spending time with the Jacksons on such a romantic occasion, was the place to be. I broke out the white chocolate covered Oreos and we proposed a toast with berry flavored water. The night was filled with laughter as we all shared stories of fun times in our past. As far as anniversary celebrations, it was never to be forgotten.

During the second day of the storm, we attempted to ascend to 16,200 feet to make a cache, but aborted the effort when Brent realized he could not see the crevasses because of blowing snow. We dropped our gear at 15,500 feet and returned to camp. The next day we made another attempt, but the snowpack was unstable, and the risk of an avalanche was too high to continue. Again, we returned to camp. The 2,000-foot climb from Genet Basin up the West Buttress Headwall to 16,200 feet elevation would be the steepest and most technically challenging section of the expedition. Midway up the route, we encountered a thirty-degree slope that was steep enough to make us alter our footsteps—either walking with our toes pointed outward like a duck, or both feet pointed sideways to sidestep up the mountainside. Both ways eased the muscles in our legs and provided some relief to our aching calves and Achilles tendons.

The real challenge, however, came on the upper portion of the route where the pitch was as great as fifty-five degrees. On this section, we utilized several hundred feet of fixed rope. Each climber grabbed the rope with a small handheld device called an ascender which could be slid up the rope but when pulled upon would not slide backward. The device allowed the climber to use their arm to pull themselves forward in support of each step. Being the first team to go above Camp Three, Brent tested and replaced fixed ropes in need of repair. It made for a very slow trek, but it was necessary for the safety of our team and the climbers that would follow us later in the season.

Our third attempt was a success, allowing us to cache our gear at 16,200 feet. I thought climbing up the fixed rope was challenging but hiking back down the fifty-five-degree slope was a far more dangerous and exhausting experience. We initiated the descent by bending sharply forward and charging down the slope. Balance in this precarious position was maintained by wrapping the fixed rope around our left arm to create friction, and using the grip of our hand to control the speed of our forward motion. In our right hand we carried an ice axe which was used like a cane for further support. Rounding out our equipment, crampons or "spikes" attached to our boots kept our feet from sliding out from under us. The descent was an extremely strenuous, full body effort. I felt such relief when I finally got off the upper section of our route and I was able to walk upright again. I hoped my quivering, fatigued muscles would recover overnight and be ready to climb the next day.

When we reached our camp at 14,200 feet, we found Pat and Mark had made it back after delivering Karen to Base Camp. They had been trapped at 11,000 feet for an extra day as the storm raged down the mountain. With our team once again united and supplies cached above us at 16,200 feet, we were set to continue our expedition on Denali.

CAMP FOUR: 16,200 FEET

I woke up on May 16th, my fifteenth day on the mountain, noting that the tent walls were still. A day with calm winds would be great for our climb up to Camp Four. I looked over at Don and found him sleeping comfortably. We were alone in our tent after another shuffling of sleeping locations occurred with the return of Mark and Pat. The interior of the tent was frosty and cold, but I could see the sun was just beginning to touch the nylon and warmth would be arriving soon. Brent served granola for breakfast, and everyone was thrilled with the menu change. I think the entire team was happy not having to face another morning of instant oatmeal. We broke down our camp and cached our snowshoes and sleds. Neither piece of equipment could be used on the steep climbs ahead.

With lighter packs and familiarity with the route, the team hiked smoothly up the fixed rope section. The group made it to the top of the West Buttress headwall around three in the afternoon. We set up camp on the exposed narrow ridge with a 1,500-foot drop to Peter's Glacier on one side and a 2,000-foot drop on the other. We spent four hours cutting blocks of snow to build a four-foot wall around our tents. When we finished, our camp was completely contained to prevent any accidental falls off the mountain ridge.

Camp Four was by far the toughest camping area to set up and at that point, I was tired, thirsty, and hungry. Brent made a culinary feast that evening that started with a steaming cup of ramen soup, followed by hearty beef stew and a large side of mashed potatoes. He finished the meal with a package of chocolate chip cookies. Although I felt fatigued from the day's efforts, I remember standing beside the snow wall eating my dinner and marveling at the view. I never tired of staring at the mountains of the Alaska Range. I found the setting to be peaceful and calming; like how one might feel sitting on a beach watching and listening to the waves. Don caught my happy vibe and quickly took a photograph. To this day, I can look at the picture and be transported back to that wonderful moment in time. After cleaning our dishes with a handful of snow, I readied myself for bed and snuggled into my sleeping bag feeling content. We were two days from the summit and the weather forecast was promising. I fell asleep filled with hope.

HIGH CAMP: 17,200 FEET

There was only a thousand feet of elevation gain to reach high camp, but crowded conditions and the complexities of the route made for an all-day effort to get there. While we were breaking down Camp Four, the Denali Team, another guided group, hiked by our tents on their way up the mountain. With nearly twenty-four hours of sunshine, climbers could begin their day at any time and this group had obviously started in the middle of the night. We caught up to the Denali team later that morning just as they were beginning another fixed rope section. They were very cautious and slower moving which forced us to decrease our pace as we followed behind them.

Awaiting my turn to ascend the fixed rope allowed me the luxury to take a few pictures of this spectacular section of the trip. I was so excited to finally be climbing a combination of snow and rock. This part of our climb had the most exposure and was just what I had envisioned the expedition would look like. Our route weaved around a large rock formation known as Washburn's Thumb. Another part of the trail was a knife-edge ridge with vertical fall lines on either side— plummeting thousands of feet onto crevasse riddled glaciers. The guides had warned us that this section of ridge line would be a turnaround point in the event of foul weather. But May 17th offered only sunshine and very little wind; perfect for experiencing the upper portion of the mountain. I found the day to be thrilling.

Once we reached high camp at 17,200 feet, I made another discovery. The air was significantly thinner at this elevation. Setting up camp was a much slower process because of the additional time required to catch our breath after each effort. I had read that the air at this altitude had 50 percent less oxygen than at sea level. The statistic did not have much impact on me, but now I could feel the meaning of those words with every move I made. When our chores were complete, Don and I walked over to the edge of the camping area to look down at Camp Three. A few tiny dots of color could be seen in the snow 3,000 feet below us. At this altitude, we now looked down on Mt. Hunter directly in front of us. The view was as breathtaking as the elevation.

At dinner, Brent let us know the weather forecast was holding and that we would attempt to summit the following day. He outlined what to take with us for the climb. Brent would have an emergency tent, sleeping bag and medical supplies. We would only need to pack our parka, all our warm clothes, lunch food, water, and, of course, our camera. Our packs would be light which was a relief because moving at this altitude was challenging enough without a heavy load to carry. And with every step we climbed, the air would become even thinner.

SUMMIT: 20,310 FEET

Brent came by our tent at eight o'clock the next morning and yelled, "Summit day. Everybody up!" After quickly consuming a hot bowl of oatmeal, we were ready to start our climb within an hour. Packing was easy having gone over everything the previous evening. I double checked the list of items to carry to the summit because I realized my oxygen starved brain was not functioning at a normal level. I noticed before breakfast that it took me an absurdly long time to tie the laces on my climbing boots. That's when I understood how oxygen deprivation was going to impact me. My brain was yelling instructions to my body to move quickly but my reaction was still in slow motion. My mantra for the day was to stay focused and aware. We all made sure to hydrate well at breakfast and then topped off our water bottles for the rest of the day. The guides told us the climb would take eight to ten hours and then another four hours to hike back down to our tents. Today I was carrying a special treat up the mountain. I had a dozen white chocolate covered Oreos left and I planned to have them power me to the top.

The route out of High Camp began with a traverse of a long hillside up to Denali Pass. The hike was in the shadow of a mountain wall and without the sun shining down on me, I felt the cold seep into my fingers. Don had a little thermometer on his pack that read ten degrees. We were fortunate that we had very little wind and lots of sunshine beckoning us forward to the ridge ahead. After a couple hours of hiking, we made it to Denali Pass and were engulfed in the warmth of the sun. While my hands warmed up, the rest of me began to overheat. When we stopped for a short break, the entire team removed their outer Gortex coats and stayed comfortable in just fleece jackets.

It took another two hours of climbing to reach an area called The Football Field; one of the few flat expanses on the mountain. From the Football Field, we could see the headwall that led up to summit ridge. Once we ascended the steep headwall, we dropped our packs and hiked another thirty minutes along the ridge line. The knife edge ridge was extremely exposed with a thousand-foot drop to the Football Field on one side and a five-thousand-foot drop on the other side. Instead of feeling fear or concern about the exposure, I was elated to be walking above the clouds and about to reach the summit of Denali with Don at my side.

On May 18, 1993, at six o'clock in the evening, Don and I were standing on the highest point of the North American Continent. With tears in our eyes, we hugged each other and our teammates and shared words of congratulations. A couple from Canada reached the summit just behind our team and offered to take a picture of our group. The photo captured our RMI Team gathered on the top of Denali with nothing but blue sky in the background. The faces of my nine teammates showed everything from exhaustion to happiness. I of course, stood there with the biggest grin on my face. I was filled with pure joy and could not stop smiling the entire time. The sun was shining brightly, and the winds were calm, but the temperature was a cool zero degrees. After spending an hour on the summit taking pictures and marveling at the view, the team was ready to start the hike back to camp. It had taken us nine and a half hours to reach the top of Denali. We knew our return trip would be a long trek as well. There was no rush or worry because we had good weather and twenty-four hours of daylight. We also knew that the excitement and adrenaline rush from our conquest would be wearing off and exhaustion would soon set in.

We made it back to our tents in four and a half hours. Hiking for fourteen hours with so little oxygen in the air made us more tired than usual.

Brent recognized we were all at our breaking point, so he had everyone climb into their sleeping bags while he heated up soup for dinner and delivered it to each tent. The hot soup helped warm up my insides and my sleeping bag warmed the rest of my body. Don asked me to hold his hat and gloves while he got himself comfortable in his bag. I woke up two hours later still holding his hat and gloves wondering if Don was cold without them. I found him sound asleep next to me, his hat and gloves forgotten as soon as he laid down. He woke up when he heard me rustling around so I handed him his gear to put on. We did not have to say a word. Just a look and a smile between us conveyed all the love, pride, respect, and admiration we had for one another.

RETURN TO CAMP TWO: 11,000 FEET

We woke to another bright and shining day which was the opposite of how I felt as I crawled out of my sleeping bag. The feeling of jubilation from summiting the day before had morphed overnight into a level of exhaustion I had never experienced. The guides always stressed that the summit was not the ultimate goal; a successful climb was being able to get back off the mountain safely. Breaking down our tent, I made a ridiculous comment to Don. "At least we only have to hike downhill." I totally underestimated the difficulty of descending the 40-to-55-degree slopes on the fixed rope sections with a full pack and tired legs. As it turned out, this part of the route would leave its mark on me for the rest of my life.

My rope team that day consisted of our junior guide Mark, Pat, and Don with me tied on last. We worked well together until the end of the first fixed rope section. The guys all hit the bottom of the slope and began their full-size steps before I had totally descended and let go of the anchored line. Being tethered to the men by the team rope, I was pulled forward much faster than I could safely walk downhill. Using the fixed rope wrapped around my left arm for braking kept me from falling on my face but not from hurting myself. I was dragged for several yards while yelling for the men to stop. The rope burned through my fleece jacket and base layer top and produced a deep three-inch long gouge in my forearm. That evening, Brent cleaned my wound with antiseptic and put a bandage on me. Over the years when-ever someone asks me about my scar, I always begin my answer by saying, "There I was on the summit of Denali..." Though the injury occurred the day after we summited, this sets the stage for the story and allows me to share one of the greatest accomplishments of my life.

After negotiating all the fixed rope sections, we stopped at Camp Three at 14,200 feet to retrieve our sleds and snowshoes we had cached and to have lunch. Personal supplies were getting low, so Brent broke out more pilot bread and we made peanut butter and jelly sandwiches from the team reserves. As we were eating, a French team came by and offered us an entire bag of PowerBars. There must have been a couple hundred bars in the bag. They said they were sponsored by the PowerBar Company, but they didn't want the food. I understood their dilemma immediately. In 1993, PowerBars were the first nutritional bars on the market. They were hard in texture and difficult to chew in warm weather but impossible to eat when exposed to freezing temperatures. In my opinion, however, the worst thing about the original PowerBar was that they were terrible tasting. The French guys said they hated them and now had to carry all those heavy bars up and down the mountain. We watched them approach every climbing team at Genet Basin and offer their bag. They could not give the bars away.

The other thing we noticed at Camp Three was the increased number of climbers on the mountain. There were now a couple dozen teams with groups of tents spread across the basin. I was amazed how much the area had changed in the few days we had been gone. Our quiet plateau of pristine snow and calming vistas was now heavily tracked and noisy with activity. Again, I was thankful that we had chosen to climb on the first available date. Our experience climbing the mountain unfolded on a private playground. We often set tracks on a route with no other footprints in sight. As many as twelve hundred people attempt to climb Denali each season. I would later read that the route up the mountain can become an eighteen-inch wide, hard packed path and that climbers had to frequently stop and wait for their turn to ascend or descend the more technical sections of the climb. I feel fortunate that my experience was nothing like that. It was probably more difficult to break trail, set fixed ropes and build walls around each camp, but I will always cherish the peacefulness and serenity that being first provided.

We hiked down past Windy Corner to Camp Two at 11,000 feet and arrived at six o'clock. Our old campsite was available and still in pretty good shape, so we leveled the sleeping areas and set up our tents. The weather was an unusually warm twenty degrees which allowed us to stand around after dinner visiting and enjoying the warmth of the evening sun. Everyone was appropriately tired but in good spirits. Our conversation turned from the summit to the next big event in all our lives: a bath and a steak dinner. Tomorrow we would reach Base Camp and be flown back to Talkeetna. A hot shower sounded like heaven to me. We parted company and climbed into our tents laughing about our excitement over the prospect of meat and hot water.

RETURN TO BASE CAMP: 7,200 FEET

The team was up early and broke down camp quickly the next morning. We were like barn sour horses who had only one thought in mind; head to Base Camp and fly off the mountain. The elevation loss for the day was only 3,000 feet but the twelve-mile route was covered in soft snow. Dawn broke with clear, sunny skies and by mid-morning the snow became slushy which made dragging sleds extremely difficult. The trek felt like walking in deep sand. The good news was that the route was well marked and chances of falling in a crevasse were quite low. The relatively safe, sluggish march allowed me the opportunity to let my mind wander and reflect on all my experiences over the last nineteen days on the mountain.

The first thing that came to mind was the majestic beauty of the Alaska Range covered in snow and shining brilliantly in the arctic sun. There are no words to adequately describe the vistas I experienced throughout the journey. I knew, no matter how hard I tried to explain, without seeing it, my family could never comprehend why I would want to risk my life climbing Denali. I was just glad Don, and I did it together and that we shared the same memories. I thought about the severe cold we endured and was happy that I had chosen the right gear to make the conditions tolerable. I was moving to the mountains of Idaho and expected there would be lots of snow and cold in my not-so-distant future. The experience of surviving outside in fifty below zero temperatures lessened my concern about Idaho winters. I was also very proud of myself for accomplishing such a large goal and for demonstrating a level of physical strength and determination needed to complete the expedition. I felt both physically and mentally tough and ready to meet all the challenges that life would throw my way.

As far as what we did right on the trip versus what we could have improved upon, let's just say two rolls of toilet paper was NOT enough. I had to use some of Don's stash. Snow is rough on the nether regions, so I was not impressed with that recommendation. In my opinion, one roll per week would have been a better idea. And along that same line of thinking, one pair of underwear and socks per week would have been nice. The aromas coming out of my sleeping bag after nineteen days without bathing was a bit much to endure. All my clothing was going into the trash as soon as I was off the mountain. There would be no way to get the body odor out of them for future use. Don went a step further. After stating, "I am not bringing this pair of underwear back to civilization!" He kept his sleeping underwear on and threw his other pair in a crevasse with the poop bag.

A few wet wipes carried in a zip-lock bag would have been a good idea. We never thought of it, but other climbers had them. I could handle not bathing but I really found I missed cleaning my hands. Snow was too rough and cold for scrubbing one's fingers. Wet wipes would have worked well but the downside was that to keep them from freezing, it would have been one more thing to store in an already crowded sleeping bag every night. Pee bottles were a necessity and Nalgene bottles worked best because you could trust them not to leak. At least that was what I told myself each night as I stuck the bottle in my sleeping bag so it wouldn't freeze. And my white chocolate covered Oreos were a great idea. I loved the cookies and found I could eat them no matter how bad I felt.

My musings came to a halt around two o'clock when our hike on the Kahiltna Glacier became unbelievably hot. Comically, everyone stripped down to their long underwear to complete the trek. I covered my face with sunscreen repeatedly and used my bandanna to protect my cheeks throughout the rest of the afternoon. Heartbreak Hill seemed to go on forever, but finally we reached base camp and made arrangements to fly back to Talkeetna.

A SUCCESSFUL JOURNEY

Don and I were on the second plane which had us arriving at our hotel at 7:30 p.m. The team made plans to gather for dinner at 9:15 p.m. at the Latitude 62 Degrees restaurant. Don and I had over an hour and a half to get ourselves clean and ready for our evening with the group. As it turned out, that was barely enough time for the scrubbing that needed to occur. I had no idea that a layer of my skin would come off in the form of sludge. It took three soaping efforts to create any suds on my body. I had underarm hair that was shocking in length and my legs once again looked like the hairy twelve-year-old girl I had once been. The small bottle of hotel shampoo barely made a dent in removing three weeks of sweat and grease from my hair. It took a surprising amount of effort to get my body back to normal.

As I stood in front of the mirror, I realized that my physique was pretty much the same as it had been when I started the expedition. As a fun experiment, Brent had all the team members weigh themselves the day before we left for Denali. He told us that most people lose between eight and fifteen pounds during the trip. When our plane landed back in Talkeetna, Brent had the scale out again for each of us to weigh. Don lost a full fifteen pounds. When he stepped out of the shower, the weight change was noticeable. I lost a whopping four pounds. That was it. Regardless, I planned to eat a big steak, a baked potato with all the trimmings and dessert for dinner. Those four pounds would be right back on before I left the state of Alaska. I had earned this celebration meal and was looking forward to it.

Dinner was a whirlwind of an evening filled with toasts, good food, storytelling, and lots of laughter. Everyone was in a great mood and thrilled to have successfully completed the trip. Feeling comfortably stuffed, we left the restaurant together and made plans to board our bus the next morning for our return trip to the Anchorage airport. Our grand adventure was about to end. While lying in a bed that felt a little too comfortable, in a room that felt a bit too warm, I reflected on the enormity of what Don, and I had achieved together. I fell into a deep sleep filled with happiness, having experienced such an extraordinary journey.

DENALI PHOTOS

1. Rest day at 11,200 feet—Drying our gear and clothing in the sun.

2. Camp 3—14,200 feet. Building an igloo to protect our cooking area from wind and blowing snow.

3. The Bandit Mountaineer—Using a bandana to keep the blisters on my face from getting any worse.

4. Just climbed past Washburn's Thumb, on our way to Denali Pass and High Camp.

5. Don on Denali Pass—exposed section of the trail.

6. View from High Camp—Genet Basin (seen below) only has a few spots of color. In just a few days time, dozens of tents will cover the area and the pristine snow will be heavily tracked.

7. Summit Ridge—Walking above the clouds.

8. Denali Summit. 20,310 ft.— May 18, 1993

The 1995 Seattle Marathon—All finishers had a commemorative medal placed around their neck when they crossed the line.

A MARATHON BIRTHDAY

EARLY IN 1995, DON surprised me by asking if we could run a marathon for his birthday. Running a marathon had been added to our bucket list a decade earlier, and now that Don was turning forty-four on November 25th, he was ready to check it off the list. Throughout the years, Don had talked about competing in a marathon "one day" just to experience running that far in a race. I was thirty-four and had no idea if my big-boned, stocky body could endure a twenty-six-mile run. But like all the other crazy things we did together, I was game to try. I answered, "Sure, but I need to train for that kind of distance. When and where are you considering competing?"

Don was always reading athletic magazines and had recently found an article in *Runner's World* featuring the flattest marathon courses in the country. One of the listings was in Seattle, Washington which appealed to Don because he loved running in the rain and thought the odds would be in his favor for a stormy race day. When we investigated further and learned the race in 1995 was scheduled for Saturday, November 25th, it was a done deal. Happy Birthday, Don!

With a new goal set for the end of the year, we began putting together a spring training program that would allow us to increase our running distance in a systematic way to avoid injury while gaining speed and endurance. Living in Sawtooth City, Idaho, surrounded by national forest, provided an endless playground of logging roads to jog. Dirt was more kind to our knees and hips than asphalt. Our regimen produced steady results, allowing us to reach our targeted goals throughout the summer and into early fall. We enjoyed running in the forest and the camaraderie of once again suffering together through interval training. It had been years since we trained for triathlons, but the physical and mental pain were still familiar. As the end of fall approached, providing fewer hours of daylight, we began running on the bike path in town after work to accustom ourselves to pavement and to keep me safe while jogging in the dark. Don always said, "Shannon can trip over a shadow!" A partially lit bike path with a very smooth surface was the best course of action to keep me upright and uninjured.

Our last long-distance training run was a comfortable nineteen miles which made me confident that I could run a full 26.2-mile marathon. Completing the race and supporting Don in reaching his goal was important to me. I smile remembering the day Don shared his "complete list of wishes" for his birthday. Running on a forested logging road on a beautiful summer day, Don announced, "I want us to cross the finish line hand in hand in under four hours, enjoy a steak dinner after the race, and make love to you for my present!"

After I stopped chuckling, I responded, "That's a pretty high energy birthday list, honey." But again, like with all the other ideas and challenges Don dreams up, I also added, "Game on!"

Don's gamble on Seattle providing a perfect, stormy race day was forecasted with favorable odds. Our drive to Washington was in cloudy weather with periods of rain. We drove halfway on Thanksgiving Day and then rolled into Seattle in early afternoon on Black Friday. Alanis Morrisette's album, *Jagged Little Pill*, had just been released, and I had a copy on cassette tape. The miles flew by as we belted out "You Oughta Know" and other tunes, singing along with Alanis the whole way.

To Don's delight, the morning of the event produced a sky filled with gray clouds and the promise of scattered rain showers throughout the day. The racecourse was a point-to-point route, not a loop, which required a bus ride to the starting area. There were thousands of people competing in the marathon, all milling around, waiting for the gun to go off. As I nervously stood with my hands pressed against an empty school bus and leaning forward to stretch out my hamstrings, Don warned me, "The officials are going to be really pissed if you push that bus over!" It took a couple seconds for his comment to register, but when the guy next to me started laughing, I finally understood what Don had said and smiled. My reaction was exactly what he wanted. The pressure of making this the perfect birthday was getting to me. I was not sure if I could keep up the pace to achieve the four-hour finish time Don had set. As if reading my mind, Don said, "Don't worry. We will just run our own race together."

With over five thousand people running the marathon with us, it took a while to reach the starting line once the gun went off and we all started moving forward. The first sixteen miles were great. The course was scenic, winding through parks and along bike trails that skirted the edges of creeks and ponds. The temperature felt perfect, hovering in the high fifties without sunshine. We had a few sprinkles of rain on different sections of the run, but never a downpour. The moisture kept Don cool and comfortable. There were intermittent aid stations along the route offering food, water, and sports drinks. We stopped twice so I could visit the portable toilet and grab a bite of a nutrition bar. Mile seventeen introduced the only significant climb on the racecourse. Though the hill was relatively small, the timing of the additional effort had a huge impact on my body and psyche. During the next couple miles, my pace began to slow, and I was concerned about not meeting our goal of four hours. I glanced over at Don running beside me—he looked as fresh as when he started the race.

I had read that there are two races in a marathon: the first twenty miles and the final 10K. The body will either embrace the last 6.2 miles or the person hits a wall and bonks. I was in the latter category after running up the hill. My spirit was willing, but my body was not responding to my mental directive to keep moving. Everything hurt and it was all I could do to take another jogging step. While I plodded along, my husband ran beside me with a stride that looked as light and effortless as a gazelle.

At the mile twenty marker, I told Don to go—to leave me and run his own pace. He reminded me that we were supposed to finish the race holding hands. After much debate, I convinced Don that I would complete the course and see him at the end, but we needed to alter our expectations for the finish line. With strong encouragement from me, Don took off to run the last six miles on his terms. And what a 10K he ran. Every mile was faster than the previous one as he increased his speed to a comfortable six-minute mile pace for the duration of the race. Don finished the Seattle Marathon in three hours and fifty-seven minutes, achieving his goal of completing the course in under four hours. I came in fifteen minutes after him. Any disappointment in not finishing together was immediately erased when I saw his big smile and felt the joy in his hug at the end of my run. I knew sending him off to fly to the finish line was the right choice.

All the marathon racers were wrapped in a lightweight emergency blanket when they crossed the line and handed a commemorative medal for their efforts. Snuggled in our blankets with the medals proudly draped around our necks, we contentedly climbed into our car and began the drive home. Laughing and recapping our day, Don reminded me that he still had two of his birthday wishes left to enjoy. Our plan had been to find a steakhouse and hotel on our way out of town and stop for the night. We were feeling pretty good post-race and made the mistake of driving too far before stopping. When we got out of the car four hours later, we could barely straighten up to stand. Walking was more of a hobble on our way up to our hotel room. A nice, hot shower loosened up our stiff muscles and made sitting more comfortable throughout our celebration meal. The steak dinner was delicious, although I am sure being ravenous from hours of running added greatly to our enjoyment. From the uncorking of the wine bottle to the last bite of chocolate birthday cake, the evening was filled with laughter and happiness. Walking hand in hand to our room, I smiled as Don reminded me there was still one item left on his birthday wish list. Despite our cramping muscles and exhausted physical condition, Don proudly fulfilled his commitment. "It was like sex, but different," he always comments when retelling the story.

To which I laughingly add, "Thank God, it wasn't another marathon!"

24 HOURS OF MOAB
MOUNTAIN BIKE RACE

THE 24 HOURS OF Moab Mountain Bike Race in 1995 ushered in what would become the largest, most prestigious annual gathering of fat tire enthusiasts. The brainchild of the concept was Laird Knight, a Mountain Bike Hall of Fame inductee, forever recognized for his impact on mountain bike racing around the world. Knight's company, Granny Gear Productions (GGP), hosted the inaugural 24 Hours of Canaan in 1992, launching a new type of competition when mountain biking was considered the hottest "extreme" sport in the nation. Capitalizing on the success of the event in the Canaan Valley of West Virginia, GGP quickly established five additional locations creating a national series of 24-hour races. One of the locations was in the remote Behind the Rocks area, twelve miles south of Moab, Utah.

Each year, an entire community sprang up in the sandy, desolate locale, allowing more than four thousand racers, support crew and spectators to spend a couple days together participating in a contest of epic proportions. Don and I felt very fortunate to have competed in the 24 Hours of Moab race during the weekend of October 9–10, 1999. We were there in the beginning—during those first few years when lighting equipment and the concept of nighttime racing was new and considered the ultimate challenge in mountain bike competitions. Although the race would only be held for eighteen years, the wild and crazy stories of competing in Moab's remarkable desert location have risen to the status of folklore with tales full of bloody shins, broken bones, red dust covered faces, and sleep deprived grins. Our experience in the legendary cycling jamboree lived up to the hype.

In 1999, Don and I were living in Sawthooth City, Idaho, located forty miles north of Sun Valley. With both of us working in the Wood River Valley, we carpooled into town daily. Driving home one evening, Don excitedly shared a conversation he had with his co-workers earlier in the day. "Doug and Lee asked us to be on their five-person team to compete in a relay race this fall called the 24 Hours of Moab. They need a woman on the team, and they asked if you would be interested." Before I could reply, he went on to say, "The race is about twelve miles south of Moab in an area called Behind the Rocks and we would camp there over the weekend. The guys said they heard it was a tough course but a fun time out in the middle of nowhere. Think you might want to do it?"

Surprised to hear Don talking about mountain bike racing when there was still snow on the ground but also intrigued by the idea, I cautiously answered, "Yeah, but I want to know more about what I am getting myself into. Twenty-four hours means riding at night which is something I've never done before. I'm open to trying it, but we don't own lights. What kind of equipment would we have to buy?"

Don shared information about bike lights from the discussion the men had earlier in the day. "Nightrider makes a new halogen lighting system that runs on a rechargeable battery. The battery can power the bulbs for a solid hour and a half; about the time we would need for a night lap on the course. Lights will be our biggest expense."

"How big is this race?" I asked.

"It's huge—more than a thousand people competing." Don paused so I could digest the enormity of the event. "Most competitors will be on a four-person team racing according to their classification of pro, expert, sport, amateur, veteran, or masters. There will also be both men and women making solo efforts. We'll be racing in the five-person category called Open Team that requires at least one woman and prohibits professionally ranked cyclists."

"So, who's the fifth person on our team?"

"The guys are going to ask Billy. He's been racing expert but might be turning professional this summer. If he delays turning pro, he would be an awesome teammate." Don said the race would start at noon on Saturday, October 9th, and end at noon the next day; the team with the most laps in twenty-four hours would win. Racers still out on the course at twelve o'clock would be allowed to complete their lap and include the finishing time as part of the team's final placement. Don also shared that the men had discussed racing strategy including what our lineup order should be and whether a person should ride one or two laps at a time to allow teammates to sleep and recover. "The guys want to go out on the trails together this summer to see how everyone performs and then decide what would work best for our team."

I could tell that Don was really excited about the idea of racing in this unique style of competition. Without any further hesitation, I agreed to join the men and then added, "I really like the idea of being on a team *with you.* We will be cycling all summer anyway, but now we have an incentive to train harder throughout the season. It'll be fun."

TRAINING

With our new goal in mind, we increased our weightlifting routine to gain muscle strength throughout the rest of winter and early spring. I loved living in the mountains and having the opportunity to ski and snowshoe, but seven months of snow and extreme cold always began to wear on me by the time spring arrived each year. With snow lingering on the ground until mid-May in Sawtooth City, Don and I decided to travel to Moab in April for a long weekend vacation with friends. Located nearly six hundred miles to our south and a full sixty degrees warmer in temperature, a cycling trip to check out the Behind the Rocks area in Utah sounded wonderful.

One of Moab's bike shops provided us with a map so that we could find the racecourse in the remote location. My first impression of the sixteen-mile loop was one of shock. Don and I had been told that most of the route was on a jeep road, so I expected the course to be fast and free of major difficulties. In a letter I would later write to my parents, I shared our discovery by saying, "The route goes over some grueling terrain that includes boulder walls, river washouts, deep sand, and rocky roads. It'll be fun, but very challenging. No easy sections anywhere!" I was downplaying it to keep them from worrying about me. In truth, I came home from our exploratory outing thinking, "How the hell am I going to navigate those steep rock gardens at night with only a headlamp to guide my way down?"

The more I thought about the terrain, the more excited I became about mastering the challenges. Shortly after returning home, I told Don we had to make plans to go back to Moab during the summer. "I need to spend more time studying the racecourse so I can safely maneuver down those twenty-foot-high walls of rock. Being able to ride the technical sections will allow us to gain time on all the other racers that have to get off their bikes and walk." I never questioned Don's and my ability to overcome the obstacles on the course. We were always interested in learning new skills and willing to lose a little skin to raise our competency level. All the racecourse was ridable; it was up to us to figure out how to become more adept at flying down rocky terrain and cycling through sand.

Don and I returned to Moab in August so we could study all the technical segments of the sixteen-mile racecourse. We made repeated efforts on the boulder walls until the descents became smooth and fast. I even sketched the entry points to the drop-offs and the best lines through the rocks so that I could memorize the approach and feel confident in my ability to safely ride down the dangerous sections at night.

We tested our lighting system a couple of times by riding familiar trails back home. A light mounted on our handlebars illuminated the trail directly in front of us and an additional light strapped to our helmets swiveled with our head, expanding the view to whatever our eyes focused on. Although the system worked adequately, the narrow beam of a handlebar light cutting through the pitch-black forest created a sense of tunnel vision that made a well-known trail feel totally unfamiliar. During our first test ride on Fox Creek Trail, a local favorite, I commented, "I can't believe how eerie this feels. Sometimes I don't even know where I am because the view is so distorted."

Don agreed and added, "The good news is that we didn't outrun our lights on the downhill. I could see okay even when we were moving fast." Overall, our lighting system worked well. Don liked his first night ride and enjoyed riding in the woods with the moon and stars overhead. He was looking forward to racing at night in the desert. It would take few more nighttime outings to increase my level of enthusiasm and comfort with cycling in darkness, but by race time, I felt confident about competing day *or* night.

BEHIND THE ROCKS

"Great song! I like the music they're playing," I commented to Don while setting up our tent. Queen's *Fat Bottomed Girls* was blasting out of speakers mounted high off the ground to allow the sound to be easily heard across the open desert landscape. An amazing little city had been erected in a high desert meadow which now had a podium stage complete with a sound system, a water truck piped to four shower stalls, a dozen portable toilets, a small medical tent, a gazebo with cycling merchandise for sale and a large, big top tent for race operations. A steady line of vehicles could be seen cresting the hill and snaking their way to the open camping area in the early morning sunshine. Within three short hours, the empty desert plateau would have every square yard of space filled with tents, cars, and RVs as thousands of racers, family members, and friends established campsites as far as the eye could see.

The team had driven down the previous day to preview the course together. Everyone managed to get themselves down the technical sections unscathed, but Billy's effort was exceptional. Watching Billy roll up to the edge of a steep rock face, dive in without hesitation, stop midway down, hold a track stand on a boulder, then hop his bike sideways to a safer line to descend again, had left me stunned and speechless. I could ride a bike but NOT like that. Although Don and I had been racing road bikes for a decade, we purchased our first mountain bikes in 1994 and were still honing our skills on dirt, rock, and sand. This was a light bulb moment for me as I realized the incredible difference between a physically strong person participating in a mountain bike race and a true elite mountain bike racer.

"Hey guys, let us help you raise the legs on the canopy," I called out as Don, and I rushed over to assist Billy and Lee with setting up the framed shelter.

Lee looked over his shoulder at me and said, "Thanks. It's so much easier to extend the support posts with four people moving the metal legs at the same time."

With the weather promising clear skies and warm temperatures for the weekend, shade from the blazing sun would become more important as the day progressed. Durance Cycleworks in Ketchum, where Billy was employed, sponsored our team, and offered the use of the company canopy over the weekend. Our sponsorship also included a discount on cycling gear allowing all of us to purchase matching outfits. The photo we took of the five of us posing in our team kit before the start of the race created a tangible memory and served to remind us that we were all in this adventure together.

RACE "DAY"

"Come on guys, it's time to go. They're asking racers to gather at the podium area," I called out to Don, Lee, Doug, and Billy. Laird Knight, who was emceeing the event, welcomed everyone and provided a quick recap of the contest rules. With the field of competitors standing tightly packed below a towering speaker, I got my first exposure to the other teams. "Oh my gosh, Don look at those girls dressed in pink evening gowns with matching wigs." Staring at the group, I added, "The one in the middle is a guy! Do you think they'll race in those outfits?" Surveying the crowd, I noticed several other individuals wearing costumes and body paint adding to a carnival like atmosphere before the start of the race.

There was also a definite feel of tension in the air as everyone was eager to get out on the racecourse. In consideration of the broiling sun and the nearing of high noon, Laird swiftly communicated the necessary information and brought his speech to an end with a final, "Good luck to you all. Have fun!"

The 24-Hours of Moab race in 1999 hosted 1,500 competitors comprised of twenty-one solo riders and 341 teams. The race series always began with a Le Mans-style start which meant 362 first lap competitors had to run a hundred yards to a large, flagged bush and back before jumping on their bike to make their first pedal stroke in the race. With a few last words of encouragement from the team, Billy headed over to the starting line to race the first lap of the course. When the gun sounded, chaos erupted along with the rise of an incredible dust cloud as hundreds of cyclists pounded the dirt as quickly as their cleated feet would allow. The open run segment served to break up the crowd of several hundred cyclists into more manageable throngs of racers leaving the starting area on their bikes. Watching riders speed away from the venue, I asked, "Did you see Billy on his bike? I saw him take off running near the front but lost him in the crowd."

Don looked over to where Billy's bike had been standing. "I didn't see him leave but his bike is gone so I know he's out there on the course." Turning to walk back to our camping area, Don commented, "Nothing to do now but rest up and wait for our turn to ride. Let's go get under our shade canopy."

The planned order for our relay team, officially named The Wicked Spuds, was Billy first, followed by Lee and then Doug. The fourth leg would occur during the hottest part of the day, so I offered to race the late afternoon lap because I handled the heat better than Don. Everyone had a fantastic first run on the course. Billy was on fire with an hour and nine-minute lap which included his Le Mans sprint. Lee, Don, and Doug were spaced between an hour fifteen and an hour and twenty-five minutes per lap. I completed my first lap in an hour and thirty minutes. I was grateful to have done the loop at a competitively fast women's pace given Moab's cloudless blue sky had allowed the temperature to soar to eighty-five degrees by four o'clock when I started. The sun's rays reflecting off the hot sand and rock were brutally warm and draining, but my familiarity with the route allowed me to move quickly through the obstacles without incident or mechanical issues.

Don was waiting for me at the timekeeper's table to exchange the baton when I arrived at 5:30 p.m. Protocol required I hand the timekeeper the team baton which allowed them to document my finishing lap time; once completed, they passed the baton to my teammate to begin their loop. These were the early days before the invention of computer chipped bands to digitally record laps and track participants on a racecourse. Rules for manually capturing lap times were strictly enforced. A lost baton resulted in a huge time penalty, essentially taking a team out of contention for a win. We fiercely protected our baton and were able to complete the race without mishap.

My late afternoon lap perfectly positioned Don so that he experienced sundown and the arrival of cooler evening temperatures in the desert. Don would later tell me, "Riding conditions were great—not too hot. The only problem I had was when the road looped around and headed west, the sun was so low on the horizon, it blinded me to the point I could only look a few feet beyond my front tire. I almost went off the trail a few times because I couldn't see where I was going." Sunset in Moab, Utah during the middle of October occurred around 6:45 p.m. which was about the same time Don rode into the finishing area to exchange the baton with Billy who would begin our nighttime rotation on the racecourse.

AS DIFFERENT AS NIGHT AND DAY

Classic rock music blasted out of the speakers all evening until ten o'clock when the sound system was turned off for the night. I had taken a quick shower after my ride, eaten a sandwich, and then laid down to rest at 8:00 p.m. hoping to fall asleep. The rhythmic beat of the songs reverberating across the desert combined with continuous crowd noise overstimulated my senses and kept me awake. My head had started to pound with the pain of a migraine shortly after my meal; creating one more struggle to overcome before I could get any rest. Don came inside our tent a little before ten. While he quietly sat down on his cot and started rummaging through his clothing bag, the music abruptly stopped. To let Don know I was still awake, I mumbled softy, "Thank God they shut the sound system down. I tried to tune out the music but couldn't."

"How's your head?"

"I took a pill a little while ago. I hope the medication kicks in soon so I can get at least an hour of sleep before my next lap," I whispered. "Thanks for going ahead of me this round."

Don leaned down and gave me a gentle kiss on my forehead. "I just want you to feel better." Changing clothes, Don provided an update on the team. "Doug is out on the course now. He should be back in about an hour. Last check, we were ahead of Smith Optics by two minutes." From the moment the starting gun sounded, The Wicked Spuds had been in a constant battle with the Smith Sport Optics team from Ketchum. For nearly twelve hours, the accumulative lap times for the rival teams had stayed within a minute or two of each other. "I'll ride next and should finish my lap in about an hour and a half, maybe less. That means you could be riding as early as one o'clock. I checked your bike. Lights are working, tires are good, it's ready to go." Once fully dressed, Don grabbed his coat to leave. "Your alarm is set for midnight so that you can wake up and be at the baton exchange on time. Try to sleep now to help your head." With another quick kiss, on my cheek this time, Don slipped out of the tent and left me to relax.

My alarm startled me awake confirming that I had fallen asleep for at least a little while. The pain in my head was no longer incapacitating; just a mild irritation that was manageable. I was surprised by how cold the inside of the tent felt when I crawled out of my sleeping bag. With the setting of the sun, the desert temperature had fallen from a high of almost ninety to a chilly twenty-nine degrees Fahrenheit. We had brought a variety of clothes including heavier full fingered gloves, booties, vests, and jackets. Not being sure how much heat I would generate racing out on the course, I dressed in removeable layers. After drinking a quick cup of coffee to warm me up and eating a nutrition bar for a few needed carbohydrates, I readied my gear and made my way to the timekeeper's table to wait for Don to arrive.

Continuously stretching, squatting, and hopping around kept me limber while I watched for the appearance of headlights in the dark as racers approached the baton exchange area at the end of their lap. When 1:00 a.m. came and went, I began to get concerned that something had happened to Don. I had been told by my teammates that night lap times were slower for everyone. Don arrived at 1:15 a.m. drafting behind another racer as they rolled into the baton exchange area together. Needing to quickly start my lap, I didn't have time to ask Don what had slowed him down. Later, he explained,

"My lights failed when I still had a few miles left on the course. They didn't just go dim, they quit! Without any moonlight at all, I couldn't see my hand in front of my face much less try to ride my bike in pitch-black darkness. I had to wait for a racer to come by and then sprint to get behind their rear wheel so I could use their lights to see the road. The man I came in with let me follow him all the way back to the start/finish area to keep from crashing!"

Our race started on a new moon night; not even a sliver of light was visible in the sky. In contrast, the stars and Milky Way were brilliantly illuminated in a twinkling, colorful celestial pattern overhead. Without any clouds to block the view, the night sky was incredible. When Don and I walked through the compound the following morning, several conversations could be heard discussing the spectacular starry night as people continued to share their amazement.

My nighttime lap did not go smoothly. I rode the eight boulder drops without incident and was pleased that I had memorized the entry points and pathways through the rocks to stay safe. But once past the rock walls, I had difficulty getting through the sand traps that had become at least a foot deep after thousands of bikes pummeled the course. Although my tires worked well during my first lap, they became so buried in some sections that I had to dismount and run with my bike to make any forward progress. When a guy passed me on his bike while I was running with mine, I wondered, "How is he surfing this deep sand? Why did I do so much better earlier today?" Later, we were told some competitors had switched to wider tires filled with less air pressure to provide more float over the soft, bottomless sandpits. It would have been a good idea but needing a second set of tires wasn't something we had anticipated.

After sprinting up a few hills, I stopped to remove some of my warmer garments all the while telling myself, "I can't believe twenty-nine degrees feels this warm. I've got to get my vest and gloves off before I burn up!" I was working hard, generating a lot of heat slogging through multiple sections of deep, loose sand. Excited to feel the firm, rocky road beneath my tires signaling the closing miles of the lap, I couldn't help but yell an exasperated, "Dang it, don't go out now!" when I realized my lights were beginning to dim.

I was using the same lighting system as Don and encountering similar battery failure after the lights were on for ninety minutes. When a rider moved to pass me, I used every ounce of strength I had left to jump on their rear tire and stay with them so that I could see where I was going. Just like Don, the strategy worked to get me safely back for the baton exchange with Billy. As my teammate rode off into the night, I thought to myself, "I am so glad my next lap is in daylight."

CLOSING STRATEGY

"Seriously? We're still twenty-five seconds ahead of Smith Optics?" I asked in total disbelief. Nodding yes, Lee told me the Smith Optics team had experienced similar lighting challenges. After twenty hours of racing, The Wicked Spuds and Smith Sport Optics were still less than a minute apart in total time. It was almost 8:30 a.m. and Don was out on the course. He had woken up feeling strong and wanted to ride his lap before mine to capitalize on racing during the cool morning hours. I was gathering up my gear to head over to the baton exchange area when Lee came over to my tent and asked, "Would you be okay with Billy taking your lap and racing next?" He explained, "Don's completing our fourteenth lap. We really want to make sure we complete our fifteenth lap before noon so we can go out on the course for a sixteenth lap. Billy's average lap time would keep us in contention for the podium, provided no one gets a flat tire or has a mechanical."

Relief coursed through me. "Absolutely!" Mild residual headache pain was keeping me from feeling one hundred percent, so not having to race was welcome news. The rules stated that racers in the Open Team division could go in any order as long as every person completed at least two laps. I was happy to relegate myself to support person and cheerleader for the rest of the race.

Lee, Doug, and I followed Billy over to the baton exchange area to wait with him for Don's arrival which came even sooner than we expected. Don surprised us all when he turned in his fastest lap time of the race; rivaling his teammates who were twenty-plus years his junior. As Billy exited the tent after receiving the baton from Don, I rushed over and gave my husband a big hug. "I'm so proud of you," I whispered. Don had left everything he had out on the racecourse and stood completely exhausted in my embrace with his arms hanging and a blank stare on his face. It would take a little while for him to recover and realize just how spectacularly he had performed. His goal had been to compete well—despite his age. He ended the day both happy and content.

Lee was set to race the last lap unless Billy was still feeling good when he came in from the course and wanted to continue riding. The entire team was standing near the baton exchange area when Billy arrived and told the timekeeper that he would keep the baton to make another loop around the course. After quickly handing him a water bottle, we cheered him on as he sped away in a cloud of dust.

There were ninety-six teams competing in our racing category with the first five finishers considered podium positions and given awards. Stray Dogs won the Open Team category by completing seventeen laps at 12:36 p.m. Billy gave an amazing effort that allowed The Wicked Spuds to place sixth with sixteen laps finishing at 12:25 p.m., only one position away from winning money and prizes. We ended our race six minutes behind the fifth place Leadville Claim Jumpers. Our silver lining was to outperform our Ketchum rival after a full twenty-four hours of close racing. Smith Sport Optics tied with team Pablo for eighth place, eleven minutes behind The Wicked Spuds.

The 24 Hours of Moab was a truly unique, once in a lifetime cycling experience. I was filled with excitement and hope every lap, whether I was cheering for my teammates or giving my best effort out on the course. Night riding produced its own set of challenges by grossly altering the look of the racecourse resulting in some exhilarating descents through the rocks. Surprise encounters with the glowing eyes of desert wildlife and the magnificent star filled sky added to the experience that riding in darkness provided. Sharing one's pain, exhaustion, and passion with over a thousand people who intimately understood the dedication and courage it took to keep racing lap after lap somehow made the effort feel more important and rewarding. The fact that these same competitors frequently offered words of encouragement, compliments, and smiles during the most difficult times made the race feel so much bigger than the sum of its parts. Don and I had not competed as Team Jackson since our last racquetball tournament in 1983. Racing as teammates made our experience even more special. It was a combination of all these memories that made the 24 Hours of Moab an extraordinary race.

24 HOURS OF MOAB PHOTOS

1 Entrance Sign to the Behind the Rocks location of the 24 Hours of Moab Race. Courtesy of Dana Pachar.

2 The Wicked Spuds—(L to R) Billy, Lee, Doug, Shannon, and Don. Courtesy of Dana Pachar.

3 LeMans Style start—Cyclists run 100 yards out and around a bush and back before getting on their bikes to start their first lap.

4 362 bikes lined up and ready for cyclists to start pedaling after the opening run. Courtesy of Dana Pachar.

5 Shannon finishing her first lap around 5:30 p.m. Courtesy of Dana Pachar.

6 Don finishing his first lap at 6:45 p.m. Courtesy of Dana Pachar.

7 Shannon giving Don a big hug at the end of his third lap—his fastest time! Courtesy of Dana Pachar.

Whittier

ALASKA

**Prince William
Sound**

<u>START:</u> Whittier

1. **Dual Head**

2. **Humpback Cove**

3. **Tiger Glacier**

4. **Nassau Fjord**

5. **Jackpot Bay**

<u>**END:**</u> Whittier

AN ALASKAN KAYAKING
ODYSSEY

AN ODYSSEY IS CHARACTERIZED as an adventurous journey filled with extraordinary events, a perfect description of our kayak trip in the Prince William Sound of Alaska. We were just plain lucky that the timing of our vacation provided us the opportunity to witness the completion of the salmon life cycle and the impact of their spawning on the wildlife in the area. We were gifted nine days of fabulous weather, allowing us to spend a great deal of time on the water interacting with several types of marine mammals and fish. Overall, the vacation felt like a National Geographic expedition, providing an up-close and personal look at nature while visiting a very wild part of the Alaskan coastline.

The trip was initiated by our friend Glenn, a professional photographer who was hired to photograph Dagger Kayaks and L.L. Bean products in the beautiful Alaskan wilderness. Glenn then asked Ed, Teri, Don, and me to join him and pose as models along with his wife, Kathcrine. Dagger and L.L. Bean provided the kayaks and a full wardrobe for each of us to wear. With equipment and clothing secured, we planned the locations to visit and made reservations for air travel, car rental, van shuttle, and the boat charter required to deliver us to our destination. The vacation took several months to organize, but all of us would agree that the rewards were worth every minute of our time. The long planning period became especially important to me and Don as life dealt us a major blow that nearly forced us to abandon our friends before our journey ever began. In true Jackson fashion, we had to navigate our way through a little adversity before starting our adventure.

OH DEAR, A DEER!

The unfortunate incident occurred on the morning of May 20, 2000, when Don decided to go for a road bike ride to Galena Summit from our home in Sawtooth City, Idaho. While climbing up the mountain, Don passed a deer in an aspen grove off the side of the road. Spotting game was a normal occurrence and part of the enjoyment of riding on scenic Highway 75. Without giving any additional thought to the deer, Don continued to the top of the pass where he turned around and began a fast descent back down to the valley floor. During that short period of time, the doe emerged from the woods and crossed the pavement to reach the thick green grass growing at the base of a rock outcropping. Standing on the shoulder, the doe was totally unaware that Don would soon return. The mountain road contained numerous curves as it snaked downhill keeping the deer hidden from Don's view until he was only a few yards away from her. Coasting at a nearly silent 38 mph, Don startled the doe. With her only escape route back across the highway, the deer's reaction could not have been worse, as she leaped exactly when Don was passing her, colliding with him, and slamming his body to the pavement before running away unscathed.

Don's impact with the asphalt was immediate; he heard the resounding crack of a bone. Shoulder pain had him gently touching his skin which outlined a very deformed clavicle. After using his good arm to free himself from his mangled bike, Don discovered he was bleeding through his torn clothing and that his helmet had cracked into three pieces and was dangling off his head by the straps. With a nonfunctioning bike, a broken collarbone, a possible head injury and extensive road rash, Don stood by the side of the road waving a bloody hand hoping a good Samaritan would help him get home. Fortunately, a man in a truck stopped and drove Don and his bike down the mountain to Sawtooth City. And that was when I received the phone call with the news, "Hey honey, a deer hit me on the highway, and I think I'm hurt."

"What do you mean a deer hit *you*? What happened? How bad are you hurt?"

"I'm pretty sure my collarbone is broken. I need to get to the hospital for X-rays. Since the fall was on my left side, I think I'll be fine driving to town." Don conveniently left out the part of the story where he had hit his head hard enough to destroy his helmet and later admitted he kept telling himself, "Don't fall asleep, don't fall asleep. . ." as he drove.

The emergency room physician examined Don for a possible concussion and ordered images of his neck and chest. Fortunately, the only broken bone was Don's clavicle which was cracked in five places and resembled the letter W. The good news was that the breaks were non-displaced and would not require surgery. The doctor explained to Don that he would have to wear a figure-eight sling to stretch and hold his collarbone in the proper position for healing. That was when Don asked the all-important question, "How long will it take for the bone to heal? Shannon and I have a sea kayaking trip planned with two other couples in late July. Will I be able to go?"

I was holding my breath as the ER physician replied, "It takes six weeks for the bones to knit and then you will need to start physical therapy to strengthen your shoulder. What day does your trip start?" When we told her our departure date and the plan to be paddling by July 23rd, she said, "Your bones should be healed by that time, but your upper body will be weakened from lack of use. You will have to paddle your way into shape while on your trip. The most important thing is to be a good patient and wear the sling, so your bone heals correctly."

Both of us breathed a big sigh of relief at the news that our trip was still a possibility. Don would be totally out of commission for six weeks while his collarbone, muscle, and skin healed. Looking at the shredded material of his arm warmers, I was glad he had put the coverings on for the ride downhill. The ER nurse spent a good amount of time cleaning the cuts and scrapes from his extensive road rash. He would be sore all over for a few weeks, especially his neck and shoulder, but he was determined to travel to Alaska, so he became the perfect patient to set the odds of a full recovery in his favor.

Don's dedication to wearing his sling worked. At six weeks, his collarbone had healed. His clavicle no longer felt smooth to the touch, but the new lumpy, bumpy ridges of bone were solid and allowed him to start a focused exercise program to strengthen his shoulder and arm muscles. On July 9th, with only eleven days left before boarding the plane for Alaska, it was time for us to attempt paddling and to learn how to safely maneuver a kayak.

Neither Don nor I had ever been in kayak and needed instruction on how to operate the boat. Ed's friend Becky, was an avid paddler and agreed to provide us with a lesson on the skills necessary for open water kayaking. Ed, Don, and I met with Becky at Alturas Lake in the Sawtooth National Forest for an afternoon of demonstration and practice. Becky owned two boats: a single and a double kayak. After a thorough explanation of how to operate the boats, we tested our new knowledge by paddling around the large lake under Becky's tutelage. By the end of the day, everyone was feeling confident in their ability to steer and control the kayaks. We also knew Glenn and Katherine were seasoned kayakers and would be there to help us if needed. With our planning complete, logistics in place and all of us healthy, it was time for our trip to begin.

NORTH TO ALASKA

It took a couple days for the six of us to fly into Anchorage, purchase perishables and drive to Whittier, Alaska where Honey Charters was holding our kayaks and would portage us and our boats to our first campsite. Expecting a late afternoon arrival, we had made reservations for the night at the fourteen story Begich Towers. Hands down, Whittier was the most unusual place I had ever visited. At first glance, the town looked run down with decaying infrastructure left behind by the US armed forces when they abandoned the area. The government established Whittier as a military base during WWII, in part, because it possessed a deep port that would not freeze in winter. Second, the two mountain ranges converging at this location trapped a semipermanent cloud cover that hid the base from Japanese bombers and kept the area free of danger.

Although Anchorage was only sixty miles away, the city could not be reached by land until the military carved a two-and-a-half-mile tunnel through the mountains to accommodate a single rail line for supplies. For more than fifty years, the train remained the only way to reach Whittier by land. Then on June 7, 2000, the tunnel was opened to motorized vehicles allowing easy access to the small community. Because of the limited width of the road, traffic moved one-way, alternating direction each hour and the tunnel closed from eleven o'clock each night until five o'clock in the morning. Just six weeks after opening, we found ourselves being shuttled through the very narrow underground passageway before emerging into the gray, gloomy atmosphere of Whittier, Alaska.

The small village involved one square mile of land in the shape of a horseshoe and was surrounded by mountain walls rising from the harbor. We drove directly to June's Whittier Condo Suites and met June Miller, the owner of the property management company. Another bizarre feature of Whittier was that the building that contained our condo rentals also housed most of the community including the town's businesses, government offices, school, church, hospital and 150 residents. The Begich Towers were originally built as military housing to accommodate a thousand soldiers. Overtime, the upper floors had been converted into multifamily apartments and sold. During our stay, only about 20 percent of the structure was owner occupied with a few dozen condominiums rented out to visitors. There was a considerable amount of uninhabited space creating an echoing, empty feeling to the place. It was a nice surprise to find the interior of our apartment in good shape with comfortable accommodations. The view was the most outstanding feature of our stay, even with heavy cloud cover. Ed and Teri had a pretty ocean view overlooking the cobalt blue waters of Passage Canal. Located on the other side of the building, Glenn, Katherine, Don, and I gazed upon a magnificent green mountainside with multiple cascading waterfalls. If one could overlook the depressing buildings, cracked asphalt, abandoned fishing boats and rusty equipment, Whittier was a beautiful place.

We decided to go exploring that evening to see what our options were for dinner. A small grocery store sold fresh shrimp, so we purchased four pounds for boiling, a few potatoes for roasting and salad fixings. Don noticed T-shirts for sale and called me over, "Look at this," Don said while holding up a T-shirt. "The Weather is Shittier in Whittier! Pretty funny." It hadn't stopped raining since we had arrived, so the catch phrase seemed appropriate and amusing.

Glenn made us all laugh when he held up another shirt featuring weather forecasts for a variety of Alaskan locations and read the caption imitating the monotone voice of the radio's tidal forecaster, "The weather is currently shitty in Anchorage, mostly shitty in Fairbanks, increasingly shitty in Homer, and shittier in Whittier."

"The local newsletter in our condo said the town only averages 133 days of sunshine per year," I commented. "Got to give the locals credit for being able to turn that gloomy fact into a humorous money-making opportunity."

Smiling with optimism, Teri added, "Maybe we'll get lucky and have a little sunshine during the next ten days!"

Despite the pouring rain, everyone's positive attitude and enthusiasm about visiting this part of Alaska allowed us to find humor in our stormy weather. Rain or shine, we would enjoy the trip. For the rest of the evening, we ignored the raindrops and shared a delicious seafood dinner filled with fun conversation and genuine camaraderie. Tomorrow was the start of our adventure. I fell asleep thinking that no matter what kind of weather I woke up to in the morning, I would bring my own slice of sunshine with me on our trip.

SHIP AHOY!

The hour and a half boat ride to our campsite at Dual Head was amazing. I grew up in Texas and had boated in the Gulf of Mexico on numerous occasions, but nothing about my previous experiences were similar to our cruise in the Prince William Sound. The waters of Passage Canal and the Marine Highway were smooth as glass allowing us to see a variety of marine life. All along the route, big fish kept jumping out of the water. Pete, our captain, and owner of Honey Charters told us we were observing migratory salmon. Noticing a pod of whales in the distance, Pete drove us closer so that we could watch them breach and create huge waves as they splashed back down on the surface of the ocean. Dolphins swam alongside our boat and easily kept pace with the craft. Now and then we noticed a head pop out of the water and quickly submerge again. Pete informed us there was an abundance of harbor seals in the area and that we would probably see many of them during our kayak trip. The ocean was alive with activity.

Mountains, waterfalls, and glaciers could be seen on both sides of the boat. Floating icebergs became more prevalent the closer we got to our drop-off point. Our goal was to camp at multiple sites during our week and a half vacation allowing us to fish in a variety of places and visit different glaciers along the way. Dual Head was centrally located and a great location to start our adventure. Pete ran his boat up on the gravel beach and extended an aluminum ladder off the front so we could disembark and form a human chain to offload the kayaks and gear. In no time, we were unloaded and waving goodbye to our captain. Our trip had officially begun.

FIRST IMPRESSIONS

My first day kayaking was filled with wonder and awe. The ocean was emerald green, extremely clear, and as calm as a lake. The glassy surface made paddling a delight as the group maneuvered along Dual Head's shoreline. Numerous bald eagles were nesting in the area and demonstrated their hunting prowess by swooping down and retrieving fish from the water. Our presence seemed to have no impact on them as they fought over food and dominance right in front of us. I had never been this close to an eagle and was reminded of their incredible size when one flew directly over Don's head, and I could see the wingspan nearly matched the length of his boat. Watching these magnificent birds, I understood why their image was selected for the emblem of our nation. Their strength, beauty, and fighting spirit are easily recognized. Spending the afternoon observing them in their natural habitat was a privilege that I thoroughly enjoyed.

The eagles weren't the only animals fishing in this part of the Sound. I was shocked by the sudden appearance of a sea otter next to my boat. The animal surfaced within reaching distance and stared at me as if trying to figure out what I was exactly. After several seconds passed, the sea otter dove under my boat and reappeared on the other side as if still trying to decide what he was encountering. Turning his head to look at me from different angles while floating on his back, he finally wiggled his nose and disappeared below the surface of the water. It was such a delight to be able to get so close to the otter. The kayak seemed to be regarded as a safe object allowing the animal to be curious but not afraid of my presence.

Paddling past a huge iceberg, I was surprised by the loud cracking noises it produced as it thawed. As a group, we had already discussed the danger in getting too close to an iceberg in case its base, hidden in the water, melted enough to make it top heavy and unexpectedly roll over. No one wanted to be taken out by a chunk of ice. With that thought in mind, I respectfully kept my distance.

There was no reason for us to be concerned with finding sources of fresh water to drink on our trip. Snow and glacial melt created an abundance of waterfalls and streams across the landscape. Approaching a waterfall from the ocean allowed us to hear the amplified, echoing sound it made and feel the invigorating mist emanating from the cascading stream. Some of the larger falls produced their own wind and created an undercurrent as huge volumes of water pushed out from the land and into the sea. On the warmest of days, we learned the breeze from a massive waterfall felt like an air conditioner vent and used it to cool ourselves off.

There was something truly magical about our first day of ocean kayaking. I went to bed that night excited about our next day's paddle into Humpback Cove which provided the opportunity to find whales and to fish for salmon. The following day held the promise for many new experiences.

A WHALE OF A FISH TALE

Our day began with a southerly cruise through Whale Bay with the goal of reaching one of its fingerlike extensions called Humpback Cove. Pete recommended the area for fishing, so upon his advice, we headed in that direction to see what we could find. Needing a mid-morning break, we pulled up on a gravel beach to stretch our legs. There was a wide, but very shallow stream snaking its way out of thick vegetation and across an open grassy area. To our surprise, there were a half dozen salmon struggling to swim upstream in the minuscule amount of water. The fish made heroic efforts to jump over exposed sections of rock as they made their way from one small pool of water to an another. We were captivated by their attempts to reach their goal and found ourselves standing on the bank cheering their successes.

A short distance away, I found a large fish huddled next to the side of the bank. Kneeling to get a closer look, the fish surprised me when it did not swim away. Reaching in the water, I ran my hand down the length of the fish, and it still didn't move. When my friends noticed what I was doing, they came over to watch me. "If I were a bear, this salmon would have been eaten. Pretty unbelievable this fish is letting me pet him."

Ed replied, "That salmon is dead on the fin. He spawned and is now exhausted and in the process of dying."

Glenn knelt to grab the salmon by the tail and then held it up for us to see. The sight was a new experience for the group. He put the fish back into the water allowing the salmon's life cycle to continue its natural course. Finding those few salmon during our break made all of us even more determined to continue our quest toward Humpback Cove hoping to locate an area where we could fish for sport.

Despite its name, Humpback Cove was not home to any whales we could find. We did, however, run into an astonishing number of salmon. The six of us paddled down the long-protected cove to its southern end where a wide freshwater stream flowed into the ocean. As I started to maneuver my kayak into the mouth of the outlet, the calm surface erupted and fish began knocking against both sides of my boat. Peering into the shallow water, I could see hundreds of salmon swimming next to me. We had found a stream loaded with fish; time to get out the rod and reel to catch dinner.

Our fishing licenses were staggered over the ten vacation days so that someone was legal to fish everyday of our trip. On July 24th, Glenn, and I both had a valid license. Don readied my pole and then handed it to me so I could cast from the bank. The fish were energetic and plentiful; jumping out of the water in every direction we looked. Glenn caught two nice size Silvers in a matter of minutes and strung them on a line to cook for Teri's birthday dinner that evening. He decided the area was perfect for photographs and took out his camera to capture me catching my first fish. What a moment I provided for Don and my friends. On my first cast, I immediately felt a fish hit my line, so I set the hook and started pulling it toward the shore. With large salmon jumping out of the water on both sides of my prized catch, I excitedly hoisted the hooked fish into the air and squealed, "No way! All these giants everywhere and I catch this puny little guy?" Meanwhile, everyone was laughing hysterically. My fish was barely as big as my hand and was desperately wiggling to be let go. While Don removed the hook from its mouth and released the little guy back into the water, I stood there shaking my head in disbelief that I could hook a smolt within a pool of huge salmon. I let Don make the next cast and he instantly hooked a good-sized Coho. He then handed me the rod to bring the fish to shore. Glenn was able to get the action photographs he wanted, and I took a few of Don posing with the fish as well. It would take some practice before I became proficient at handling my fishing pole, but a week later, I would be the one catching the "king" salmon of the trip.

JUST THE TIP OF THE ICEBERG

After two days of camping at Dual Head, we decided to pack up and paddle to a completely different environment within Prince William Sound. We spent an entire day in our kayaks traveling through an area called Icy Bay to reach a cove where the spectacular Tiger Glacier was located. Maneuvering through Icy Bay was quite an ordeal because of the incredible number of floating icebergs. The tide pulled ice from both Tiger Glacier and Nassau Fjord which converged in Icy Bay creating a formidable section of water. The dimensions of the icebergs varied from jagged pieces the size of a small car to chunks the size of a house. The wind blew from the top of the glacier down through the cove adding a headwind for us to battle. At times the gusts were so strong that when I quit paddling for a short rest, my boat quickly began to drift backward. The wind was gusting strong enough to create white capped waves and force icebergs to collide. For several hours, the group concentrated on navigating through the rough waters to avoid being pinned between large blocks of ice, until we safely reached the other side of the wide bay and pulled up on shore for a much-needed break.

As if rewarding us for our efforts, Mother Nature broke up the clouds and provided rays of sunshine to brighten the rest of our day. The wind calmed and the temperature rose, providing much nicer paddling conditions into Tiger Glacier Cove. We arrived at our campsite in early evening and immediately understood how the area got its name from the loud, explosive roar that was produced when an ice sheet calved and fell into the sea. The sound became an irregularly cadenced lullaby to fall asleep to that night.

THE "PANTYGONIA" BUSH

We slept until the sun's rays warmed our tent and emerged to discover beautiful blue skies overhead. Without any threat of rain, the gang decided this was the perfect day for washing both our bodies and our clothing. Fifty yards from camp was a large stream containing pools of water deep enough to dunk oneself for bathing. Although I knew the stream originated from a glacier, it was not until I squatted down to wiggle my fingers in the water that I realized the temperature was barely above freezing. Ed was the only person that submerged himself in the frigid waters. Don and I bathed standing on the bank, using our bandannas for washcloths and a cooking pot for rinsing. I still experienced an ice cream headache while pouring the extremely cold water over my head, but after three days of camping, it was worth a little discomfort to be completely clean.

Dressing in the last of our clean clothes meant it was time to do laundry. All our gear consisted of quick drying fabric that would only need a few hours of sunshine to dry and be ready to pack. We hand-washed our clothes and decided to drape the items over the branches of a nearby bush in lieu of setting up a clothesline. It wasn't until all six of us had hung our garments together that we realized everyone was wearing Patagonia brand underwear. We found ourselves laughing at how many pairs of "panties" were airing in the breeze. Teri said, "This isn't a clothes drying bush, it's a *pantygonia* bush." We all chuckled at her clever comment. The term stuck and became part of our vocabulary; each utterance evoking the special memory of our fun time together at Tiger Glacier.

Glenn capitalized on our gorgeous sunny day by taking several photographs. We kayaked as close as we dared to the base of Tiger Glacier so Glenn could stage a few shots contrasting the size of our boats to the massive wall of ice. We witnessed the incredible power unleashed by the calving ice as it displaced enough water to create huge waves that kept the ocean churning; never allowing calmness to prevail in the cove.

After our photo session, we paddled to the shore and enjoyed a nice lunch on the beach. While fishing, Don discovered an area where huge slabs of flat rock were tucked in the mountainside, protected from the wind and free of bugs. He led us to the special place to relax and enjoy the afternoon reading, fishing, and writing in our journals. Most of us were lulled to sleep by the distant rumble of the glacier and the warm embrace of the sun while lying on the smooth rock platforms. A few hours easily slipped by in this tranquil setting.

As early evening arrived, I made the announcement, "It's five o'clock somewhere and I have a surprise for everyone, Kalua over ice! I just need some help chipping away at this iceberg to create our drinks." Ed started hacking at a chunk of ice that had been set ashore by the tide earlier in the day. He scraped away the salty exterior to reach the clean, clear pellets a few inches from the surface. Working together, we filled everyone's glasses with cubes and liqueur.

Glenn expressed his approval, "What a flash of genius. This is world class ice and perfect for making drinks!"

His comment prompted a lively discussion about the formation of the perfect ice cube and the age of our iceberg. Ed explained to the group that glacier ice was monomineralic rock that transformed from snowflakes. "As fallen snow compresses to become more dense and tightly packed, the process removes the air, and the light fluffy crystals change into hard, round ice pellets over time."

Don added, "The clearer the ice, the older the ice. This iceberg could be as old as 30,000 years. Maybe a mammoth pooped on the snow that made the ice pellets in our drinks!"

Don's statement caused moaning and exclamations of "*eww*" from everyone until Glenn made the witty rejoinder, "Good though." Everyone started laughing as we all associated his response with the punchline of a joke told earlier in the trip.

Our laughter turned into a round of toasts. "To great weather," "To great wildlife," "To great friends and fun!"

Our first four days of vacation had offered spectacular scenery, unparalleled fishing opportunities, and extremely unique sights from our kayaks. Don and I went to bed excited about what we might yet find exploring Alaska's coastline.

BUGS, BISCUITS, AND BIG RAINDROPS

Our goal for the following day was to camp near the Chenega Glacier in Nassau Fjord. The paddle out of Tiger Glacier Cove through Icy Bay was very pleasant for the first few miles until we arrived at the entrance to Nassau Fjord. This section of Icy Bay had presented dangerous waters during our paddle two days earlier. When we arrived at the southern edge of the broad fjord inlet, it was choked with impenetrable ice. Blocked but not deterred, we crossed to the other side of the wide opening and discovered a narrow passage of ice-free water along the northern shoreline leading toward Chenega Glacier. In close single file we navigated our way past a myriad of iceberg sentries to safely reach the black sandy beach of Beam Campsite deep in the heart of Nassau Fjord. A thirteen-foot tide was forecasted that evening making it necessary to set up our tents quite a distance inland on the flat, expansive camping area. We also had to haul the kayaks up on the ebony-colored beach and secure them with tie-downs to prevent them from floating out to sea with the outgoing tide.

Chenega Glacier was a towering mass of ice. The wall face was more than five times the size of Tiger Glacier. Falling ice sheets created waves that rippled across the entire width of the fjord depositing an incredible number of icebergs on our beach. Within fifteen-seconds of hearing a thunderous boom, waves began to break upon the shoreline in front of our tents. After dinner, we created "theater seating" by organizing our camp chairs in one long row to provide the best viewing of the show. Glenn described it best when he made the comment, "It's a parade of ice!" We spent the evening being entertained by Chenega Glacier and all the floating icebergs. Ed broke out a bottle of Bushmills and poured it over "mammoth ice" to create another outstanding drink. The stories and laughter flowed as smoothly as the icebergs and whiskey until late in the evening.

When Don and I woke up, we instantly realized the weather had dramatically changed. Sunrise normally occurred around four o'clock, but our camp was still shrouded in darkness at nine in the morning. We were not surprised to find gray clouds covering the sky when we crawled out of our tent. No one complained about the imminent rain. We had been gifted five gloriously sunny days and expected a change in conditions. Using a large tarp and our paddles for support poles, we set up a shelter to protect us from inclement weather. Our timing was perfect, as raindrops started falling we were enjoying our breakfast of oatmeal and biscuits. The baked biscuits were fluffy and delicious. They put a smile on our faces despite the gloomy outlook for the day. We all repeatedly thanked Glenn and Katherine for bringing their Dutch oven and creating such wonderful baked goods throughout our trip. Fresh made scones, brownies, cakes, biscuits, cinnamon rolls, and hearty one dish meals had been such a treat while camping. Our original menus were great, and the addition of baked foods and fresh salmon made our meals extraordinary.

Bathing the previous night, Don and I had seen salmon in the small stream next to camp. Thinking there might be good fishing nearby, Don and Glenn decided to brave the downpour and paddle along the shoreline in search of a salmon run. As a safety precaution, the men took one of the handheld radios with them to stay in contact throughout the day. While the men fished, Ed, Teri and I played several exciting hands of gin rummy.

Teri had packed a deck of cards, providing the opportunity for a fun and competitive afternoon of games.

When Glenn radioed to let us know he and Don were heading back to camp, sans fish, we emerged from the tent to start preparing our preplanned dinner meal. Ed had gathered driftwood the previous evening and tucked it under the tarp before the rain showers started. To conserve fuel, we built a fire to heat water for hot beverages, cooking, and the final rinse of our dishes. Glenn's keen eye for capturing perfect pictures had him staging an impromptu modeling session as he commented to everyone, "I think this country is particularly beautiful after a rain like this; with the mist just hanging in the trees." With a pause in raindrops, he quickly took photos of the group in front of the campfire with the shoreline full of icebergs and Chenega Glacier in the background. An image of Don, Teri, and me sitting around the campfire would soon be published in *Backpacker Magazine*.

Just like the saying "every cloud has a silver lining," the positive side of enduring an entire day of rain was the vast reduction of insects we had to contend with throughout the evening. The presence of bugs is an expected part of any Alaskan wilderness experience and ours was no exception. Don and I wore head nets much of our time on land. Mosquitoes and biting flies continuously attacked making the effort of eating meals somewhat difficult and downright comical looking at times. I became a master at executing the necessary steps for ensuring a bug bite free meal: swat the netting, lift the cover, take a bite, and then quickly lower the rim before bugs gained access to my face. Over the course of our trip, the pattern became routine, and the movements performed without thought.

Katherine was the only one of us to have an acute reaction to a bite. During breakfast, a bug crawled under her head net and bit her on the lip causing the area to swell to an alarming size. Fortunately, we had a small pharmacy of medications with us to combat basic illnesses, pain, and allergic reactions. Katherine took a couple Benadryl tablets and slept while the rest of us fished and played cards. By dinner time, the swelling was almost gone, and her lip looked close to normal. I found it interesting that our two glaciated campsites had more bugs than the first moderately warm camping location. I thought the colder temperatures and cooler breezes flowing down the ice would reduce insect activity, but that theory was not true in our case.

Our camp's cold and stormy setting provided us with a nice surprise just after dinner. Large ice barges were floating a short distance beyond the shore and black dots could be detected covering their surface. Using binoculars, we discovered the black dots were hundreds of harbor seals that had climbed on the ice to spend the night. Unsure if the weather had caused them to congregate or if they gathered for some other unknown reason, we watched their interactions and enjoyed their company before retiring for the evening. Drifting off to sleep, my last thoughts were about the two beautiful glaciers we had visited and how exciting it had been to kayak in such close proximity to the thundering ice giants and their fallen icebergs. I had enjoyed the uniqueness of the icy locations but was ready to trade the cold environment for a more temperate climate in search of a great fishing hole.

HITTING THE JACKPOT IN JACKPOT BAY

We truly felt like we had hit the jackpot when we kayaked into Jackpot Bay. The area was picturesque and teeming with wildlife. Every paddle stroke brought new encounters with animals all along the waterway. Harbor seals had kept pace with us in the early morning. The seals seemed very curious about my boat and swam back and forth underneath my kayak, surfacing to stare at me for a few seconds before diving back underwater. They finally abandoned my side when the ice transitioned to the warmer waters of Dangerous Passage, our entry route into Jackpot Bay.

Ingress to Dangerous Passage was through an expansive bay where the open view allowed us to spot humpback whales breaching in the deep waters of the nearby marine highway. We were close enough to see their flukes and the mighty splashes they made but far enough away to feel safe. Soon after spotting the whales, five porpoises surfaced and began swimming in unison beside me as I paddled across the open stretch of water. I never realized how large a marine mammal they were until I was able to measure them directly next to my kayak and found they nearly matched in length. After scrutinizing the kayaks, they sped past the group and headed out to sea.

Our midday lunch stop was along a random grassy beach. A black bear surprised us when he stepped out of the vegetation while we were filtering water from a stream. He wasn't aggressive and quickly retreated into the thick bushes making us think he had been shocked to see us as well. We had seen bear prints at our campsite at Tiger Glacier and had diligently followed protocols for camping in bear country. We knew bears were in the vicinity but today confirmed their presence and reminded us to remain vigilant in how we handled our food.

Eagles and otters greeted us on our approach to Jackpot Bay and once again, the waters became glassy and calm in the more narrow, protected channel. Salmon were jumping out of the water as we paddled to our campsite. Their presence, along with the otters and eagles, gave us hope that this would be a grand fishing location. The bay was large and comprised of fingerlike coves providing a multitude of areas for us to explore. We camped on a rock jut at the mouth of Jackpot Creek located on the northern end of the bay. Although not in our original plan, we would spend the last four nights of our vacation at this location because, as Don so eloquently stated, "Every time we leave camp, we discover something spectacular here."

THE BONANZA

Our camp at Jackpot Bay would be nicknamed "Fish Central" because of the colossal number of salmon that had congregated in the area. Everyone was able to experience the exciting feeling of reeling in one of these mighty fish. There seemed to be at least three species of salmon in the location: Chinook (King), Coho (Silver), and Chum (Dog). All three were large and fought fiercely once hooked on a line. Catching far more fish than we could consume, we quickly became catch and release anglers. Fresh salmon was incorporated into the menu for dinner each evening with side dishes added from our packed provisions.

On our first day, Glenn caught a Silver, Don caught a King, and Ed caught a Chum. We decided to cook the Silver and the King, releasing the Chum back into the sea. Though both fish were very tasty, the King was the most delightful of the two. Interestingly, there was absolutely no fish scent to its meat. The King fillet was significantly more red than the other, both raw and when cooked, and had a texture that resembled a tender steak. By contrast, the Silver tasted and smelled exactly as expected and had a little flakier texture. A distinction I never would have made except for the unique circumstances provided by this trip. They were both good but different.

We found our best fishing hole during an early evening exploration of Jackpot Creek. After paddling a hundred yards upstream, we came upon a series of rapids that required us to portage our kayaks. A pool of water could be seen in the distance encouraging us to continue. Our effort was reward-ed with the discovery of a deep pond full of salmon. It was in this location that Teri caught her first fish, a huge Silver that provided a culinary feast during our celebration of her success as an angler. The pond allowed me to hook the largest fish caught during the trip; a Silver Salmon that may have broken records had we been able to weigh the giant. As of the year 2000, the record for a Silver in the Prince William Sound was twenty-four pounds. When we purchased our licenses, a Fish and Game officer told us that the Silver Salmon were above normal size because many spent an extra year at sea before returning to spawn. We took several photos to document the catch and then released the massive Silver back into the stream so it could continue to spawn and pass on its outstanding genetics. Even though my fish wasn't a Chinook, I still claimed to have caught "The King" salmon of the trip because of its enormous size!

Probably the funniest moment we experienced on the trip was watching Teri being pulled around the pond in her kayak by the salmon she hooked on her line. Ed videoed the comical scene, along with us laughing, as Teri circled the pond uncontrollably powered by a Coho. It took a surprising amount of time for the fish to tire out and allow Ed to paddle close enough to help Teri free her line. Every time he drew near, the salmon furiously swam away, dragging Teri across the water. Years later, I still find myself smiling upon the memory of Teri's entertaining boat ride.

HISTORY COMES ALIVE

Living in the Sawtooth National Forest of Idaho and near the Headwaters of the Salmon River, I was familiar with the history of salmon in the area. The Salmon River, Redfish Lake, and Redfish Creek were named after the thousands of Sockeye (Red Salmon) that used to return to these waters to spawn. Stories claimed that during the 1960s there were so many fish "the waters turned red" and "you could walk on the backs of the fish to cross the streams." With the construction of eight dams, less than one hundred Sockeye returned to Redfish Lake in 1999. I often wondered what it would be like to see all those fish spawning in the sixties. Our trip to Jackpot Bay would provide a visual of what Idaho might have looked like forty years ago.

On the morning of our third day, we paddled south to explore a large cove at the opposite end of the bay. There was a large stream that snaked its way through a grassy plain before depositing its mineral rich water into the sea. Numerous eagles were congregated in the area alerting us that there were probably salmon nearby. We beached the kayaks and walked inland to see what we could find. That's when I experienced my 1960 history lesson on spawning salmon. The fish were lined up across the width of the stream. The females were digging redds in the gravel while the males fought for the right to fertilize the eggs. There were thousands of fish in the small stretch of water. It would have been impossible to walk across the shallow riverbed without stepping on one.

About seventy-five yards upstream, the terrain climbed steeply causing the waterway to cascade over rocks and logs. Although many salmon struggled to maneuver over the natural fish ladders, a majority succeeded in the effort to reach their natal hatching grounds. We spent a few hours watching the spawning process; intrigued by the determination and fortitude of this incredible fish. The eagles, otters, and black bears feasted on the easy prey. With all the obstacles and predators to overcome, Don and I knew we were watching a truly amazing feat as these salmon ended their long journey and successfully completed their life cycle. I came home with an even greater appreciation for those few remaining sockeye that swam over nine-hundred miles to reach Redfish Lake.

ANYONE SEEN MY BOOT?

The location of Jackpot Bay provided the best visual perspective of the changing tide levels and created a few memorable moments during the trip. We had been warned by everyone we encountered to not underestimate the rising tides. In the words of more than one local, "Watch out for high tide! It will surprise you." We had a small booklet from the National Oceanic and Atmospheric Administration that contained tide tables for the Prince William Sound area. The publication listed the time for both high and low tides throughout each day.

The highest tide during our trip was fifteen feet, nine inches which occurred on our third night at Jackpot Bay. We thought our tents were set up high enough on the peninsula to be safe, but Glenn and Katherine's tent became partially submerged while they were sleeping. When we saw Glenn the next morning, he asked, "Have you guys seen my hiking boot? It was sitting in our tent's vestibule, but I think the tide took it out to sea." Sure enough, he found it forty yards away when low tide occurred. The boot was waterlogged, but at least he had a matching pair again. Our camp at Jackpot Bay sat on a high rock outcropping with a steep drop to the ocean during low tide. There were several large rocks around the area where we camped that completely submerged below the waterline when high tide came in. Fifteen feet was a substantial height and watching the rocks disappear in a matter of minutes was astonishing.

The speed of the incoming tide caught us by surprise and caused us to nearly lose our kayaks on a handful of occasions. During a bathroom stop on our paddle to Jackpot Bay, Katherine beached her boat, and during the few minutes it took to relieve herself, her boat took off into the ocean, forcing one of us to paddle out to retrieve it for her. Don was also caught off guard when he turned his back on his boat for less than two minutes until Teri yelled to him to run and catch his kayak before it headed out to sea. The locals had been right to warn us about the tidal changes. We learned to always keep a keen eye on our boats.

A FEW SURPRISES

In addition to fishing for salmon, we brought a crab ring hoping to enjoy a fresh crab dinner one evening. While Ed was cutting the heads and tails off the salmon he had caught for dinner, Glenn asked, "Why don't you set the crab ring tonight with the fish heads?"

Ed looked up at Glenn and shook his head. "We don't need crab for dinner tonight."

Glenn sarcastically queried, "If Thomas Jefferson would have had that type of attitude, do you think there would have been a Constitution?"

Ed smiled widely as he responded, "Thomas Jefferson wasn't even at the Constitutional Convention! He was in France flirting with the mademoiselles."

"Trick question," Glenn quipped without missing a beat. "If Benjamin Franklin would have had that kind of attitude, do you think he would have discovered electricity?"

Ed laughed out loud. "Ben Franklin did have that kind of attitude. He wrote a book called *Fart Proudly*."

At this point, all of us were laughing at the quick-witted conversation. Our entire trip had been filled with these types of humorous discussions. One liners and the exchange of clever banter had us smiling throughout our vacation together. For me, our continuous laughter was just as strong a memory as the wildlife we experienced together during the trip.

Ed did end up setting the crab ring that evening. Although we never got to enjoy a crab dinner, we did catch something unique. When we hoisted the ring from the ocean floor the following day, a huge sunflower sea star, the size of a car tire, was feeding on the fish heads attached to the net. The unusual starfish was peach toned in color and had sixteen legs. Adult sunflower sea stars have sixteen to twenty-four legs and can grow thirty-six inches in diameter. Ours seemed to be a hungry young adult that did not want to let go of the bait. We cut the fish head loose from the netting and placed them both into the shallow water. A unique characteristic of the sunflower sea star is their ability to travel a meter per minute, much faster than a regular starfish. Within a very short period, the sea star and the fish head were out of sight.

The only time we encountered other people was the last evening of our trip. A Forest Service biologist and three interns arrived at our campsite, hoping to stay at our location. We explained we would be leaving the next morning, so they decided to camp only a few hundred yards away allowing them to easily relocate upon our departure. During our discussion, we mentioned our crab ring and that we had tried crabbing but had been unsuccessful. That's when the biologist told us there were no king crab in Jackpot Bay.

Ed quickly responded, "We thought there had to be crab living in these waters because we found shells on the bank during low tide."

"Those shells were from our field trip last month," one intern sheepishly confessed. "We purchased the crab in town for dinner. Sorry our shells tricked you into thinking you might get some crab for dinner."

Our response was a series of moans as we realized a king crab dinner had never been a possibility. At least our crabbing efforts had been rewarded with the catch of the sunflower sea star. Not a king crab dinner, but a good memory just the same.

Both Glenn and Don had been successful in catching fish earlier in the day which prompted a conversation within the group about our menu for the last night of our trip. "Let's build a fire and grill salmon steaks for supper," I suggested. "The weather is great, no rain or wind. Seems like a perfect evening for a campfire."

"We'll probably never have the opportunity to eat salmon this fresh again so we should enjoy it while we can," Don added. Everyone agreed with the idea and looked forward to spending the last night filling their bellies full of fresh fish. Having exhausted our supply of firewood, we all decided to kayak the shoreline to find dry kindling for a fire. Don found a fallen dead tree and was able to saw off several small branches, quickly creating a pile of wood that would meet our needs for the evening. Utilizing bungie cords, we attached limbs to Teri's boat until it looked like a beaver dam floating across the bay.

During our late afternoon return to camp, a strange stillness could be detected in the air. Unbeknownst to us, a storm was rolling in and we were experiencing the calm before the storm. The other peculiar thing we noticed was the emergence of thousands upon thousands of jellyfish in Jackpot Bay. I had grown up playing on Texas beaches and fishing in the Gulf of Mexico, but I had never witnessed anything close to the bloom of moon jellyfish we saw that afternoon in Jackpot Bay.

Don stopped paddling on his way back to camp and was staring intensely into the ocean when Glenn came up beside him and asked what had caught his attention. "The water is so clear and calm, the jellyfish look like galaxy formations floating in deep space," he answered.

"So, Don, did you ever drop acid when you were younger?" Glenn asked. Laughing together, the two shared Don's observation of the thousands of jellyfish with the rest of us later at dinner. Leave it to Don to put a unique perspective on the jellyfish encounter. Adding levity to a situation seemed to be his specialty throughout our trip.

Ed set up his tripod and took a group photo of us lined up in our camp chairs eating dinner. The photo captures us all with happy smiles even though the skies had started to darken, the wind had picked up and the smell of rain was in the air. The changes around us added to the realization that our grand vacation was ending. The following day would include a quick breakdown of camp and a speedy paddle to our pickup spot about six miles away. We had no way of knowing that getting back to civilization would be the most challenging part of our adventure.

A FITTING FINALE

We pushed out to sea the next morning through crashing waves on the shoreline. Jackpot Bay was no longer calm. Large swells were moving on the horizon, and once we entered Dangerous Passage, whitecaps began to break over our boats. We paddled hard moving parallel with the shoreline and kept an eye on each other to ensure everyone remained upright in their boats. We had given ourselves extra time to travel to our pickup spot which made me feel better when I saw Katherine head to shore for a much-needed break from nerves and too much morning coffee. The rest of us followed suit and spent a few minutes on the sand stretching and studying the map to verify our current location and the distance we still needed to kayak.

We successfully reached the pickup point by our target time of noon. While we stood on the beach waiting for Honey Charters, the weather continued to deteriorate. When rain started hammering the coastline, we set up a tarp and huddled underneath it to stay dry. We knew our situation was growing more serious but instead of focusing on the brewing storm or the fact that we might have to camp in place, the group looked on the bright side: everyone was together, no one was hurt, there was adequate food and fresh water nearby. We were okay. In fact, after standing a few minutes nestled close together, I broke out in the song from the *Monty Python and the Holy Grail* movie, "Always look on the bright side of life!" Glenn, Ed, Katherine, and Teri chimed in with the whistling part of the song. Laughter erupted and then we all started belting out the rest of the song together. One tune transitioned to another, and before long I found myself entertaining my friends by singing and acting out the entire Hershey's Chocolate commercial, "There's nothing like the face of a kid eating a Hershey's bar. A face as happy as it can be ... Hershey, the great American Chocolate Bar!" Ed caught my one woman show on video as well as everyone's laughter. A little frivolity improved our spirits and quickly passed the time; we continued to sing a variety of songs and jingles throughout the early afternoon.

Before long, Ed directed our attention to a small aluminum boat heading our way from the Marine Highway. When the boat ran ashore, the six of us formed a human chain and swiftly loaded the kayaks and gear. We made it aboard the craft, but there would be no smooth sailing on the ride back to Whittier in eight-to-ten-foot seas. Our captain, Brooke Whippe, tried to "ride the trough" by steering the boat through the calmer water found between the big waves but he was often forced to crest the top and free-fall eight to ten feet before hitting the ocean surface with a painful smack. The repeated pounding was hard on our bodies and required us to hang onto the bench to stay seated. Fortunately, the boat had a covered cabin as waves continually crashed over the top deck. Nothing could be seen out of the boat windows but a wall of water. Brooke later told us, "Had the ocean been any rougher, we would have been camping together somewhere along the coastline." Normally, the boat ride would have taken an hour and a half. We cruised into Whittier harbor after two-and-a-half hours of battling the seas; a little beat-up but whole.

June Miller, the property manager, picked us up at the dock and delivered us to our condos. Returning to civilization and specifically, taking hot showers, settled our nerves and energized us to gather for a celebration meal at the local Chinese restaurant. Our odyssey had come to a close, but the moments we shared during the adventurous journey will always be remembered.

1 Whittier Harbor—Begich Towers in background. (L to R): Teri, Katherine, Ed, Glenn, Don, and a member of Honey Charters.

2 Honey Charters boat—The covered cabin would become very important on the return trip to Whittier when eight to ten foot seas crested over the top.

3 Our first day—beautiful clear, calm waters of Dual Head Campsite. Courtesy of Ed Cannady.

4 Paddling to Humpback Cove. Waterfalls all along the route. Courtesy of Ed Cannady.

5 Evening light with Don in silhouette—Marine Highway in background. Rocks will completely submerge with high tide. Courtesy of Ed Cannady.

6 Navigating past icebergs in Icy Bay on our way to Tiger Glacier. Courtesy of Ed Cannady.

7 Exploring the shoreline in Tiger Glacier Cove. Courtesy of Ed Cannady.

ALASKAN KAYAKING PHOTOS (2 OF 2)

8   Tiger Glacier—paddling as close as we dared to the roar of calving ice. Courtesy of Glenn Oakley.

9   Don kayaking past a constant parade of ice in Nassau Fjord. Courtesy of Ed Cannady.

10   Don enjoying the campfire in Nassau Fjord. Courtesy of Ed Cannady.

11   Exploring one of the many streams flowing into Jackpot Bay. Courtesy of Glenn Oakley.

12   Shannon with her "king-sized" silver salmon caught in Jackpot Creek.

13   Jackpot Bay—Enjoying a grilled salmon dinner on the last night of our trip. Seating area completely submerged by the rising fifteen foot tide within an hour of this photo being taken. Courtesy of Ed Cannady.

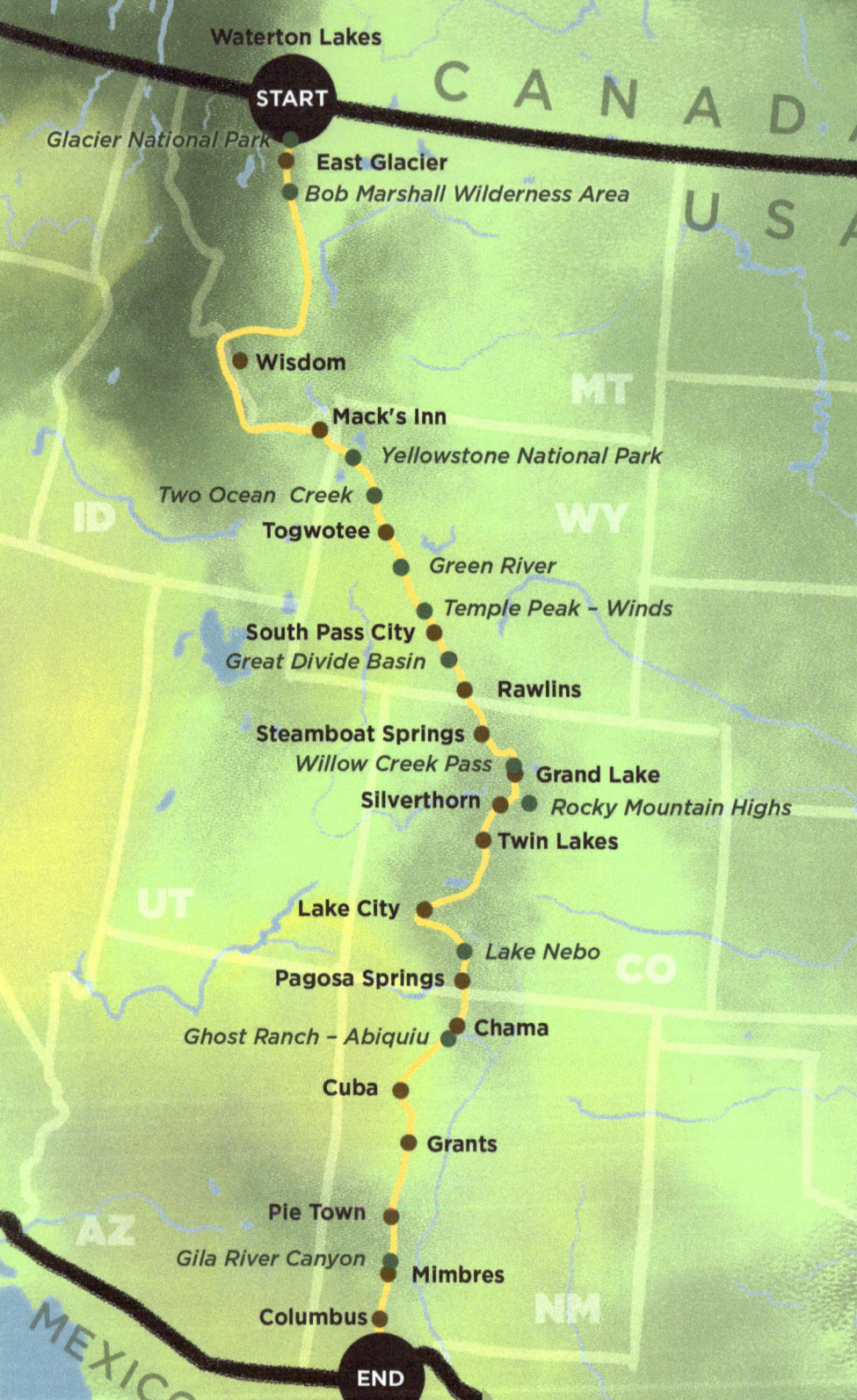

Waterton Lakes

START

CANADA
USA

Glacier National Park

• **East Glacier**

• *Bob Marshall Wilderness Area*

• **Wisdom**

MT

• **Mack's Inn**

Yellowstone National Park

ID

Two Ocean Creek •

• **Togwotee**

WY

Green River •

• *Temple Peak – Winds*

South Pass City •

• **Rawlins**

Great Divide Basin •

Steamboat Springs •

Willow Creek Pass •

• **Grand Lake**

Silverthorn •

• *Rocky Mountain Highs*

• **Twin Lakes**

UT

Lake City •

• *Lake Nebo*

CO

Pagosa Springs •

Ghost Ranch – Abiquiu •

• **Chama**

• **Cuba**

• **Grants**

AZ

• **Pie Town**

Gila River Canyon •

• **Mimbres**

Columbus •

NM

END

MEXICO

THE CONTINENTAL DIVIDE TRAIL

THE HEART OF THE MATTER

My heart began to beat with a noticeable flutter while I was Nordic skiing on a cold, crisp day in January 2002. I was wearing an exercise watch which displayed a heart rate of 265 beats per minute. "That can't be right. Something must be wrong with my chest strap." Of course, it had to be an equipment error. It never occurred to me that perhaps something could be wrong with my heart. As the week progressed with more training sessions on the snow, I experienced several more episodes of a hummingbird flutter in my chest accompanied by a shortness of breath and a leaden feeling in my limbs. I could no longer deny that something was seriously wrong with me. It was time to seek professional help.

In the year 2002, the book *Haywire Heart* had not yet been written, and atrial fibrillation and ventricular tachycardia were not prevalent diagnoses. It would take another fifteen years for doctors to understand the correlation between endurance athletes and heart electrophysiology issues. Thus, my experience with doctors and the battery of tests they conducted was filled with frustration, confusion, and a horrible misdiagnosis.

My EKG, sonogram, and stress tests were all normal—my heart arrhythmia would not present in a clinical setting. It was not until my primary care physician had me wear a Holter monitor at home that I was able to show what was going on inside of me. Connecting the machine to my body, I returned to the ski trail and pushed myself as hard as I could go. Intervals or climbing a steep hill on my Nordic skis had caused the irregular heart rate to occur. After several pole strokes, I felt the initial flutter, pushed the start button on the device and kept climbing. After the first event was captured, my heart had still not converted to a regular sinus rhythm, so I pushed the button again to capture another minute of data. Knowing the Holter monitor held three events, I repeated the process until the machine's data storage was full.

Later, I transmitted the information stored on the Holter monitor to a central data collection service via the telephone. About a minute after completing the data transfer, I answered my phone and found a very nervous young man on the line.

"Shannon, you need to get to the emergency room right now," he said. "I'm sending your data to the ER physician on duty at the hospital."

After explaining that I was in my office at the local hospital, I calmly walked through the double doors to the ER and found Dr. Robert Hall working. As he reviewed my results, he started shaking his head from side to side. "If you were a seventy-year-old man, you would be dead," he bluntly stated. "This episode would have killed you out on the snow."

His harsh comment froze me in place for a few seconds. When I finally absorbed the news, all I could do was ask, "What should I do?"

Dr. Hall said he would make a referral to Idaho Cardiology and that I should be seen by a cardiologist as soon as possible. His last words to me were a forceful, "Do not go skiing!"

I requested a copy of the faxed report, and although I could not read the EKG study, that was not necessary to interpret the findings. The page was black. It reminded me of a movie scene where a person is given a lie detector test and they provide false statements. My report showed a heavy line of up and down scribbles that were never ending for a full three minutes. I had been skiing without a regular heartbeat; just a quivering of my heart muscle. I was lucky my heart had converted back to a normal sinus rhythm at the end of the episode. It could just as easily have stopped. I sat stunned, thinking to myself, "What now?"

In Boise, I had another series of tests, including an MRI. The cardiologist told me the results of the tests determined I had right ventricular dysplasia, a rare and fatal disease in which the wall of the heart develops fat and scar tissue until it no longer is able to beat. The ventricular tachycardia I had experienced was how the disease initially presents itself. My prognosis was frightening; a heart transplant was needed. In the short term, it was suggested that I limit my activities and have a defibrillator implanted in my chest wall to correct any irregular sinus rhythm episodes that occurred while waiting for a donor. Physically, I had gone from skiing up steep mountain trails to being unable to climb up a set of stairs without imminent threat of a heart attack.

As I was reeling from the shock, Don acted. He quickly determined we needed a second opinion. He looked up the top ten heart hospitals in the country and found that Texas Heart Institute was ranked number seven. But, more important than its ranking, Dr. Ali Massumi was on staff. Dr. Massumi had written the first research papers on right ventricular dysplasia in 1982. He was touted as the best physician to diagnose and treat the disease.

When Don made the phone call to schedule an appointment, he was told Dr. Massumi had a six-month waiting list for new patients. The devastating news from the surgeon's assistant made Don very emotional on the phone. He talked about the importance of our relationship and said, "Shannon is my best friend. She can't die!" The lengthy discussion left both of them in tears but when Don hung up the phone that afternoon in March, I had an appointment the following week with Dr. Massumi at the Texas Heart Institute in Houston.

Don's ability to connect and convince a total stranger that our future together warranted her opening an appointment slot for me was quite heroic and probably saved my life. His love for me at that moment was a tangible thing. Surrounded by his care, I felt protected and knew that together we would fight to get through this ordeal.

I got a highly specialized cardiac MRI at the Texas hospital and the findings provided an entirely different diagnosis. I had ventricular tachycardia but no indication of ventricular dysplasia. "What a relief," I thought, but then realized I could still die from a heart attack while my heart was fluttering during an episode. With this new diagnosis, ablation surgery was scheduled for the following week.

The challenge of the ablation procedure was to get my heart cells to irregularly "fire" and cause an arrhythmia while in a controlled environment. Up until this point, my tachycardia had only presented during intense exercise. To improve our chances of success, Dr. Massumi told me he would not use any type of pain killer or numbing medication during the surgery because he wanted me conscious, in pain, and anxious. Inserting tubing through the femoral artery in my leg up to my heart without any pain killer did the trick. In addition to a large leather strap across my torso, four people had to hold me down to keep me from jerking uncontrollably during the insertion of the needle and catheter.

The stimulants atropine and inosine were introduced into my system along with electrical stimulation over the course of a couple of hours. As the surgical suite began to fill with people in white lab coats, I realized my case was perhaps a bit of an anomaly. At one point, there were eight physicians staring at the wall of monitors. I was an athletic forty-one-year-old woman and not the usual ablation patient. My thoughts were confirmed when Dr. Massumi directed the resident standing beside my gurney to inject another dose of atropine.

The resident responded, "We are not following protocol because of her background, correct?"

"Shannon, you can take it, right?" Dr. Massumi shouted from the wall of monitors.

"Yes, just do it!" I screamed. There were tears leaking from my eyes and my body was flopping like a fish on dry land as I thought, "How do I help; what can I do?" And then the idea came to me to re-enact the Boulder Mountain Ski Race in my mind—one kilometer from the finish line. Skate skiing was where my heart had always presented in the past. I was already gasping for air as adrenaline coursed through my body from the large doses of drugs and the electrical stimulation to my heart. It was easy to get into the mindset of the race and envision a skating motion with my arms, legs, and core working hard to propel me to the finish. My goal was to synchronize my mental state with my heavy breathing and pounding heart. "Go harder. Go faster. Give it everything you've got. Go. Go. Go!"

Finally, my heart presented with an arrhythmia that pinpointed the problematic cells requiring eradication. Dr. Massumi leaned over me on the operating table, looked into my eyes and said, "We got it, Shannon! The cells are mapped. I am going to give you Versed now so you won't remember this next part because it will be quite uncomfortable."

The last thing I remember thinking was, "How can it be worse than what I just went through?"

The ablation was a success, but Dr. Massumi could not offer a long-term prognosis. During my last visit with him before leaving the hospital he stressed, "We do not know what causes the ventricular tachycardia or if it may reoccur, but don't be scared to participate in all your athletic activities. Go out and live your life!"

As I traveled back to Idaho the second week of April 2002, my mind was a whirlwind of thoughts. I was so thankful for my husband who had relentlessly pursued my getting access to a specialist in the field of cardiac electrophysiology. I had thought my life was over, but because of Don, I was able to make plans for our future. I wanted to celebrate with a special event. For more than a dozen years, Don and I had often talked about hiking the Continental Divide; a 3,100-mile trail that stretches from the Canadian border to Mexico, passing through Montana, Idaho, Wyoming, Colorado, and New Mexico. Together, we decided to follow our dream and make hiking the national trail our goal for the coming summer.

THE CONTINENTAL DIVIDE TRAIL

Most people take at least a year to plan an adventure of this magnitude, but Don and I had only seven weeks to put our trip together. The joy of being healthy once again made planning fun instead of overwhelming. The first step was to expedite an order for hiking guidebooks on the Continental Divide Trail (CDT) written by Jim Wolfe. In 1985, the author published a collection of five books that masterfully organized a descriptive narrative of the entire route, listed all the topographical maps needed for the 3,100-mile hike and provided addresses for locations along the trail that would accept and hold resupply boxes for thru-hikers. The books provided us with all the information needed to create our itinerary, including how far we would have to walk each day and how many days we would need to travel to reach each resupply point. With laser-like focus, we obtained all the maps, food, clothing, and equipment needed and distributed these items into boxes to be forwarded to us throughout the trip. When we left home the first week of June 2002, we had twenty-nine boxes sitting in our living room positioned in the order of our itinerary. We would depend on our friends to routinely ship the boxes, approximately one week prior to our scheduled arrival, so the supplies would be waiting for us when we needed them.

THE DEVIL IS IN THE DETAILS

There were several memorable experiences during our seven-week planning period. One of the activities that surprised me was just how long it took to fold and pack 409 topographical maps. Two of our friends joined us for dinner one evening and assisted us with the endeavor. Don and I had torn apart the CDT Guidebooks and then stapled together the pages that described each five to eight-day section of our itinerary. With our friend's help, we combined the guidebook pages with the corresponding topographical maps and folded the materials to fit into a gallon size Ziploc bag. The four of us folded maps for an hour and a half—six hours of combined time—to complete the project. I never expected this simple step to be so time consuming.

Costco shopping took on an entirely new dimension while purchasing non-perishable foods for the CDT because of the volume of product we needed to buy. Don and I started our grocery list by determining how many ounces of cereal we would consume each morning for breakfast and the amount of dried fruit, nuts, crackers, nutrition bars, and cookies we wanted daily for snacks. Once we decided on quantities for each day, we multiplied that number by the number of hiking days on our itinerary. As an example, we allotted ourselves one cup of cereal every morning. Our itinerary included 122 hiking days, so we multiplied 16 ounces (8 ounces for each of us) by 122 days to obtain a total of 1,952 ounces of granola. Quaker Oats Granola comes in a 28-ounce box. Do the math (1,952 ounces divided by 28) and we needed to purchase sixty-nine boxes of granola to feed ourselves breakfast throughout the trip. In similar fashion, we calculated the need for forty cases of nutrition bars, sixty bags of dried fruit and so on. In total we ended up with four large shopping carts of food. All the items were then repackaged and distributed into each of the twenty-nine resupply boxes.

In addition to the food, maps, and guidebook sections, we also packed extra film, camera batteries, sunscreen, new socks, shirts, underwear and even shoes in our resupply boxes. We did our best to estimate when the weather would warm up in the summer and grow cold in the fall so, we would have the correct type of gear for the season at hand. At one point in the process, I asked Don, what he thought of a long sleeve bright yellow top for our box at Pagosa Springs, Colorado. "It will be October and hunting season, so I want to make sure I am visible on the trail. The weather should be a bit nippy, right?" Don just sat silently looking at me as I stared back at him and allowed the weight of my comment to sink in. It was early May, and we would still be hiking five months from now. In that moment, we both began to truly comprehend the enormity of our goal.

After a few more seconds had passed, Don smiled before replying, "It will be perfect!" I smiled back, feeling calm and knowing we were ready to take on the challenge of the Divide.

Not all our planning went well. In fact, our shakedown camping trip two weeks before our departure date was an absolute disaster. Don and I purchased two pieces of equipment for the trip that we were very excited about using: a GPS and a lightweight tent. In the year 2002, a GPS was a relatively new gadget on the market. Don had been studying the instruction manual. Imagine our surprise when the coordinates we entered for a known trail junction a half mile to our north was shown to be 12,000 miles to the south. With a very perplexed look on his face, Don asked, "What just happened? How can that be?"

Obviously, we had a lot more learning to do. As it turned out, there are alphabetical zones that correspond to specific latitudes of the globe. We discovered they were printed on the bottom left-hand corner of the topographical map. During our first effort, we had incorrectly set up the GPS with a zone in South America. Once we figured out our mistake and changed the setting to North America, the unit worked perfectly.

Staying on course would always be our top priority on the CDT, however, limiting the amount of weight we carried on our back was also important. Carrying a light backpack increases hiking speed and daily mileage because it makes the effort so much easier. As Don and I made a list of essential equipment, we realized a very light tent could reduce our load significantly. With this thought in mind, we purchased a two-person trapezoid shaped tent. It was extremely lightweight but what we learned that trial night in the forest was that the shape was not conducive to spending any length of time in the tent. The profile was so low that there was barely enough head room to sit up straight. When we tried to change clothes, the narrow width and sloping foot box design made the effort impossible with both of us inside. And forget trying to stuff your pack inside the tent in inclement weather. I got up the morning after sleeping in the tent and said, "No way are we taking this tent on the Divide. Can you imagine being stuck in that thing for a couple stormy days? There isn't room to move, much less protect our gear!"

Don's response was more to the point, "That tent is a pain in the ass. It should be called a hemorrhoid, not a trapezoid!" From then on, the tent took on the name "The Rhoid." Fortunately, we found a replacement in the form of a lightweight teepee style tent. The design felt roomy and provided a lot of head space. We were content with our new home away from home.

All our planning allowed each of us to carry an ultralight pack that weighed a mere seventeen pounds when loaded with personal clothing, navigational gear, and camping equipment. When a week's worth of food and two liters of water was added, each pack totaled thirty-two pounds.

Our itinerary began at the Canadian border and ended four miles south of Columbus, New Mexico at the Mexican border. Our friends, Ed, and Teri, offered to drive us to Glacier National Park and join us for our first week of hiking. We thought that was a great way to start our adventure. On our way out of town, we mailed the first three resupply boxes; Ed and Teri would send all the others throughout the rest of our journey. Those first three boxes would never be seen again.

CDT MANTRA: THRU-HIKERS MUST BE FLEXIBLE

To say that our trip began with difficulties would be a massive understatement given the disaster that plagued us from the very first day of our adventure. As planned, our friends drove us up to the Canadian border of Waterton-Glacier National Peace Park with the intention to hike the first few days of the trip with us. We knew a snowstorm was expected to hit Glacier National Park and prepared ourselves by taking snowshoes, ice axes, and crampons for the first section of the trail. What we were unprepared for was the eight feet of snow that hammered the park the day before we arrived. Apparently, the national weather center was just as surprised by the record snowfall. Their lack of warning left all the businesses, lodges, park service personnel, and road crews unable to manage the massive volume of snow and resulting destruction. Most lodges were forced to close because the roads could not be cleared for staff to get to work. The scenic highway just outside the park had so much snow and water runoff that a few sections buckled and broke apart creating three-to-four-foot gaps in the asphalt. The restaurants that were able to open had to boil water because the sewer system backed up from the overflowing rivers, creeks, and flooding streets. Ranchers had stranded cattle all over the rangelands surrounding the park which lured the grizzly bears to venture beyond the park boundary for an easy meal. Glacier National Park had become a dangerous, impassable mess with no hope of a hike in the woods.

Don and I spent the next forty-eight hours at Glacier Park Lodge in East Glacier, assessing the situation and attempting to find a hiking solution. There, we met another six CDT hikers who were also stranded in the storm's aftermath. One individual, Ron Vaughn, let us know he was a triple crown thru-hiker, meaning he had already completed the Appalachian Trail (AT), the Pacific Crest Trail (PCT) and the CDT. He looked at me and very condescendingly said, "If you are going to be a thru-hiker, the first thing you have got to learn is to be FLEXIBLE! Travel south and start your hike." Ron's attitude made me angry. To me, Ron had given up too easily. Hiking the *entire* CDT was my dream, and I could not just abandon it. This grand adventure was a bucket list item for me and Don and represented much more than a walk in the woods. I had to try and fight for my goal. While the other six individuals headed south to begin their trip, Don and I had our friends drive us to Piegan Port of Entry on the Canadian border to begin our hike. We walked eighty miles along Highway 89 and Route 49 which circumvented the park and allowed us to technically say we had started our journey IN CANADA.

After our multiple day highway march, we spent the next week trying to find a way across the Bob Marshall Wilderness Area just south of Glacier National Park. The melting snow from the record storm created raging rivers and creeks that were impossible to ford. After a couple false starts and reroutes post holing through thigh high snow, we admitted defeat and took a train and bus ride to the Montana/Idaho border to continue our adventure from a more southern location. Before boarding the train, I vowed that I would return to experience the famed CDT-Highline Trail and the following summer, Don, Ed, Teri, and I hiked through the heart of Glacier National Park completing the goal.

YELLOWSTONE NATIONAL PARK

Our bus ride took us to West Yellowstone, Montana, just outside Yellowstone National Park which seemed like the best place to restart our journey after Mother Nature destroyed our plans for Glacier National Park. Natalie, a dietitian I worked with at the hospital, had moved on to a new job as the caretaker of a private fishing camp located at nearby Mack's Inn, one of the resupply locations on our CDT itinerary. I had given Natalie our resupply box back in May before we left Sun Valley. Natalie picked us up at the bus stop and drove us to the trailhead where this section's guidebook and maps began. Don and I were excited to be hiking again and ready to experience Yellowstone National Park away from all the tourists and crowds.

We obtained all our necessary backcountry camping permits from the Park Service Headquarters. Our permits determined the distance we traveled between camps. During our first few days, campsites were only eight miles apart allowing us to walk at a very leisurely pace and enjoy the scenery in the park. Surprisingly, a large portion of the CDT route went through miles of burned forest. The remains of charred pine trees, resembling blackened telephone poles, covered the landscape as far as the eye could see. The 1988 Yellowstone Fire burned 800,000 acres, slightly over one-third of the park. I remembered reading about the fire, but the numbers did not register until I saw the extent of the devastation with my own eyes. Green grass with small bouquets of colorful wildflowers were now growing on the hillsides. There were also waist high pine trees dotting the landscape. Rationally, I understood that fire helped the ecosystem by removing deadfall and diseased trees within the forest, but selfishly, I was very saddened that I missed seeing the gorgeous old growth forest of early Yellowstone.

Our days in late June 2002 were filled with clear blue skies. Walking without shade through the blackened, limbless trees made our hike exceptionally hot in the glaring sun. No deer, elk, or bison could be found grazing on the hillside grasses. The land was noticeably barren of any life until the evening hours when the forest came alive with mosquitoes. Having traveled to Alaska on three different occasions, I thought I was prepared for the insects, but none of my previous experiences came close to what we endured on our hike through Yellowstone. One clear night, we slept without our rainfly. Our tent body, or nest, was constructed of screen material which was wonderful for viewing the stars and the night sky. But the hordes of mosquitoes that blanketed the netting was unnerving to me. The sound alone was eerily loud. I kept thinking, "Please don't let there be a tear in the netting!"

Around midnight, I woke up and realized I needed to pee. Now I had to venture out with the mosquitoes to relieve myself. In preparation, I put on my loose-fitting nylon jacket and wind pants. I hoped the garments would protect me from the clouds of insects. I even put on my head net so my neck, face, and head would be unreachable by the swarm. All my moving around made Don stir, prompting me to ask, "Would you help me with the zipper on the door, so the mosquitoes don't fly in the tent? And please be ready to help me get back inside." Don did as I asked and managed the nest door. I was covered with clothing except for my hands, the tops of my feet and my big white butt cheeks. I knew I was in trouble the second I dropped my drawers. Swat. Pause. Swat. Pause. Swat, swat, swat. Pause. Slap, slap, slap, slap, slap, slap, slap. "I am being attacked. Oh no, they're biting me!" At this point, Don started laughing. He was not sympathetic to my situation and thought the whole ordeal was pretty humorous. There was a full moon, allowing him to clearly see me spanking my own bottom trying to keep from getting bitten.

Though I urinated as quickly as possible, I was bitten numerous times. I dove back inside the tent even more nervous about the mosquitoes than before. We spent a few minutes using our flashlight to find and kill a few strays that had entered the tent with me. Crawling back inside my sleeping bag, I saw a shadow come really close to my face just beyond the tent netting. I whispered, "Did you see that thing that just flew by the tent? What was it?"

Don sat still for a minute, looking all around our tent. A moment later, another shadow passed overhead. "It's a bat! The bat is eating the mosquitoes!" One bat soon turned into dozens.

Although I was thrilled by the prospect of the bats devouring all the mosquitoes, I asked, "Can a bat's radar detect our tent netting?" I worried that one might get caught in the fabric and rip a hole in it. The bats repeatedly dove next to our tent screen as they feasted on the thousands of mosquitoes. They were nearly silent in flight; we could only hear a slight fluttering of their wings as they gracefully avoided colliding with the tent.

When I woke the next morning, our nest was undamaged, and between the bats and the freezing temperature, the mosquitoes were gone. I felt immense relief that I could pack my head net and avoid the frustration of having to battle bugs all day. With just a small amount of insect repellant, we were able to hike comfortably on a narrow pathway through thick grasses and bushes. Although an abundance of mosquitoes returned when the sun went down that evening, their numbers were more appropriate for springtime conditions. We never encountered the heavy swarm and thick blanket of insects that had clung to our tent nest again.

BEAR AWARE

Yellowstone provided a few unique experiences because of the presence of grizzly bears. There is an element of heightened awareness when hiking through grizzly country. Having backpacked in Denali National Park and the Arctic Circle of Alaska where we encountered many of these massive bears while armed, I seriously questioned whether we would survive an altercation using only a can of bear spray as our defense. It was imperative that we avoid surprising the animals on the trail, and we had to be careful not to attract them to our campsite. Throughout the day, Don and I spoke loudly and even shouted to each other when walking through thick brush or around blind corners on the trail. In the evenings, we strictly adhered to establishing our camp in a triangular fashion. We set up our tent at one point, cooked at another and hung our food at the third ensuring each point was at least seventy-five yards apart. No food was ever brought into our tent. Sweet smelling products like toothpaste, sunscreen, Chapstick, and biodegradable soap were also packed with the food items and hung up high at night.

The campsites in Yellowstone required the hanging of food and provided bars constructed for the purpose in lieu of trees. To use the bar, we tied one end of a long length of parachute cord to a rock and threw it over the cross-bar. Replacing the rock with our food bags, we hoisted them up high where the bears could not reach them. We thought our plan was pretty solid until the third campsite. Don was standing next to the bear bar getting ready to toss the cord when he stopped and called me over, "Look up at the top bar. Do you see the claw marks?"

I was stunned. "Holy cow! How did the bear do that?" There were huge claw marks where a grizzly had crawled up the side log and over to the middle of the top bar to get someone's food. The bar was at least twenty feet off the ground—about the height of a two-story house. Obviously, hanging food was a deterrent but not completely out of a hungry bear's reach.

THE GEYSERS OF YELLOWSTONE

Seeing a variety of geysers along the CDT trail was another unique element of hiking in Yellowstone. Our route went through Shoshone Lake Geyser Basin and Heart Lake Geyser Basin where there were several boiling cauldrons of water in vibrant colors of blue, green, pink, and golden yellow. None of the hot springs spewed like Old Faithful but I never stepped off the main trail because I was uncertain about the stability of the fragile crust surfaces surrounding the basins. Many animals are killed each year by falling into the boiling pots. With that knowledge, I kept a respectful distance. "I wonder what the early American explorers thought the first time they saw one of Yellowstone's boiling pots?" Don asked at a particularly beautiful turquoise basin.

"I don't know, but these colors are amazing. I'm sure they were as impressed then as I am today."

Our trek through Yellowstone National Park ended with a walk through heavily forested terrain. The trail led us past the headwaters of the famous Snake River to a remote campsite on the southeastern boundary of the park. Once again, we were completely alone at the campground and enjoyed having the soothing sounds of the flowing creek and the picturesque setting to ourselves. We wouldn't have known we were exiting the park, were it not for a small sign that read: Leaving Yellowstone National Park. The lack of fanfare and crowds prompted me to ask, "Do you realize we only saw six people while hiking for five days in the park?" Before Don could reply, I went on to comment, "We passed two CDT section hikers and four campers at Heart Lake. That's it. It seems so strange that a couple million people visit Yellowstone each season, but it only takes hiking a few miles away from any road and the park is a secluded, quiet place."

Don spent a moment thinking about what I had said and then responded, "We saw a Yellowstone that very few people ever experience."

PARTING OF THE WATERS; A PERFECT DAY

Before leaving home, Don and I had watched a couple videos about hiking the CDT. During one interview, a thru-hiker said, "The weather is guaranteed to be perfect 20 percent of the time." They laughingly went on to say, "The rest of the time the days will be too hot, too cold, too wet, too windy, or too buggy. But 20 percent of the time, your hiking experience will be absolute perfection." That information was helpful because it provided a realistic assessment of what to expect day to day on the trail. As a thru-hiker, I readily accepted the daily weather challenges and was grateful when we finally got a perfect day. The next section is taken directly from my journal; a verbatim expression of what I thought was a perfect day out on the trail. Upon reflection, it had nothing to do with the weather.

"Happy 4th of July—A Perfect Day!"

"The day began in the Bridger-Teton National Forest with a ford of Mink Creek and a 1,200 foot climb out of the valley. The climb ended on a spectacular plateau at 10,000 feet elevation. There were lakes and 360-degree views of mountains. The Tetons were magnificent. I tried to take a couple pictures, but I'm sure the camera was not able to pick them up. They were fifty miles away. Climbing up and across Two Ocean plateau, we were able to view the devastation of the high-elevation tornado of 1987, the only F4 tornado recorded in Wyoming history. The storm uprooted over a million trees in the Teton Wilderness leaving a swath over a mile wide. Also, on our hike up, we could tell we were following a bear cub and mother. This little guy had to be only a couple months old. The little prints looked like a baby's mitten. So cute and so small. The large patches of bear scat we found were fresh on the trail, so we sang and spoke loudly for most of the hike.

After leaving the plateau, our trail headed down a thickly vegetated hillside where balsamroot, lupine, and paintbrush were in full bloom. We saw a doe with two baby fawns hiding in the colorful flowers. Then we ran into two herds of elk with two little calves as well. They were adorable. We descended to a high alpine meadow on the Continental Divide where the actual *Parting of the Waters* was located. Two Ocean Creek divides with half the water flowing 3,488 miles to the Atlantic Ocean and the other half traveling 1,353 miles to the Pacific Ocean. It was interesting to see the creek split. Don scooped a handful of water out of Atlantic creek and threw it into Pacific Creek just to defy nature. As we walked our last mile, a large rain cloud came over us. With it were very strong winds. We had entered a burn area and all at once, trees began to crash down all around us. We ran quickly to an open meadow and watched the trees fall. Pretty wild to see. Then, within minutes, the rain stopped, the wind stopped, and we continued to walk. Nature is grand. A fitting event for our perfect day."

IN GOD WE TRUST

There were a few occurrences throughout our hike that defied logical explanations. Situations where I asked myself, "Is this a coincidence? Or is someone watching over me?" One experience will always stand out as a day my prayers were answered.

In 2002, the Continental Divide Trail was not a continuous 3,100-mile trail. The CDT was more of a suggested route that attempted to link up 1,000 miles of existing trails through various national forests, parks, Bureau of Land Management (BLM) lands, and wilderness areas. The rest of the route (approximately 2,100 miles) was split evenly between jeep roads and roadless, trackless terrain known as cross-country travel. After retrieving our resupply box at the Cowboy Village Resort near Togwotee Pass in Wyoming, Don and I had to hike 125 miles to our next resupply box with most of the first sixty miles being cross-country.

Finding water sources was always my biggest concern. Oftentimes, the maps we used would lead us to dry creek beds or springs that no longer had flowing water. Such was the case on our second day in the wilderness. After leaving camp that morning, we hiked for nearly eight hours without finding any water. The jeep road that we had been following, ended at the top of a hill and left us with miles of uninhabited land in all directions. We plotted our location on the topographical map using our GPS and then took a bearing with our compass to a stream located on the map. But once again, all we found was a dry creek bed.

Late in the afternoon, with my water bottles empty, I was growing very nervous at not being able to locate a water source. The next option for water on the map was many miles away. With only a few hours of daylight remaining, I worried we would not reach the next creek before dark. After another hour of hiking, I started to panic. Don was my rock and kept telling me, "Calm down, Shannon. We are still okay. You're doing great. Just keep walking and we'll find water." I was so thirsty and as I realized all our water sources could be dry, the more parched I became. But I kept moving and somehow kept pace beside Don.

We were crossing a small meadow along the bottom of a hill, when I looked ahead and saw a strange green patch of grass. As we drew closer, I could not believe my eyes. There was a tiny spring with cold clear water seeping out of the ground. I was so relieved, I started to cry. After drinking our fill and refilling our water containers, we used our GPS again to plot our location on the map. That was when we realized two things: The spring was not shown on the map, and we had accidentally walked off course. I will always believe I was guided to that location to find a providential water source.

Our trip had at least a dozen more incidents where dire or dangerous situations arose, and each time, Don and I came through unhurt and able to continue our hike. I would like to think that Don and I are very resourceful individuals, and our positive outcomes were a result of our physicality, knowledge of the land, and our belief that together we could overcome any challenge presented to us. And while all those things are true, there were times when I could not help but feel the presence of a higher power on our journey. Throughout our hike, I realized that dangerous weather was balanced with a beautiful rainbow or sunset, challenging terrain was always tempered by an abundance of animals or wildflowers and exhaustion was lifted with a unique encounter with wildlife. I came home a more confident and happier person and my faith and spirituality were strengthened because of our experiences on the Divide.

AMERICA THE BEAUTIFUL

When asked the prettiest place on our journey, two spots come to mind: the Green River flowing along the base of Squaretop Mountain, and Temple Peak in the Wind River Range. We hiked through these two areas on a single 125-mile section from Togwotee Pass to the Big Sandy Lodge in Wyoming.

After successfully navigating the sixty-mile cross-country stretch in the Bridger-Teton National Forest, we entered the Gros Ventre Wilderness and began hiking through the Green River Valley. The Green River is aptly named, being a rich shade of jade. When I first laid eyes on it, I stopped and asked Don, "How can that river be so green? It is such an incredible color." We were both in awe of the beautiful river. The date was July 12th, the height of the growing season, and the entire valley was lush with grass, wildflowers, and wildlife. Standing on the riverbank, we heard coyotes yipping in the distance. Within a few minutes, two large deer came running in our direction. We assumed the coyotes stirred them up. They were magnificent bucks which added to the picturesque view.

After hiking an entire day along the Green River, we climbed over Vista Pass and entered the Wind River Range in western Wyoming. The entire landscape dramatically changed into an endless view of lakes, rock, sparsely growing pine trees and towering granite peaks. It took us four more days of hiking to reach Temple Peak at the southern end of the mountain range. Each day, our route took us over two or three passes with daily elevation gains of 8,000 to 10,000 feet. I had routinely hiked up Baldy, our ski mountain back in Sun Valley, which has a 3,000-foot elevation gain. Hiking in the Wind River Range, I would tell myself, "You can do this Shannon. It is just a Baldy climb!" And then I would repeat the phrase a couple more times before the day would end.

The landscape of the Winds was unlike any other mountain range in the entire length of the CDT. Standing on one of the mountain passes, our view was filled with dots of shimmering blue lakes. "No problem finding water sources in the Winds," I told Don. After four days of hiking, we reached Clear Lake and looked upon Temple Peak in the background. Don took a picture of me walking through wildflowers by the blue lake, gazing up at the granite walled valley and our trail to Temple Pass. Moved by the beauty of the place, I told Don, "I hope we can come back here one day and take a more leisurely hike to explore the Cirque of Towers and other mountain peaks in the Winds. This place is amazing."

The Wind River Mountains and the Gros Ventre Mountain Range were diversely different. Hiking the lush green mountains of the Green River encompassed all the elements of a perfect walk through the woods. In stark contrast, the towering granite rocks of the Wind River Range turned out to be an equally wonderful experience.

There were many other locations on the Divide that deserve an honorable mention for their beauty or uniqueness. In the San Juan Mountains of Colorado, Lake Nebo was striking with its turquoise color framed by the fall foliage of late September. The San Juans were not jagged granite but rather smooth, rounded, grandiose peaks of dark colored rock set against a golden ground cover. Ghost Ranch in Abiquiu, New Mexico showcased seemingly painted sandstone mountains in shades of red, orange, pink, and white all set against a desert landscape of piñon pines, cactus, and scrub brush. And near the end of our journey, the Gila Mountains of New Mexico surprised us with green pine trees nestled in red volcanic rock throughout a narrow canyon that contained the Gila River. The Gila River Canyon was twenty-one miles in length with the CDT crossing the water seventy-eight times. The Gila was a true oasis sprouting out of the desert sand and the location of the world-famous Gila Cliff Dwellings. There were so many spectacular places along the divide that I could never list them all, but the locations mentioned above have the distinction of motivating one of us to capture them on film.

DUMB AND DUMBER—ACROSS THE GREAT BASIN DESERT

We had read that the Great Divide Basin, with its 123-mile stretch of barren land intersecting the famous Oregon Trail, would be one of the biggest challenges on the CDT, and it did not disappoint. I was most afraid, exhausted, dehydrated, beat-up, and burned-out on this section of the journey. My nerves started to fray two days before we ever got to South Pass City on the northwestern edge of the Basin. After leaving the Wind River Range, we encountered four CDT thru-hikers traveling south to north and each of them had a tale to tell about their recent experience crossing the desolate landscape. This was a drought year and finding water, or rather not finding water, was all anyone wanted to talk about. One CDT hiker named Jed suggested we hire someone to cache water for us like his girlfriend did for him. Then Pete told us he carried nine liters of water (an extra seventeen pounds) and had to ration the supply over a twenty-five-mile stretch between water sources. The last thru-hiker we spoke to was Ishmael, who after claiming extensive experience hiking both the AT and PCT, warned us that the Basin was drier than normal. He gave us the name of a BLM person to contact, Ray Hansen, who provided updates on current water sources and then left us with these ominous words, "I nearly died out there. It is life and death dangerous."

As the ground beneath our feet transitioned from dirt to sand, my feelings of mild concern transformed to a state of anxiety. Working myself into a bit of a panic, I said, "I know you call me a water hog, but I am really scared about not having enough water. I did not survive a heart problem to die of thirst in the desert!"

Don just calmly looked at me and said, "We are not going to die in the desert. We will check out the situation when we reach South Pass City and make a rational decision on how to cross this section of the trip."

We retrieved our resupply box at the post office in South Pass City, made phone calls to the BLM regarding current water sources and investigated options for caching water along the trail. As the day wore on, so did my nerves. Ray Hansen was on vacation for nine days and no one else at the BLM had any information on water sources in the desert. The only rental vehicles available were seventy-seven miles away in the city of Lander and nobody working at the South Pass City State Historical Site was able or willing to drive to the middle of the desert to cache water for us.

Sitting at a shaded picnic table eating a snack and discussing our situation, Don looked up and smiled at the couple hiking out of the desert and heading our way. A friend of ours back home had a sister, Marcia, who was hiking the CDT from south to north. Marcia and her husband Ken were using the same handmade, thirteen-ounce backpack we were carrying. When Don saw the packs, he called out, "Are you Marcia and Ken?"

The couple abruptly stopped and said, "Yes! How do you know our names?" When we explained how we identified them, Marcia shouted, "Oh my gosh, you guys are Don and Shannon!"

Ken and Marcia were just completing their hike through the Great Divide Basin and said they could tell us the exact GPS location of all the water sources so we could navigate the desert safely. They confirmed there was one waterless thirty-mile section at the very end heading into Rawlins. Don and I figured we could carry an extra gallon of water using our camp shower bag, affectionately named Mr. Blue Belly, rationalizing the additional weight would be offset by the food we would consume by that time.

We were all so excited to meet each other and share stories from our trip that we hitched a ride to Lander with a member of the museum staff commuting home from work. After getting a hotel room and cleaning up, we met for dinner and spent the next several hours talking about our adventures. As we parted ways at our hotel door, hugging like old friends, we thanked Ken and Marcia again for the water source coordinates and gave them our bear spray that we no longer needed. Once again, when my fears were at their worst, these wonderful people appeared in my life to allay all my concerns. I went to sleep feeling relieved and at peace that Don and I could make it through the Great Divide Basin safely. Now I was excited to see the desert.

The formal CDT route out of South Pass City and into the Great Divide Basin followed a single-track trail for several miles until it converged with a jeep road that crossed the Oregon Trail. Our goal was to hike at least twenty-one miles each day which required us to carry enough food for six days of camping. Water was not a concern on the first day, but extreme heat became an issue by mid-afternoon. The arid landscape coupled with the warmth of the sun radiating off the sand created an oven like environment. By mid-day, we had hiked fifteen miles to Sweet Water Bridge where we crawled underneath the structure to rest for a few hours. The small thermometer hanging from my backpack dropped from 105 to 91 degrees in the shade. Mormon Spring, our goal for the day, was another eight miles away.

We started hiking again in the cooler evening hours and set up camp just before dark. The landscape was flat and barren with only rock and sagebrush surrounding us. Brushing our teeth, we noticed dark clouds rolling in from the south. We had a few extra tent stakes and used them to hold the fly more securely in the loose sand. I set a few larger rocks on top of the stakes as an additional precaution. Within seconds of crawling into our sleeping bags, the wind picked up and started whipping the sides of our tent. In a short amount of time, a lightning storm rolled over us. *Crack. Bam. Boom!* Thunder and lightning began a rhythmic patten overhead. I timed the intervals between the flash of lightning and the explosion of thunder and never completed the phrase, "1,001, 1,002." The roar of the thunder was deafening as it reverberated through the tent. "Ouch!" I yelped. "I just got shocked."

"Get away from the aluminum tent pole," Don shouted. "Make sure your body is on the sleeping pad."

As I pulled the foam mat toward the perimeter of the tent and away from the center pole, I noticed my hair had begun to frizz out around my head. "Oh my gosh, you can see the static electricity in the air!" The lightning was bright enough to totally illuminate the inside of the tent. When Don tried to fall asleep, he had to pull his sleeping bag over his eyes to block the lightning flashes that were so bright they hurt his eyes through his eyelids. We laid in our bags listening to the intense rumbling of thunder for nearly three hours. I fell asleep thinking this was the most amazing storm I had ever experienced.

The next three days of hiking in extreme heat impacted my body with a domino effect of issues. Wearing ankle-high gators kept small pebbles and debris out of our shoes but trapped body heat and caused welts to form all around the lower half of our legs. By the second afternoon, Don's feet had swollen a couple sizes larger than normal, so we limited wearing our gators to only the cool morning hours. All our clothing was made of nylon or a blend so it would dry quickly. Unfortunately, with prolonged sweating, wherever the nylon clothing touched my skin, I developed a rash. A nylon pack laying against a nylon shirt over nylon shorts pressed against nylon underwear was a disaster. Reapplying sunscreen periodically throughout the day kept our skin from burning, but all the welts and rashes made any sun exposure very itchy and uncomfortable. Consuming enough water to replace the increase in sweat production was a challenge. No matter how much I drank, my body could never cool down and I always felt slightly nauseated. As my extremities became swollen from the heat, I grew more miserable.

Don and I used Marcia's GPS coordinates and were successful finding water. With five additional days of record-breaking heat, the quality of a few sources had deteriorated since Marcia and Ken had visited. Hay Press Reservoir had become a cow watering hole. Don took one look at it and said, "Oh man, it's 50 percent piss, 25 percent shit, and 25 percent water!" We both knew we could not reach the next water source without more fluid, so we filtered the putrid water and added iodine tablets to our hydration bladder to improve our chances of not becoming ill. The next two springs had become such small seeps we had to creatively use our cooking pot to collect enough water to filter. Disaster struck at the last watering seep when the side seam of our pump cracked apart when we tried to filter out the excessive impurities in the water. With a slight shake of his head, Don tore off a small section of duct tape we carried wrapped around our hiking pole and placed it over the small hole in the side of the pump. We were in the middle of the desert, and it would have to do until we reached civilization. The next water source was a faucet used to fill a large tank for ranging cattle. Just like Marcia had promised, the water was cold, clear, and wicked good.

The wildlife we encountered had changed as dramatically as the landscape. The desert was home to wild mustangs who appeared to be thriving in the environment. Small herds of three or four roamed together foraging for food and water. Each group we saw always had a baby colt in their midst and the adults appeared well fed and healthy. They were feisty animals who saw us as a threat to their water cache. At one of the seeps, a stallion approached us and reared up on hind legs and then false charged to drive us away from the area. Don and I had already filled our containers with water by the time the horses arrived, so we willingly retreated and started hiking on down the road. I understood exactly how precious that water was to those animals.

"Look, Don, it's a horny toad!" I could not believe my eyes when I found a horned lizard on the desert road. I had not seen these toad shaped creatures, with skin that formed horned protrusions over their eyes, since I was a kid. I used to play with them and remembered they became very docile if you flipped them over and rubbed their bellies which was the only soft place on their body. Smiling, I decided not to try that tactic with my newfound friend and left him to scurry away.

The desert did not have mosquitoes but was instead filled with flies. One type of fly we named "the vampire fly." These insects were slightly smaller than the common house fly and had a mottled brown and cream body with big red eyes. Their most prominent feature was their bite which would draw blood much like the familiar horsefly. But unlike the horsefly, the vampire flies traveled in silent hordes and would unsuspectingly ambush us as we hiked by. We came to recognize gullies, washes, and low-lying areas as their habitat and literally ran through these sections to avoid the swarms. Each of their bites seemed to contain venom, or at least a chemical that reacted with my skin to form, yet again, another welt. After four days in the desert battling the heat and the bugs, my skin was a lumpy, bumpy mess of welts and rashes.

It is often said that bad luck comes in threes and on our fifth day of hiking, I experienced three monumental setbacks. At our mid-morning break, I sat on my rubber sleeping pad and then somehow, after relieving myself and stretching, walked off and left it laying on the ground. It took me an hour and a half to realize my mistake. We didn't have enough water to make a three-hour round trip to retrieve the pad. Sleeping on the hard surface of the tent floor was not going to be fun, but I knew it was the right decision. Shortly after realizing my idiocy, the sky became cloudy, and rain began to fall. Four hours later, it was still drizzling when Don and I arrived at what had been touted as the very best water source in the desert. In shock, Don and I stood and stared at the empty water trough. We had been told the solar pump provided a steady flow of fresh water from a deep well, however, without sunshine, the motor was silent. We desperately looked for a manual switch but could not make the equipment function. The trough had holes drilled into the bottom creating a drain to keep the water from becoming stagnant. The remaining water on the ground was in puddles mixed with cow manure and urine. We had a couple pints of water in our hydration packs, but not enough to hike thirteen miles to the next water source which we had been warned was of poor quality. As we tried to filter the disgusting fluid out of the deepest puddle, our pump disintegrated into what looked like a leaky faucet with water spurting in all directions. In a last-ditch effort to mend the pump, Don took a lighter and held an open flame to the plastic hoping that it would melt, and we could mash together the sides of the pump. As direct fire only made the crack widen, Don and I looked at each other and just shrugged. We silently loaded our gear, put on our packs, and started walking down the road under a gloomy cloud of sprinkling raindrops.

Taking an inventory of our current situation, I realized we were down a sleeping pad and a functioning water filter, we were forty-three miles from Rawlins, and only had two pints of water left. On the positive side, I was soaked from the rain and my body felt cooler, so I needed less water to drink. My frustration was mounting about the same time Don started telling me a story. "Antelope, like people from many native cultures, are known to have dug down a couple feet into the sandy floor of a dry wash or creek bed to find water."

Though Don was quite animated and excited to provide details on the many ways to find water in the desert, I was flabbergasted and yelled, "You want me to start digging in the dirt!" It was obvious that we were not in the same emotional place. I was panicking, but Don was enlivened and thrilled to face a new challenge where he needed his wits to survive. We had polar opposite reactions to the same moment. After my outburst, I decided it would be best if I tried to remain silent and kept on hiking.

The clouds broke up allowing the sun to come out in late afternoon. At the end of a thirteen-hour hike, we arrived at Bull Spring, our last water source. The spring, which was located on the side of a small hill, was no more than a tiny trickle of water flowing over the dirt surface. Don and I studied the seep and came up with a plan. Three feet from its source, the stream ran over a protruding rock lip with just enough height to hold a cooking pot on its side and slowly collect a few ounces of water. After letting the dirt and rocks settle in the bottom of the pot, we poured the water into our hydration pack and repeated the process until our reservoirs were full. We then added an iodine tablet to make the water safe to drink. Using this method, it took us several hours to collect enough water for our dinner and next day's hike.

To cheer me up, Don gave me his sleeping pad and refused to let me sleep on the hard tent floor that night. As we readied ourselves for bed, a small herd of mustangs joined us at the water hole. They whinnied and tossed their heads, communicating with each other. I fell asleep thinking they were celebrating, relieved as I was, to find water in the desert.

Our map and guidebook indicated we had thirty miles still to travel. The first third was along the CDT Trail to the southern edge of the Great Divide Basin and then a ten-mile walk on a dirt road to reach Highway 287. From there we would walk the final ten miles on asphalt to reach our resupply box in Rawlins, Wyoming. I was so ready to be out of the desert, I got Don up, packed and walking before sunrise. The CDT trail was well signed and easy to follow allowing us to make good time. Mineral-X dirt road provided something of an optical illusion. We thought we could see where the road terminated, but like a mirage, no matter how long we hiked, the end never grew closer. After an hour, Don looked over at me and said, "I feel like I am walking on a treadmill. My feet are moving but I'm not going anywhere." Mineral-X road was a ribbon through a visually indistinguishable expanse of land. Without a terrain feature to measure our progress, the hike felt much slower than usual.

The monotony was broken with a nice surprise as a couple of mountain bike riders rolled by us in the early afternoon. The three men waved and kept pedaling. "Why would those guys be out here cycling?" I asked.

Noticing they were carrying packs on their bikes, Don responded, "They may be mountain biking the Great Divide Mountain Bike Route (GDMBR). I think this is part of the official course through the Great Divide Basin." A short time later, another cyclist rode up alerting us with the familiar *Brringgg, Brringgg* of his bell.

The man slowed and called out to us, "Are you two CDT thru-hikers?"

After we answered yes, the rider told us he was from Liverpool, England and was attempting to complete the GDMBR in just over a month. He said he was surprised that we were the first CDT thru-hikers he had run into on his journey. I explained the two routes were diversely different because for the most part, we were hiking on high-elevation trails where mountain bikes were not allowed. "Only the Great Divide Basin provides a section of the CDT where all of us can have fun in this hot, sandy playground together." He laughed at my analogy and assured me his time in the desert had been a lot easier than ours. Mountain bike cyclists were able to quickly cover the 123 miles limiting their exposure to only one or two days in the arid landscape. The Englishman rode away signaling his departure with the ring of his bell.

Watching the cyclist quickly fade into the horizon, Don commented, "I am so jealous of him having a bike right now!" I totally understood the feeling. We were both overheated, tired, thirsty, and ready to be in town. When we reached the asphalt of Highway 287, I decided to try hitchhiking. The official CDT route crossed the highway and continued south but our plan was to go to Rawlins, get our resupply box and spend the night.

A rancher picked us up and took us to the Rawlins, Wyoming post office. As Don and I started to climb out of his truck, he asked, "Do you know what we call CDT hikers in Wyoming?"

Looking over my shoulder while sliding off the seat, I half grinned and asked, "No, what do you call us?"

The older man chuckled as he answered, "Dumb and Dumber!"

I laughed along with him at the punch line of the joke and then commented, "Yeah, there were a few times I felt just like that in the desert. Thanks again for the ride. Appreciate you picking us up."

With a parting wave, the rancher pulled out of the parking lot and drove away. Don and I had successfully crossed the Great Divide Basin of Wyoming. But at what cost? My mind was a tsunami of emotions as I remembered the challenges we had faced while surviving the last six days of hiking. I was seriously considering going home. I spent the next twenty-four hours processing everything we had experienced in the desert as I made my decision whether to stay on the trail.

MOMENT OF TRUTH

With our resupply box in our arms, we walked to a nearby hotel to stay the night. The blast of cold air on my face upon entering the room felt amazing. Showering for an incredible length of time, I luxuriated in shampooing my hair and scrubbing my body clean. I was so appreciative of the little conveniences we take for granted in our daily lives. I missed washing my hands with hot running water, showering, using a real toilet, air-conditioning, sleeping in a comfy bed, not having to battle the bugs, being protected from inclement weather, and never having to worry about finding water. I was only six weeks into our hike and the difficulties of the trail had become overwhelming. When I voiced my doubts about continuing, Don replied, "Shannon, I really want you here with me. But if you are so unhappy and don't want to go further, I will help you get back home." With a sigh and a slight shake of his head, Don went on to say, "I am not leaving the CDT. I want to complete the trail even if I have to do it alone. Think about what you really want to do and make your own decision."

This was my moment of truth. I needed to analyze my emotions and decide my future. Reflecting on all the experiences of our hike, I realized the challenge of the CDT was 95 percent mental. A person had to have the will to complete the trail because the journey was so formidable. The physical demands of the CDT were brutal. I thought back to our first four twenty-mile days walking around Glacier National Park and how humbling those hikes had been. Casual exercise of jogging, cycling, and skiing throughout the winter had not prepared me for our goal. Sheer tenacity had kept me moving for the last month, enduring the strain of ten-hour hikes carrying a thirty-pound pack. Now, I could comfortably repeat the effort for many days in a row. My reflection in the mirror strikingly displayed how my body had suffered the physical transformation of getting in shape by losing weight and gaining muscle. The woman staring back at me was lean and powerful looking. Early in our journey, a thru-hiker named Denny Fixmer, made the comment about hiking the national trails, "You either get strong, or you go home." Although it takes both physical and emotional strength to tackle the

Divide, a strong sense of willpower was responsible for the initial success of my journey.

So now that I was physically able to meet the demands of the CDT, why was I struggling to continue? After spending a few hours wrestling with this question, a paradigm shift occurred in my perspective of the trail. Mother Nature may have tormented us with rain, blustery wind, extreme heat, and insects, but we were also gifted with calm sunny days, colorful wildflowers, and glorious vistas. I recognized I had exchanged my comfortable mattress for a sleeping bag under a canopy of stars with a fascinating view of the Milky Way and night sky far away from the bright lights of the city. And although the wind gusts were frustrating, they had inspired great conversations about the jet stream and the developing formation of storms. I remembered one specific time when Don remarked, "The clouds are moving so quickly in front of the sun it seems like a light switch is being turned off and on repeatedly."

"I think the sky looks like a video on fast forward with the clouds sailing over us so rapidly," I had responded. "It doesn't look real."

Immersed in nature and surrounded by wildlife, I understood how fortunate Don and I had been to observe the behavior of the animals while sharing the forest, desert, and water. The trail had made demands but had generously rewarded us with grandeur. I finally realized there had always been a balance; a "give and take" with every difficult step completed. Did I really want to abandon all the wonderful opportunities the trail still had to offer? My nerves were frayed from exhaustion. Too many days spent worrying about water, not sleeping, and walking great distances in the heat had taken their toll on me. I needed to rest and recharge. I drifted off to sleep still sorting through my feelings on whether to continue hiking the Divide.

As was my usual habit, I rose with the sun the next morning. After a full night of deep sleep, I felt rested and clear headed. My decision became obvious as I thought about the reality of returning home alone. There was only one answer that would truly make me happy. I had to follow my heart which meant my choice was to stay with Don. Only by his side would I find genuine contentment. Sharing all the memories of the journey was far more important to me than the creature comforts of home. With my decision made to continue the hike, Don and I went shopping to restock our packs with a new water filter, foam sleeping pad, and food. I persuaded him to stay another night at the motel, allowing us to eat a few more meals and get additional rest to fortify myself for the next section of our adventure.

TRAIL ANGELS

"Oh no! What happened to my underwear? Don, do you see it anywhere?" As Don and I stood scanning the northwestern horizon and the mountain ridge we had just walked, a gust of wind forced me to take an unsteady step and the answer became clear: my underwear was somewhere in eastern Colorado on its way to Kansas. Darn. In the early morning light, I had washed our clothes at a stream crossing and hung the wet garments on my pack so the sun and slight breeze could dry them as we hiked throughout the day. I obviously had not paid close enough attention to the increasing wind that had easily picked up my undergarment and transported it beyond visibility. There was nothing I could do. We would reach the resort town of Grand Lake in three days. I could purchase another pair at one of the local shops, but until then, I had to make do with the underwear I was wearing. Again, the mantra came to mind: "thru-hikers have to be flexible." Make a new plan and just keep walking.

In the late afternoon, our route took us off the high mountain ridge by way of a perilous rocky descent. Most of the day was spent hiking without a trail, making progress slow while navigating the difficult terrain with a compass. I was very happy to finally reach a rough jeep trail at the bottom of the mountain which would hopefully take us to an established Forest Service road that connected to a designated CDT trailhead. That was the best information we had from the guidebook and maps. Our general direction of travel was southeast which was where Grand Lake was located so I was comfortable with our current situation. My only concern was that the route lacked any sources of water for miles, and I was almost out.

As Don and I were walking down the dusty Forest Service road, I could hear a distant motor that seemed to be growing nearer. Looking over my shoulder, I suggested, "Let's stand here for a minute and see if this motorcycle rider will stop to talk to us. Maybe this person will know of a water source nearby."

Don reluctantly slowed his steps and then paused to scan the horizon behind us where the bike was growing larger as it came into view. I waved my hand to say hello and the man on the bike cut the engine when he got within twenty feet and slowed to a stop. He also called out, "Hey guys, sorry about the noise of the bike. I'm sure it's detracting from your hiking experience!"

I must have stood there for a few seconds with a stunned expression on my face because his greeting had been so thoughtful and pleasant. Don was quicker to respond, "No problem, but thanks for your consideration."

I asked the man, "Are you, by any chance, from around here? Do you know if there is a stream or a creek nearby or if this road will cross water anytime soon? We are heading to the Willow Creek Pass Trailhead but are almost out of water."

He thought about my question and then answered, "This dirt road goes another three to four miles and then intersects Highway 125. No water from here to the highway. On the other side of the pavement is the trailhead for the Willow Creek Pass Trail and there is a creek but it's at least four miles into the woods. You're quite some distance from any water sources. Where are you hiking from?"

Don answered with our standard explanation that we were hiking the CDT and had been walking for a few months starting in Canada. Don went on to describe our route for the day and how it had started with an exceptionally beautiful sunrise up high on a ridge near Muddy Pass and continued cross-country with extreme elevation gains and losses to the top of Parkview Mountain (12,298 feet) and then back down to our current location. "Because of all the ups and downs and being off trail, we were moving a little slower than we anticipated." Looking over at me, Don said, "Looks like we will be walking in the dark to reach water."

With my shoulders slumping in disappointment, I turned to the man on the bike and told him, "We best get moving along. Have a good ride, and thanks for the information!"

As the motorcycle rolled on down the road, Don and I started hiking and formulating a plan for the rest of the day. About fifteen minutes later, we heard the rumble of an approaching motorbike. It was the same guy we had been talking to earlier and again, he turned off the bike and rolled to a stop. He offered to bring us a couple gallons of water from his nearby home if it would help our situation. Don thanked him and said, "That would be awesome. Not having to worry about water allows us to camp almost any-where along the trail."

The man told us his name was Paul Brown and that he would leave two gallon-jugs of water at the Willow Creek Pass Trailhead just a few feet past the sign. "Can't miss it," he said. Again, we thanked Paul for his help and watched as he rode on down the road. With big smiles on our faces, Don and I started hiking down the Forest Service road, excited about our surprise water cache and the prospect of making camp soon.

I had delayed eating my afternoon snack because I did not have much water to wash the food down. But with the knowledge of water being avail-able soon, my stomach started growling in earnest. Don was hungry as well, so we stopped to sit on a log and ate some cheese crackers. While we were munching, Don said, "I hope Paul comes back with not only the water he promised but also carrying a hot cherry pie. Wouldn't that be great?"

I rolled my eyes and chuckled. "I think you may be hallucinating there, buddy. But keep dreaming if it makes you feel better."

We made it to the trailhead in just under an hour. We did not find any water or any sign of Paul. However, within a few minutes of taking off our packs, a Ford Explorer pulled in and Paul stepped out of the car. "Hi guys. I have two gallons of water with me. I am happy to leave them with you, but I also wanted to offer you another option for the evening. I just spoke to my wife, and she agreed with my idea. We would like to extend an invitation to stay at our place for the night. We are offering you dinner and a bed in a separate cabin on our property in exchange for an evening of conversation about your CDT adventure. We have a seven-year-old son, and I would really like him to hear about what you two are doing and some of the highlights of the CDT trail. We will feed you breakfast in the morning and then I'll drive you back to the trailhead, so you won't have any additional mileage to hike from our house. Would you guys be up for that?"

I looked at Don to gauge his reaction and responded to Paul. "Thank you for the generous offer. We would love to meet your family and share stories about our experiences on the Divide. Sounds great." And with that, we put our packs in the back of the SUV and let Paul take us to his cabin in the woods.

During our conversations that evening, we learned that Paul worked in the timber industry out of Fort Collins, and his wife, Barb, was a case worker at the local hospital. As often as possible, they spent vacations, long weekends, and holidays at their cabin. Their son, Harrison, would be going back to school soon so this was a short vacation before the start of the new school year. Paul told us he had grown up in New York and had always wanted to hike the AT but like so many people, gave up the dream as "life" got in the way of the goal. He was interested in how we put our itinerary together and how we were resupplying ourselves during the trip. Barb asked us to share the most beautiful places we visited and the most challenging parts of our trip. Harrison did not quite know what to think about our hike. "Why would you want to do this?" he asked. His perplexed look made us all chuckle in unison.

The evening was outstanding. The Browns decided to take us out to dinner at a little restaurant in the nearby town of Rand. The seafood restaurant was named *The Rand Yacht Club,* although it was not close to any body of water. I ordered the coconut shrimp plate and Don had fish-n-chips. Both meals were delicious. We had told Paul about Don's hallucination on the trail when he hoped Paul would bring us water and a cherry pie. Paul secretly went back into the kitchen to ask the chef at the restaurant if they had any cherry pie available for dessert. We were so touched at the sincere effort that Paul made to ensure we had a special evening. I felt so grateful to have met this wonderful family.

The next morning, the Browns made a huge breakfast of pancakes, sausage, and a fresh fruit bowl of watermelon and cantaloupe. Barb even fixed a pot of hazelnut coffee just for me. I was in heaven. Everything tasted so good. I helped with the dishes, and Paul and Don mapped out our route for the day. Paul was very knowledgeable about all the trails in the area. He provided us with a great deal of information regarding our next two days of travel to Grand Lake.

As promised, Paul drove us to the Willow Creek Pass Trailhead. We hugged goodbye then donned our packs. I felt like I had made new friends and was surprised at how close I had grown to these individuals so quickly. We exchanged addresses with the Browns hoping to keep in touch. Little did I know at the time, twenty years later I would still be exchanging letters annually with Barb and remembering our wonderful visit to their treasured cabin in the woods of Colorado.

Back in early 2000, I read a book called *Where the Waters Divide* by Karen Berger. It tells the story of Karen and her husband's journey hiking the Continental Divide in 1990. Karen often spoke of what she called "trail angels." The name represents the amazingly kind and generous people that thru-hikers encounter on the route; a perfect example being Barb and Paul Brown. Don and I met numerous individuals with whom we developed an immediate connection. We rarely had to hitchhike because folks offered to drive us to and from trailheads once they heard we were hiking the CDT. Others reacted to our story by offering us food, sunscreen, and bug repellant as gifts to help us on our journey and to participate in our adventure. There really was something magical about these encounters. Undoubtedly, a highlight of our journey was the many wonderful people we met along the way.

ROCKY MOUNTAIN HIGHS

The ninety-six-mile, five-day section between Grand Lake and Silverthorne, Colorado provided the quintessential Continental Divide hiking experience; miles of high-elevation, knife edge ridge line and the opportunity to summit numerous peaks. When I first pictured walking the Continental Divide, I imagined us hiking on the crest of the Rocky Mountains for weeks at a time;

but a vast majority of the CDT only climbs up to the passes between peaks and follows trails cut into the sides of the mountains for easier, safe passage. But this special segment provided all the challenges, views, and excitement that I had desired.

The mountains of Colorado had the highest elevations of all the states we traveled through. The day after leaving Grand Lake, we started climbing the High Lonesome Trail and quickly rose above 10,000 feet; an altitude we would not drop below during the next four days of hiking. From my mountaineering experience on Denali and Mt. Rainier, I knew the effects of high altitude and could feel my body struggling to consume enough oxygen with each breath. The mind and body slow down with less oxygen in the air, requiring additional focus to complete each task and every step along the trail. This was especially true on this section of the CDT which included a large portion of cross-country travel scrambling over talus rock and boulders. During the last two days, we would climb three major passes: Rollins, Rogers, and Berthoud, and summit four peaks: James (13,294 feet), Eva (13,200 feet), Flora (13,191 feet) and Parry (13,391 feet). High-altitude backpacking would provide us with amazing scenery and a few surprises along the way.

"Oh my gosh, Don, look at the view!" There was a slight haze of smoke on the horizon that marred the picture I was taking with my camera from James Peak, but to my eye, the panorama was nothing short of spectacular. My eyes started to fill with tears as I whispered, "Can you believe we hiked all of those mountains as far as you can see?"

Standing at the summit of James Peak, the second highest point on the CDT, Don and I had a 360-degree view of all the surrounding mountains as well as the ridge that formed the Continental Divide. Marveling at the sight, Don said, "It's incredible how far we have hiked." Then to bring some levity to the moment he added, "I think I'll make a contribution to both watersheds." A few seconds later, Don had me laughing when he urinated aiming his stream from one side of the Divide to the other.

While he was finishing his business, I located the summit register for James Peak. After reading a few of the most recent entries, I wrote the date; August 15, 2002, and a quick note that said, "How far, how high, you never know until you try," followed by our names and CDT thru-hikers. We sat for another ten minutes and enjoyed a nutrition bar, reading a few more comments in the registry. As we readied ourselves to leave, Don asked me for the camera and took a photo of me looking out at the mountains of the Continental Divide with the knife edge ridge line as part of the background. That picture would become one of my favorites because of the strong emotional memories it evokes of our day on James Peak.

We started down the mountain on a faint path of talus rock heading to a blue spot on the map named Ice Lake. The entire day had been spent ascending or descending on rock and as late afternoon approached, I asked, "Do you think we are going to find a level area where we can pitch our tent?" I had not thought about making camp until that moment.

Looking around us and being the eternal optimist, Don responded, "It might be challenging but I'm sure we will figure something out."

As usual, I had been preoccupied with concerns about finding water. Hiking exclusively on mountain tops and ridge lines meant significant water sources were likely to be well below us and difficult to reach. Throughout the day, I had kept a hopeful eye out for any depressions in boulders where snowmelt might have collected. We had filtered water from this type of natural birdbath once before on the trip after shooing away the bathing bird.

As evening approached, we rounded a very large rock outcropping and found a welcome surprise before us. A patch of grass was growing on a small jut of land just below the ridge line of the mountain. The good news was that this precious area was level and provided enough room to set up our tent. The bad news was that our tent was now perched on the side of a cliff and only a few feet away from the zippered doorway was a five-hundred-foot drop to Ice Lake. Astoundingly, we had found a place to camp and our water source at the same time. Don headed down to filter water and left me to finish unloading our packs. When my chores were completed, I took advantage of a few minutes of leisure time to take pictures of our campsite and write in my journal, enjoying the alpine glow of the setting sun.

The watch I was wearing had become an important piece of equipment providing not only statistical data of elevation gains each day, but also the current altitude, a compass, and a basic alarm clock to wake me up each morning. The watch indicated we had climbed a total of 9,000 feet that day and were currently camped at an altitude of 12,500 feet. The distance traveled was fourteen miles, and it had been a hard hike scrambling over rock and boulders at an altitude ranging from 10,000 to 13,294 feet. The information obtained from my watch made me feel a little better about gasping for air all day as it validated the difficulty of our effort.

I was finishing my journal entry as Don arrived back at camp carrying water for our dinner meal. He had also filled four hydration packs for our hike the next day, and to my delight, a bursting Mr. Blue Belly, which would allow me to wash before going to bed. I was so excited, I gave Don a hug and said, "Thanks for hauling all the extra weight back up to camp. I'm so excited about washing off the sunscreen and sweat tonight." Mr. Blue Belly was a gallon water bag covered in dark nylon that absorbed the heat from the sun. We sat the bag on a rock and let the last rays of sunshine hit it so that after dinner, we would have slightly warm water for bathing.

Don got out our camp stove to start boiling water for our freeze-dried dinner. The stove struggled to light and then sputtered and spewed as it tried to produce a strong flame. "What's wrong with our stove?" I asked.

"I don't know," Don said, adjusting the gas opening. "It's been working fine and has plenty of gas."

"I just wrote in my journal all the stats from my watch. This is our highest camp—12,500 feet. Do you think the altitude is affecting the stove?"

Don looked up at me with surprise. "We are at 12,500 feet? That's got to be the problem."

The stove hissed for another minute and then died and would not restart. Although the water never reached boiling, it was hot, so we poured it into our freeze-dried entrée package and let it sit. We ended up eating lukewarm Sierra Almond Chicken for dinner. It was not a great meal but it did fill us up, so our stomachs stopped growling and we could sleep.

We quickly cleaned ourselves by spritzing off with tepid water from Mr. Blue Belly. A bandanna makes a great washcloth that dries incredibly fast. We then donned our one change of clothing for bedtime. After crawling into our sleeping bags for the evening, we reviewed our map for the next day's hike. Tomorrow we would summit three peaks including Parry Peak (13,391 feet), the highest point on the CDT. The map also contained a section labeled "Unidentified/Exposed Trail." Looking over at Don I asked, "What does that mean?"

"I am guessing we will travel cross-country for part of the route and have to deal with exposure at some point," he replied. I drifted off to sleep excited about the opportunity to climb the big mountains and wondering what challenges lay ahead.

While we broke down camp the next morning, the wind started to howl. I was thankful we were able to load our packs without losing any gear over the side of the cliff from a big gust of wind. Once we started walking, Don excitedly asked, "Did you feel the tremor?"

"What tremor? You mean like an earthquake?"

"Yeah, I felt it early this morning."

With my eyebrows now nearing my hairline, I could not really respond. We had slept with our tent only five feet from the edge of a cliff. I truly didn't need to know about the tremor!

Most of our early morning route was cross-country and followed the ridge line heading to Parry Peak. Around mid-morning, we encountered a short fifty-yard section of trail that climbed over and around exposed rock cliffs. There was a several hundred foot drop on either side of the scramble. Our summit of Idaho's tallest mountain came to mind. "This feels just like Chicken Out Ridge on Mt. Borah back home. Only today, we have crazy wind trying to rip me off the face of this boulder." The wind had steadily increased throughout the morning and at that moment was buffeting me and my pack as I clung to creative hand holds across the precipice. As usual, Don moved like a spider and scurried with ease through the perilous area. Once safe on the other side of the outcropping, we continued our walk toward the highest mountain on the CDT.

We found the summit register atop Parry Peak and wrote August 16, 2002, and "That which does not kill us makes us stronger," followed by our names and CDT thru-hikers. Given the terrain we were navigating, the comment seemed appropriate to me.

As it turned out, the physical effort to climb Parry and the two remaining peaks was not our biggest challenge. The wind had grown to gale force level causing us to struggle to remain upright. I was leaning forward, and even with the additional weight of my backpack was still being blown backward. Placing my pole firmly before stepping was the only safe way to move forward because when the gust died abruptly, the pole kept me from face planting on the rocky terrain. We had no way to measure the actual wind speed, but the fact that we were repeatedly blown off the trail and constantly driven to misplace our footing led me to believe this day had been one for the record books. Although I was still impressed with reaching the tops of Mt. Flora and Mt. Eva, I was also very glad to end the day at Berthoud Pass where a restaurant provided us shelter from the wrath of Mother Nature. The small resort town of Winter Park was located at the bottom of Berthoud Pass, so Don and I hitchhiked to town and got a hotel room where we could ride out the rest of the storm in comfort. I loved this high-altitude section of the CDT and was looking forward to hiking the rest of the mountains in Colorado, although I hoped to have a little less of a breeze.

THE INCREDIBLE SHRINKING
MAN. . . AND WOMAN!

"Hot, fluffy pancakes stacked high, dripping with melted butter and warm maple syrup. That sounds so good right now!" I was talking about food again during our hike out of the woods to the Wolf Creek Pass trailhead. Our plan was to hitchhike to Pagosa Springs, Colorado to pick up another resupply box. Whenever we got close to a town stop, all my thoughts turned to food. We had been on the trail for three months and I had lost twenty-five pounds of body fat. I felt physically fit, but my hips and thighs had slimmed down from a full size 12 to a tiny size 4. I had not been this small since I was thirteen years old in middle school. There was nothing normal about my physique or my appetite. I was ravenous all the time. A very kind trail angel, named Brian

Burgess, stopped along the highway, and gave us a ride to Pagosa Springs. When asked which restaurant served the best breakfast, he told us about the Irish Rose on Main Street and then proceeded to drive us to their front door. After thanking Brian profusely for the lift, we carried our packs inside to enjoy a large mid-morning brunch.

The wonderful aroma of coffee wafted through the door when we entered. Everything on the menu looked great, but I knew my heart was set on pancakes. I ordered an omelet that came with hash browns and a pancake. I asked that the short stack be changed to a full stack. Andrea was the name of our server, and she offered the warning, "Oh no, honey, you won't be able to eat all that. Our side pancake is as big as a large dinner plate. A full stack is three of those monster flapjacks."

I smiled at Andrea. "I really think I can handle it. Appreciate you giving me a heads up, but if I can't eat it, I won't hold it against you!"

Satisfied that I understood the amount of food I was ordering, Andrea walked away after replying, "Okay then, I will put your order in and bring you more coffee while you wait."

Coffee was something I desperately missed on the hike. We did not have the room or the desire to carry more weight so coffee was one of the first things I had to give up on our trip. I thoroughly enjoyed every cup of coffee at each town stop and often drank a half pot with a breakfast meal.

With a slight smirk, Andrea delivered several heaping plates of food to our table. It took no time at all for me and Don to consume every crumb in front of us. When Andrea came back to refill our mugs, she stood by our table with big eyes and a stunned expression on her face. I smiled and sheepishly said, "I was so famished. Breakfast was delicious. Thank you."

After a small shake of her head, Andrea began clearing the dishes. "Well at least you guys don't have to worry about lunch now." Once she was out of ear shot, I started to giggle. I was already thinking about lunch, and I had just finished breakfast. Food was on my mind all the time and I could eat embarrassing amounts at each meal.

Don and I checked into our hotel, washed our clothes, and then went grocery shopping to resupply our food bags. We picked up a half gallon of

Starbuck's Java Chip ice cream, and sat on the curb and shared the entire container. Our snack was over 1,000 calories apiece. For dinner that evening, we each consumed a medium Domino's Pizza, half an order of bread sticks and a half liter of soda. Pizza, hamburgers, and traditional breakfast fare were the focus of our meals. We craved foods that were salty, greasy, and loaded with calories.

On the trail, our daily food allotment weighed two-and-a-half pounds and provided 2,500 calories for each of us. Unfortunately, we were hiking nearly a marathon in distance and burning 5,000 calories a day. A pound of body fat is equivalent to 3,500 calories. At the end of a six-day hiking section, we would have a deficit of 15,000 calories and have lost a little over four pounds. Most of our itinerary included sections of six days or more between town stops so this massive weight loss campaign had been going on all summer. Our menu was made up of concentrated calories that did not require refrigeration. Breakfast was granola with powdered milk. Mid-morning and afternoon snacks included nutrition bars, peanut butter crackers, Fig Newtons, dried fruit, and mixed nuts. Summer sausage and cheese could last up to forty-eight hours and was often included for lunch during the first couple days on the hike. We carried jerky and peanut butter for lunch meals later in the week when the cheese and sausage were gone (vacuum packed tuna and chicken were not available in 2002). Dinner was a freeze-dried entrée and side dish that we shared. We would top off supper with three or four Oreo cookies for dessert. Sometimes we would carry an extra entrée for additional calories, but this required carrying more weight in both food and fuel to prepare the item. Our lightweight packs were designed to carry a maximum of thirty pounds comfortably. After packing all our gear, we were limited to carrying approximately six days of food between the two of us. Adding food weight stressed the durability of the pack causing seams to tear and made the strap design painful on our shoulders and hips. For this reason, Don and I had to carefully consider any additional food item against the consequences of carrying it.

The challenge to balance calorie intake with energy expenditure was not unique to us. Every CDT thru-hiker comments on their excessive weight loss and the struggle to eat enough food to keep moving. Don and I were putting some type of food item in our mouths every hour when we were on the trail. We routinely hiked for sixty to ninety minutes and then stopped, and sat down to eat a snack. After stretching for a couple minutes, we put our packs back on and began walking again. Don and I had learned that a rest break lasting less than five minutes was not enough, but one lasting more than fifteen minutes was too long, causing our muscles to become stiff. A regimen developed over time that allowed us to comfortably cover many miles between campsites.

We returned to the Irish Rose the next day for another big breakfast. Andrea was working again and this time, did not hesitate to bring me all the food I requested. We struck up a conversation with her about living in Pagosa Springs, and she asked about the backpacks we had with us the previous day and wondered what we were doing. When we explained that we were hiking the CDT, she understood why we were so hungry. Looking us over, Andrea said, "You both are so thin, I couldn't understand how you could eat so much and not gain any weight." Throughout our leisurely breakfast, Andrea asked a few more questions about hiking the CDT. She seemed intrigued by the short stories of our adventure. When we stood up to leave, Andrea came over and gave me a hug and presented me with an Irish Rose bandanna as a souvenir of our time together at the restaurant. She thanked us for sharing our entertaining tales from the trail. Andrea and the other servers wished us a safe journey to the southern border and told us to "Come back and visit" as we walked out the door.

It was late morning when we loaded our backpacks, checked out of our hotel room, mailed our travel box to ourselves for later use and began our hike toward Wolf Creek Pass. Our route took us by the Malt Shoppe restaurant where the aroma of French fries and grilled meat had us salivating and our stomachs rumbling again. After polishing off a loaded burger, fries and a chocolate milkshake followed by a mocha at the coffee shop next door, we were ready to make our way down the road. I stuck out my thumb to hitchhike. Within a matter of minutes, a college student who had seen us at the coffee shop, picked us up and drove us twenty miles to the trailhead.

Pagosa Springs was a terrific town stop filled with trail angels and an array of delicious food. Perhaps one day we really will go back and visit.

ALL GOOD THINGS COME TO AN END

"You're asking what my proudest moment was in high school? Hmm, okay, I have a story," I replied. "Once a year, high school band members had the opportunity to try out for the All Valley Band which is composed of the best musicians from the fifteen Rio Grande Valley towns of southern Texas. A panel of judges held blind auditions that evaluated song performance, ability to sight read sheet music and knowledge of scales. Eight saxophone positions were available, and I placed fourth out of a hundred competitors. As a freshman, it was a real honor to make the All Valley Band and I was proud to represent The Edinburg Band program."

Don smiled. "That was a great story. Why haven't you ever told me that?"

"I don't know. We never really had a reason to talk about my band days. So how about you? What was your proudest moment in high school?"

"The time my best friend Jerry and I drove to Florida during spring break of our senior year to be tested for our black belts in karate."

"Oh my gosh, I didn't realize you and Jerry got your belts at the same time or that you had to travel so far for it. That's awesome you guys were able to make it happen!"

Don and I spent hours having these kinds of exchanges on the CDT. It seemed my husband created questions from an endless list of heartwarming topics that included proudest moments at different ages, highlights from family vacations, best Christmas, best surprise present, most fun scouting activity, most fun athletic effort growing up and best birthday. The laughter, good feelings, and deeper understanding of one another that resulted from these discussions added to our relationship. Surprisingly, I had been married to Don for twenty years and was still discovering new things about him. With these types of conversations, we were never bored hiking the CDT.

Our route through New Mexico alternated between desert terrain of juniper trees, piñon pine, and scrub brush or high forested plateaus filled with ponderosa pine and aspen trees. Both landscapes were beautiful and offered interesting flora and fauna. I learned very quickly that most every plant or bush in the desert was covered with thorns to protect itself. It was imperative that I watched where I stepped and was cognizant of brushing against low growing vegetation to avoid a scratch from something prickly.

Rattlesnakes became more prevalent in the New Mexico desert. Don was nearly struck by one while searching for a spring in a rocky wash thirty miles from Pie Town. Our GPS led us to a dry creek bed and although we did not find any water, we did find the snake. The consequences of a rattlesnake bite so far from civilization would have been dire. After that episode I became much more vigilant in evaluating every feature of the landscape that might harbor a snake.

Once again, we found ourselves surrounded by cows. Wyoming and New Mexico seemed to have the most cattle freely roaming the land. After leaving the spectacular Gila River Canyon, we headed through desert terrain toward the small town of Membres. Most of the land in New Mexico was privately owned, but The Nature Conservancy held some acreage on the Membres River where we were allowed to pitch our tent. This lovely campsite along the river would become extremely memorable for me and Don. At first glance, the setting was picturesque with a stream of gurgling water and ponderosa pine trees dotting the riverbanks. However, upon closer inspection, we were challenged to find a small area not covered in cow pies where we could set up our tent. Totally disgusted I commented, "I have never seen so much cow shit in one place. Can you imagine what is in that river? Maybe we should filter and add iodine tablets to our water."

"Good idea," Don said. "I'm going to go scout up and down the riverbank to see if there is an area that is less polluted."

Unfortunately, the excrement was widespread. After much inspection, we did find what we thought was an acceptable site and set up our camp. In the end, despite the safety precautions taken, we somehow allowed our drinking water to become contaminated. Ten days later, Don developed a case of Giardia that was likely contracted during our night on the Membres River. Lucky for us, his symptoms did not present until we were back in

Idaho. We ended our trip without realizing the souvenir we were carrying back home.

As part of our camping routine, I filled Mr. Blue Belly and set him in the sun to warm up for bathing after dinner. Later, when I hung him on a tree limb to more easily manage the water spout, the branch broke and the bag fell. The weight of the water in the bag caused the plastic liner to split when it hit the ground. Distraught, I yelled out, "I just killed Mr. Blue Belly! He dropped out of the tree and broke apart. I feel terrible. He's been a part of our hiking adventures for twenty years. I can't believe I destroyed him!" Although I knew I was being silly for getting emotional over a water bag, I also realized in that moment that there were years of good memories intertwined with that single piece of camping equipment and that Mr. Blue Belly had become an integral part of my experience on the Divide. And with a flash of insight, I also understood I would not only miss making memories with the water carrier, but I would soon miss making memories with Don on the CDT. My acute sense of sadness was a realization that all good things come to an end and that our adventure would be over soon.

When I expressed my thoughts to Don, my enthusiastic partner told me, "Just enjoy the moment, Shannon. Our journey isn't over yet." Keeping that calming notion in mind, Don and I spent a pleasant evening camped on the riverbank listening to the braying of cows mixed with the sound of the flowing river.

The next morning, we had a mile-long hike into the town of Membres to retrieve our resupply box at the post office. The postal worker started a conversation with us about the dangers of hiking in the mountains on our way to the border of Mexico. This was the second time we had been warned about escalating cartel activity in the area and their use of the mountain trails for smuggling illegal drugs into the United States. The first time, the conversation was initiated by a BLM employee, Jim, that was staying at the Wilderness Lodge B&B south of the Gila State Monument where we had stopped for a night. Jim had been quite concerned that we would be on the same trails as the cartel members and had encouraged us to change our itinerary to a safer route. Hearing the cautionary tone of the Post Office employee, we thanked the man for his advice and decided to review our maps at breakfast for a safer corridor of travel. We concluded that by sticking to backroads, we could hike thirty-two miles to Faywood Hot Springs and camp at a designated campground for the night. From the hot springs, we would have a twenty-six-mile highway walk to Deming where we could get a hotel room and then do a thirty-four mile walk the next day to the Mexican border. Our new plan forced us to endure three days of hiking on asphalt, but it seemed like a better alternative to the mountains.

Arriving in Deming in late afternoon, we found a hotel downtown and got a room for the night. The air-conditioning was a welcome relief from the late October sun that radiated off the pavement during our hike. The logistics of ending our trip weighed heavy on my mind. Don was adamant about hiking every mile to Mexico. I felt more pragmatic about the end of the trip and decided to let Don finish the adventure solo. While he was on the road to Mexico, I planned to take the hundred-mile shuttle to the El Paso Airport, rent a car, make reservations to fly home, drive to the mall to purchase luggage for our gear, return to Deming and then drive south toward Mexico to pick up Don at the border. The distance from Deming to the border was thirty-four miles. I told Don I was going to pick him up wherever I found him along the highway. I would later learn that my comment encouraged my husband to move quickly. He was determined to reach the border before my arrival to chauffeur him back to the hotel. After eating a quick breakfast, Don struck off at a fast clip before sunrise carrying only essential items and minimal weight.

When I returned from my day of errands and just before heading south toward Mexico, I picked up a McDonalds's to-go order with a hot Quarter Pounder with cheese, fries, and an icy Dr Pepper. Don packed only nutrition bars for food along the way and barely enough water for the distance. Knowing he would be hungry and thirsty; I was excited to surprise him with the fast-food treat. We had been apart for about eight hours and in my head, I had calculated how many miles Don should have completed walking at a speed of three miles per hour. I started looking for him along the sides of the road when my trip odometer read twenty-four miles. I did not see him anywhere. Four miles per hour is a very fast pace for hiking in boots with a pack. At that speed, I should have found Don at the odometer reading of thirty-two miles. There was still no sign of Don. This section of highway was not a warm, fuzzy type of place. All the buildings had chain-link fences surrounding them with bars over all the windows and doors. If the structure was a house, it had a pit bull roaming in the yard. I was growing more concerned with each passing mile. With a great sense of relief, I finally spotted him just before the border. He had walked an incredible four and a half miles per hour and had reached his goal of completing the Continental Divide Trail on October 17, 2002.

I hopped out of the car and took a picture of Don standing under a sign that read "Mexico Border 1/2 mile." When I gave him a hug of congratulations, he said, "You smell so clean and look so fresh. I can't wait to take a shower!" He reacted even stronger to the aroma of the surprise food. "Oh my gosh, you got McDonald's. Those fries smell so good." After taking a big drink of Dr Pepper, Don said, "This tastes awesome." Later he would tell me that he had gotten so overheated and hungry, the cold soda was the perfect beverage to cool him off and give him a much-needed jolt of caffeine and sugar.

On the drive back to Deming, Don devoured his meal and shared the highlights of his hike. He too, had noticed the increased security measures. Don told me he had felt safe walking, and that several border patrol cars had passed by him throughout the day. He went on to say, "We made the right choice to walk the roads to the border. I'm happy with how we decided to end the trip." Later that night, we celebrated the completion of our goal with a beer and Mexican food at Cano's restaurant across the street from our hotel.

Our hike on the Continental Divide Trail was a remarkable five-month adventure. Being immersed in nature for such a great length of time allowed us to feel part of the landscape and to experience a connection to the mountains and wildlife. Though the trail tested our physical and mental strength, we found that we flourished along the journey with each other's support. When Don is asked what he loved most about the trip, he always answers, "Simplicity of purpose." Gone were all outside intrusions and worries. He embraced the solitude and peacefulness of a long walk in the woods.

For me, the journey was a celebration of life. Fears that my heart prob-lem might return faded with each step I took on the trail. Completion of the trip gave me confidence that I was truly healthy and that once again, Don and I could continue to focus on our dreams and goals. With a strong desire to fulfill the promise I made to myself back in early June, we began making plans to hike the Highline Trail through Glacier National Park the following summer.

Statistics of Don and Shannon's Hike on the CDT	
Days of trek	122
Miles hiked	2,287
Shortest day of hiking (miles)	8
Longest day of hiking (miles)	34
Estimated elevation climbed (in feet)	295,000
Pairs of shoes used per person	4
Weight loss (in pounds)	15–Don 25–Shannon
Days of rain	42
Days of snow	2
Grizzly bears seen	1
Cows seen	5,000+ (too many to count)
Cases of giardia	1
Days we got lost for more than 1 hour	10
Total cost of trip	$8,000
Cost of maps and guidebooks	$1,000
Hot showers taken during trek	24
Top 3 items missed/most talked about on hike	1. Coffee 2. Hot water 3. Pancakes

CONTINENTAL DIVIDE PHOTOS (1 OF 3)

1   Piegan Port of Entry on the Canadian Border—Don and Shannon begin their Continental Divide Trail hike on June 16, 2002.

2   Parting of the Waters—Where Two Ocean Creek divides to become Atlantic and Pacific Creeks.

3   Green River Valley, Gros Ventre Wilderness, WY.

4   Squaretop Mountain in the Green River Valley, WY.

5   Island Lake—Wind River Mountains, WY.

6   Clear Lake with Temple Peak in background, Wind River Range, WY.

CONTINENTAL DIVIDE PHOTOS (2 OF 3)

7   Great Divide Basin, WY. We hiked across 123 miles of barren land with five nights of camping in record heat and drought conditions.

8   CDT Laundry Day— Washed our clothes and hung them on our packs to dry in the sun and wind while hiking.

9   Summit of James Peak, CO. Shannon gazing at all the mountains already climbed.

10   Camping near Parry Peak, CO. Tent perched on tiny patch of grass at 12,500 feet. A 500 foot drop to Ice Lake is just to the left of the tent.

11   Don and Shannon on the high plateau of Snow Mesa (11,500 ft.) in the La Garita Mountains near Spring Creek Pass and Lake City, CO.

12   Don's favorite spot—Lake Nebo, San Juan Mountains, CO.

CONTINENTAL DIVIDE PHOTOS (3 OF 3)

13 Don and Shannon on the CDT near Pagosa Springs, CO. It was hunting season. I am wearing the yellow top from the resupply box I packed in early May.

14 Shannon on the CDT near Ghost Ranch and Abiquiu, NM.

15 The Gila River Canyon, NM —The trail was 21 miles long and crossed the Gila River 78 times.

16 Don completed the CDT at the border crossing four miles south of Columbus, NM on October 17, 2002.

MEXICO BORDER
½ MILE

Made it!

CANADA

USA

START

**Wedge Canyon Fire
52,974 Acres**

**Trapper Fire
19,150 Acres**

89

Many Glacier

Saint Mary

**Wolf Gun Fire
10,700 Acres**

GLACIER
NATIONAL
PARK

**Robert Fire
57,570 Acres**

89

Kiowa

West Glacier

**Middle Fork
Complex
10,997 Acres**

2

END

East Glacier

Great Bear Mountains

Hungry Horse Reservoir

**Rampage Complex
23,497 Acres**

2

Nimrod

GLACIER NATIONAL PARK

THE CONTINENTAL DIVIDE TRAIL

Patiently standing in line to obtain our backcountry camping permits at the Apgar Visitor Center in Glacier National Park, the ranger behind the counter glanced up at us and did a double take as he recognized Don, Ed, Teri, and me. "Oh my gosh, I remember you guys! Do natural disasters follow you wherever you go?" the ranger named Mike asked our group. Without waiting for a reply, Mike went on to say, "You were here for our record snowstorm last year and now we have forest fires threatening Glacier. Maybe you guys should think about skipping a visit to the park next year!"

Mike's emphatic commentary was a surprise but not unwarranted. Coincidentally, he was the same Park Service Ranger that had worked extensively with the four of us the previous year when we had made our first attempt to hike the Continental Divide Trail (CDT) through Glacier National Park. A record eight feet of snow had fallen a few days before we were scheduled to start our 120-mile trek in June 2002. Reluctantly, Mike had granted us permits along the CDT but only after much discussion regarding our collective wilderness experience and preparedness for winter travel.

It was now July 18, 2003, and the Wedge Canyon Fire was burning on the northwestern boundary of Glacier's North Fork Area. The fire's rapid growth and threat to one of our nation's treasured parks made it the highest priority fire in the country. Our plan was to begin on the Canadian Border at the Waterton Lake Trailhead sixty miles east of the fire. The combination of distance and the granite walls of the Continental Divide mountains was considered adequate protection from danger and allowed Mike to issue us backcountry permits for an eight-day hike on the CDT. No one could have predicted that within five days, one fire would increase to six, four major park lodges would be evacuated, and the Going-to-the-Sun Road would be overcome by raging flames as Glacier experienced the largest and most destructive fire in its history.

The start of our journey seemed perfect, beautiful weather with sunny skies and very little wind. The hike along the four-mile length of Waterton Lake provided picturesque views of the surrounding mountains and lush forest, all beautifully reflected on the mirror like surface of the water. Several eagles delighted us with their presence as they soared effortlessly above the lake hunting for their next meal. After being away for eight months, Don and I were glad to be back on the trail. I found I had absolutely no anxiety about starting this adventure because everything about our trip felt familiar and routine. We were using the same lightweight packs, equipment, clothing, and menu on our hike with planned mileage well below our daily average on the CDT. All I felt was joy to be hiking in Glacier National Park and sharing the experience with my friends. Unfortunately, this amazing feeling of confidence and euphoria would only last for eight hours.

BUGGED BY A BUG

"Hey, Shannon, could you come over here a minute?" Don called out. We were brushing our teeth several yards from camp to keep any bears that might be attracted to the sweet smell of toothpaste from being lured to our tent. As I approached Don, I noticed he had a very concerned look on his face and looked a little pale. "What's up?" I asked when I got close to him.

"I've got a problem and I'm not sure what to do about it. I felt a bug bite me while we were eating dinner. It must have crawled up my pant leg after we washed earlier. I didn't think much about it at the time but now I seem to be having a serious reaction to the bite."

"Where did the bug bite you?" Don answered my question by pulling the elastic waistband out from his belly and pointing inside his pants. We had washed the sunscreen and sweat from our bodies earlier by the stream and instead of putting on our dirty clothes, we donned loose-fitting nylon wind pants and jackets to eat our meal. Don wasn't wearing any briefs and planned to change at bedtime into the clean pair of long johns he wore only while sleeping. When I looked inside Don's pants, his penis looked normal except the head was two times larger than usual and had developed blisters that resembled a cauliflower floret. "Oh, my God!" I yelled. "What the hell happened? Did you actually see a bug? What kind of bug could do that!" Ed heard my outburst and came over to where Don and I were standing to see what was going on. "Ed, you've got to look at Don's penis!"

Ed's eyebrows rose in comic exaggeration as he looked at me and started to shake his head back and forth. "No Shannon, I don't need to look at your husband's junk!"

"He got a bug bite and is having a terrible reaction. We've got a serious problem!" About that time, Don pulled the front of his drawers down so Ed could see the red, blistered skin that was continuing to swell.

Ed's reaction was a short bark of laughter before saying, "Oh dear! That's not good. I think you better take some Benadryl before the situation gets any worse." Don was always hesitant to take medications, but with much encouragement from both me and Ed, Don took a couple pills. He then laid prone across the shallow stream, dangling his package in the very cold water to reduce the swelling.

Neither Don nor I slept well that first night of camping. Although we both worried about his genitals, our focus was on different aspects of his health. I worried the swelling would close Don's urethra and not allow him to urinate or the blistered skin would become raw and infected. Don expressed his concern succinctly, "I don't want my penis to turn black and fall off." What a relief it was to hear him whisper the words, "Oh, thank God!" at dawn the next morning. When Don woke up, the first thing he did was pull his sleeping bag down along with his long johns and look at his crotch. The swelling was gone, and the texture of his skin had returned to normal. The release of stress that swept through our tent was palpable. Don was going to be okay, and we could all continue our hike.

Although we never determined the specific insect that caused such a horrible reaction, Don, and I both became quite careful about where we laid our clothing, shaking items before putting them on, and most importantly—closely inspecting our underwear. The bug bite incident would become a funny story for the four of us to tell in years to come. However, it would not be the only serious surprise we encountered during our journey through the park.

I SEE EWE

On the second day of our trip, we climbed up on the Continental Divide and traveled several miles on Glacier's famed Highline Trail. By noon, we reached the Ahern Drift where a large area of snow accumulates and covers the route year around. After kicking deep steps into the snowpack to safely maneuver ourselves over the treacherous terrain, we decided to scramble off trail for a few hundred feet of altitude gain to reach Ahern Pass. There was still an amazing amount of snow covering the pass and blanketing a majority of Ahern Peak rising before us.

Settling on a rock ledge for a lunch break, we heard small pebbles cascading down the upper granite wall of the mountain. That's when all of us spotted a half dozen bighorn sheep that had been watching us climb to Ahern Pass. The four ewes had a couple lambs with them, and the youngsters entertained us throughout our meal by displaying their agility and prowess climbing the escarpment. "Look at that little one run!" I commented to Don. "How can they move so sure-footedly on a sheer cliff face? Those ledges must be only an inch or two in width. It's amazing how they can jump and climb up something so steep." Don agreed with my assessment, and together we laughed at the animal's antics on the icy slope before us. The young sheep slid down sections of snow, chasing each other, only to run uphill again after reaching the bottom. Just like children, the lambs seemed to have fun playing in the snow and made continuous loops on the hazardous terrain.

Our hike back down from Ahern Pass to the Highline Trail provided wonderful views of the mountains to our west in the Livingston Range. We could see smoke clouds in the far distance where the Wedge Canyon Fire was located, but the sight that caused us concern were the puffs of smoke directly across the valley rising above the crest of Flattop Mountain. These smoke plumes were new.

WHERE THERE'S SMOKE, THERE'S FIRE

We arrived at the Granite Park campground in early evening and immediately realized we were going to have a problem with the size of the campsite. The area was supposed to sleep four people but was not adequate for two separate tents. Camping outside the defined boundaries was strictly prohibited. Teri and Ed's tent had a more accommodating rectangular floor plan than our tepee style tent. It was a very tight fit, but we all squeezed into the single structure for the night. In addition to sleeping like sardines, the campsite would be remembered for several reasons.

The Granite Park campsites were in high demand because of their prominent location at the intersection of three extremely popular trails: The Continental Divide Trail, the Loop Trail from Logan Pass (Going-to-the-Sun Road), and the Swiftcurrent Trail out of Many Glacier. Permits were granted for only one night and the four campsites were completely booked throughout the summer. Lacking a natural water source, a faucet with potable water was provided along with a designated meal prep area and food hanging pole. To limit high traffic abuse to the surrounding vegetation, all camping activities were conducted in a small area that no longer contained a single blade of grass and consisted of only rock and powdery dust within its perimeter. The proximity of the four campsites magnified the sounds of coughing, sneezing, snoring, and tent zippers throughout the night. Though the campground was overused, the spectacular scenery made up for any discomfort.

Perched near the top of the Continental Divide at an elevation of almost 7,000 feet, the panorama of the Livingston Range was magnificent. We spent a good deal of time admiring the views while setting up camp and enjoying an early dinner. It was during this period that we noticed the wind had increased dramatically and the smoke we had seen earlier was darker and more abundant on the horizon. Then, as evening turned to night, the four of us watched a line of fire ignite and burst pine trees into pillars of flame as it slowly burned on a course heading to our location. The fire was small in size and too far away to pose any immediate threat to us, but its growth was cause for alarm. I fell asleep feeling a bit of anxiety and was glad the next day's route would lead us past the Granite Park Chalet and then on to camp at Many Glacier, where we would be surrounded by civilization and updated fire information.

When dawn broke the next morning, the winds were calm and smoke from the fire had settled in the valley below us. No longer being able to see any flames or billowing plumes of smoke rising into the sky, we calmly broke down camp and hiked a short mile to reach the Granite Park Chalet where we met Chris, a National Park Service employee. Chris was a wealth of information and explained that in addition to the Wedge Canyon Fire burning in the northwest, lightning strikes had started the Wolf Gun and Trapper Fires. What the four of us observed the previous day was the Trapper Fire's blowup from an estimated 400 to 4,000 acres. Chris said, "A park service ranger is staying at the Fire Lookout on top of Swiftcurrent Mountain and radioing fire activity reports to us here at the Chalet. As a precaution, a park service trail crew just finished helping me set up the fire hose." Granite Park Chalet was equipped with a pump system that could deliver water from a spring fed reservoir one quarter mile away to a 3,000-gallon water tank located behind the building. Chris also told us that the chalet was not being evacuated and there would be almost thirty guests staying at the lodge that night. With this new information, we felt much more relaxed and continued our hike toward Swiftcurrent Pass and Many Glacier.

There was surprisingly little smoke in the air; especially on the eastern side of Swiftcurrent Pass. The photos we took show a slight bit of haze but not enough to mar the majestic view of the Divide. Standing on the edge of a cliff at Devil's Elbow, Don looked tiny in contrast to the massive, mountain wall of granite behind him. The picture captured the uniqueness of the glaciated mountain ranges in the National Park.

After an eight-mile descent, we arrived in Many Glacier. Our friend, Mary, who worked as a member of the Park Service seasonal staff, was living in employee housing at Many Glacier and offered us an area to pitch our tents just outside her cabin. She had been instrumental in helping us coordinate travel logistics by shuttling our car from Waterton, Canada to East Glacier where the vehicle now waited for us at the end of our hike through the park. Mary had access to radio information being shared by the park rangers. She let us know there were currently no evacuations, but everyone was on high alert and monitoring the movement of the three fires in the Livingston Range. The Trapper Fire's advancement toward Swiftcurrent Pass had slowed and offered some hope that it might turn in a more northeasterly direction avoiding both the campground and chalet. The positive news allayed our concerns, allowing us to enjoy our evening together.

Our route on July 22nd headed south along the eastern flank of the Continental Divide mountains. With an expansive wall of rock and numerous glaciers between us and the flames, we felt safe from any potential threat. We stopped for lunch beside the incredibly clear turquoise waters of Grinnell Lake sitting at the base of Grinnell Glacier. It is hard to believe that within twenty-four hours, the beautiful scene before us would be filled with choking gray smoke and the mountain tops would no longer be visible from the trail. The most destructive day of fire on record in Glacier National Park would begin the next morning on the opposite side of the Divide.

After enjoying a leisurely break at Grinnell Lake, we continued our hike up Cataract Creek, passing two notable waterfalls on our way to Piegan Pass. The smaller Feather Plume Falls fell in delicate ribbons, dropping hundreds of feet down a cliff face while Morning Eagle Falls vied for attention with its immense size and roaring sound. Our route took us past a special section of the Continental Divide called The Garden Wall. When we stopped to filter water from Cataract Creek, I asked, "Have you noticed the shape of the mountaintops?"

Don nodded. "They kind of look like home."

"That's what I was thinking. Most of the other mountains we've seen had rounded tops, but these peaks are jagged like a saw. They look a lot like the Sawtooth Range, just more colorful."

Composed of polychromatic rock, the Garden Wall displayed a wave of vivid colorful layers. Additional decorations of snow and icy glaciers made its presentation even more striking. All the mountain peaks within Glacier were quite pretty, but these felt a little more endearing to me. The photo of me and Don filtering water would be the last picture we would take with smoke-free, clear blue skies as, once again, fire started chasing us through the park.

IGNORANCE IS BLISS

Our campsite for the night was at Reynolds Creek Campground located a mile south of the famous Going-to-the-Sun Road that runs through the middle of the park and over the Continental Divide via Logan Pass. The next morning, our thirteen-mile hike started in a southeasterly direction along Saint Mary Lake heading to Red Eagle Lake. On July 23rd, while Glacier's most catastrophic fire event was occurring nearby, we walked away from danger the entire day and remained oblivious to the chaos that was happening only a few miles away.

By mid-morning, the winds picked up to a steady twenty to twenty-five mph with gusts of forty mph causing the Trapper Creek Fire to explode. Flames overran the Loop Trail, the Going-to-the-Sun Road and then raced uphill to Swiftcurrent Pass. The ranger at the Swiftcurrent Mountain Lookout reported on the advancing fire line with instructions to immediately close The Loop Trail and the Highline Trail to Logan Pass, as the fire was going to overtake them quickly. Chris, the Park Service employee we had met at the Granite Park Chalet, would later describe that all he could see was heavy black smoke and he could hear a jet engine noise coming toward him and the chalet. The pump system had a few problems when initially turned on, but the water was flowing and protecting the historical structures as the fire raced in his direction. Many of the Chalet guests fled early in the morning, but forty individuals were trapped at the location when they could not get themselves to safety. Chris's expertise with the hose would be required to keep them from danger.

At Many Glacier where Mary was still located, darkness had descended at noon. The smoke completely obscured the landmark views of Swiftcurrent Mountain and Grinnell Peak. One of the rangers working at Many Glacier provided a visual of the destruction when he reported, "Heavy ash and debris is falling at the Many Glacier Ranger Station, including pinwheeling pine bark larger than a Texas license plate and burned out sticks larger than a thumb's diameter."

A new human-caused fire was detected in the early morning hours of July 23rd at the western entrance to Glacier. The Robert Fire, as it was named, quickly grew out of control consuming much of the Apgar Mountains and threatened the McDonald Valley, as it rapidly moved along the northern side of McDonald Lake.

By four o'clock in the afternoon, the Trapper Fire spread into the center of the park causing a mass evacuation of tourists on the Going-to-the-Sun Road. A train of cars sped over Logan Pass fleeing flames that engulfed both sides of the highway and completely burned The Loop Trailhead along with an abandoned bike and a car left in the lot. Michael Ober, a Park Service ranger working the late afternoon shift, described the events this way, "When we arrived at The Loop it was dark, eerily dark. If there are hikers up on the trail. . . well, there is nothing we can do. Fire is on both sides of the road licking at anything combustible with a hungry crackle. Short canopy runs are happening both below and above the parking lot; brush and ground fuels are burning steadily and burning branches, large and small, are falling all around, debris is everywhere, layers of burned pine needles like thousands of fallen soldiers litter the road surface."

Meanwhile, Ed, Teri, Don, and I were having a great time on the trail to Red Eagle Lake south of all the mayhem. The wind was blowing out of the southwest directing the smoke away from us. Occasionally we could smell smoke in the air, but the forested path we were hiking was down on the valley floor. It was sheer coincidence that the only day our itinerary lacked a high mountain pass was the same day that pandemonium erupted throughout the northern half of the park. We never gained enough elevation to detect the billowing smoke clouds, and remained blissfully unaware of the disaster unfolding around us. Later I would realize just how fortunate we had been to schedule our trip on the exact dates we selected. A delay of just one day would have forced us to cancel our entire trip. We were among the last hikers to see the Livingston Range in all its glory and without the moonscape like devastation from the burn.

Our campsite at the foot of Red Eagle Lake was exceptionally beautiful with Split Mountain and the Continental Divide as a backdrop. We were surprised to have the campground all to ourselves that evening and briefly wondered if the fires were discouraging folks from backpacking in the wilderness. Setting aside our concerns, we thoroughly enjoyed a very pleasant evening in a gorgeous lake location.

The spread of the four major fires slowed overnight but continued to advance. While we slept comfortably and without worry, the ranger at the Swiftcurrent Lookout stayed awake all night and described her experience this way: "Night fell and finally I could see the fire appear through the smoke as a thousand points of flame and torching trees. It was like looking at the Milky Way on a clear evening. So humbling. The sheer area of land that the fire had traveled over since 2:00 p.m. the afternoon before was enough to inspire awe." The general manager of the Park Lodges called a meeting at 4:00 a.m. with her staff and instructed them to immediately evacuate the Swiftcurrent and Many Glacier Lodges. The Trapper Fire had breached the pass and everything in the Swiftcurrent Canyon, including the historical buildings, were in imminent danger. Very few park service staff slept as well as we did that night.

TRIPLE DIVIDE PASS

Our route on July 24th started with a hike through very lush, green vegetation along Hudson Bay Creek. This section of trail looked and felt like prime bear country urging us to spend the entire morning repeatedly yelling, "Yo, Bear" to be heard over cascading waterfalls and rapids. Don seemed to struggle with the ability to project his voice causing me, Teri, and Ed to laugh at his weak attempts to yell. With his melodic, "Ho, Ho, Ho Bear" sounding more comedic than powerful, the three of us ultimately took over most of the necessary shouting.

By midday we had climbed to Triple Divide Pass and found one of only two places on the entire 3,100-mile Continental Divide Trail where a single source of water branched to ultimately reach different ocean destinations. Don and I had visited Two Ocean Creek while hiking the Divide in the Teton Wilderness of Wyoming the previous year. The famous "Parting of the Waters" stream split before our eyes with half the water flowing to the Atlantic Ocean while the other half gurgled over rocks on its way to the Pacific Ocean. Now standing on Triple Divide Pass, we were able to see how the glacier and snow fed stream trifurcated creating Pacific Creek to the west, Atlantic Creek to the east and Hudson Bay Creek flowing north to Canada's Hudson Bay and then on to the Arctic Ocean. This remarkable location possessed the unique status of being the only place in the entire world where one water source drained into three oceans.

The views from Triple Divide Pass were as impressive as its geographical significance. Although we were able to detect some smoke in the valleys and on the northern horizon, the green mountainsides and snowcapped mountains created a beautiful panorama that demanded our attention. Unbeknownst to us, the centrally located Trapper Fire was no longer the only serious threat in the park. The smoke we were seeing was also from the human-caused Robert Fire that had moved along McDonald Lake requiring both the Village Inn and Lake McDonald Lodge to begin evacuating all guests. The general manager for all the lodges in the park made this statement that evening, "I can't believe what has happened today. I am sure that never before have four hotels on two sides of the park had to be evacuated in the same day because of two different fires."

July 24th was also Teri's birthday. Don and I had carried a card with us for the occasion and were happy to help Teri celebrate her special day with our little surprise. We camped at Morning Star Lake for the night and shared the location with a few other campers. We all enjoyed a nice evening together made even more memorable when Teri broke out a package of coveted cookies she had carried for the duration of the trip and shared them with everyone. The cookies were outstanding and were quickly consumed by all of us staying at the lake.

PITAMAKAN PASS—AN EXCEPTIONAL DAY

The second longest section on our itinerary was a fourteen-and-a-half-mile hike over two mountain passes from Morning Star Lake to Two Medicine Campground. After climbing six miles, we reached Pitamakan Pass, the highest point (8,100 feet elevation) on Glacier's Continental Divide Trail and the most stunningly beautiful scenery of the entire trip. My first few steps over the top of the pass had me shouting, "Look at the view!" Pitamakan Overlook showcased the Nyack-Coal Creek Area in the southwestern section of the park. The numerous mountain peaks were part of the Lewis Range; an amazing vista of cathedral towers surrounded by healthy forested valleys beckoning to be explored. We took numerous photos from the observation point where Don stood in stark contrast against towering walls of rock and blankets of dark green. This outstanding moment of our journey sparked many conversations about returning to Glacier for more hikes in the years to come.

The three-mile trail from Pitamakan Pass to Dawson Pass was a series of small climbs and gradual descents that skirted the base of Mt. Morgan and Flinsch Peak before descending steeply into Bighorn Basin. That afternoon, I made the comment to Don, "This place is so amazing! I hope the camera captures its beauty." The scenery on this fourteen-mile section of our itinerary motivated us to take more pictures than on any other day of our hike.

The last five miles into Two Medicine Campground was a moderate downhill hike with a loss of 2,000 feet of elevation. We arrived at our campsite tired and hungry but thrilled by the pretty places we had visited during the day. Unfortunately, as Don and I slept soundly that night, lightning strikes started two new fires on the southwest side of Glacier: the Middle Fork Complex Fire and the Rampage Complex Fire. Both fires would impact the picturesque scenery of the Nyack-Coal Creek Area and bring the number of active wildfires in the park to an overwhelming six blazes. Again, we were among the last people to see the amazing views from Pitamakan Overlook without a mosaic of burn patches scarring the landscape.

Our hike out of the park the next day was uneventful. The trail was on the eastern side of the Divide and prevented us from being able to detect smoke from the smoldering new fires on the western side of the Rocky Mountains. We easily found our car in East Glacier parked exactly where Mary described leaving it for us. After loading all our gear, we started our drive back to Idaho. Don and I were happy to have finally achieved our goal of completing the Continental Divide Trail through Glacier National Park and had enjoyed the journey even more because we had shared the experience with friends.

Weeks after returning home, we learned more about the 2003 Glacier National Park fire season and realized just how fortunate we had been to complete our adventure. Six major fires burned more than 135,000 acres of forest, impacting 13 percent of Glacier's total area. From mid-July through September, hundreds of firefighters labored for weeks on end to minimize damage to the park and save Apgar, West Glacier, Park Headquarters, and the irreplaceable historic lodges. Finally, on September 8th, heavy rains helped bring the most destructive fire season in Glacier's history to a close.

GLACIER PHOTOS

1. Waterton Lake Trailhead. CDT starts at the Canadian Border.

2. Don standing on the cliff edge at Devil's Elbow on the hike from Swiftcurrent Pass to Many Glacier. Courtesy of Ed Cannady.

3. Filtering water from Cataract Creek below the Garden Wall. Courtesy of Ed Cannady.

4. Hiking through the Waterton Valley. Courtesy of Ed Cannady.

5. Hudson Bay Creek on our way to Triple Divide Pass—"Yo bear!" Courtesy of Ed Cannady.

6. CDT Trail from Pitamakan Pass to Dawson Pass.

7. Pitamakan Pass Overlook with views into the Nyack-Coal Creek Areas. Courtesy of Ed Cannady.

RIDE ACROSS AMERICA

WE'RE RIDING TO SEE MICKEY MOUSE

"How is it that you and I have such a knack for starting big adventures while Mother Nature is having a temper tantrum?" I ranted to Don. "Last year we were chased by fire through Glacier, the year before that we had a record snowstorm and flooding in Montana for the start of the Continental Divide Trail, and this year, we have a heatwave hitting San Diego on the first day of our cycling trip across the country. Seriously, I feel like a magnet for disastrous weather."

Don laughed at my observation. "It wouldn't feel like a Jackson bucket list item if we didn't have a little adversity. Besides, like I always say, the worst of times are the best of times. These are the moments you will always remember."

As I started to climb a steep hill with the hot afternoon sun beating down on me, I commented between gasps of air, "If I don't die of heat exhaustion before I make it up this hill, I guarantee you I will never forget this day of riding for the rest of my life!"

Don and I had talked about riding our bicycles across the United States for decades and in 2004, we decided to bring the goal to fruition. As an added incentive, Don promised to drive to Orlando, Florida after we pedaled to the Atlantic Ocean, so I could check off another personal bucket list item: vacationing at Disney World. My husband would endure five days of Mickey Mouse and friends so I could enjoy the theme park. But first we had to survive the record heat that had engulfed southern California and Arizona. Normal high temperatures for the month of May averaged 70 to 75 degrees in San Diego. We were riding in 95-degree heat, and it was forecasted to rise above 100 degrees the farther inland we traveled.

Our decision to ride across the southern tier of the country was determined by our jobs and caretaking responsibilities. The month of May is considered "slack time" in the resort town of Sun Valley, Idaho so requesting approval for a six week leave of absence from work was easier this time of year. Additionally, we managed property in exchange for lodging and the homeowners were in residence in May making our presence unnecessary. With our window of opportunity dictating an early spring departure, the best route to avoid snow and icy roads was the southern half of the nation.

Adventure Cycling Association created bicycle touring maps for three different routes across the country: the northern, middle, and southern tier. The maps identified the safest corridors of travel utilizing backroads, city streets with bike lanes, and bike paths when available. The maps also provided lodging information and local emergency phone numbers. Although Don and I had a cell phone for our trip in 2004, the modern convenience and information provided by a smart phone had not yet been invented. With Don agreeing to a Disney World vacation at the end of our ride, our route along the southern tier was solidified. We jokingly called our adventure "The toothbrush and credit card ride to see Mickey." There would be no heavy packs filled with camping equipment on our bicycles. We carried a minimum amount of gear in a single wheeled trailer which Don pulled behind his bike and planned to use hotels and restaurants for support along the way. Traveling in this manner would allow us to move quickly across the country. Our route was 3,200 miles in distance, and we hoped to reach our destination in a little over one month.

CALIFORNIA

We began our Ride Across America on the unusually warm morning of May 4, 2004, by dipping our fingers in the Pacific Ocean at the San Diego marina and then riding on a bike path that led away from the beach and into the city. The first day of our journey was overwhelming for a variety of reasons. I had not ridden in city traffic for years and found the hustle and bustle of cars and crowded roads to be stressful. We safely maneuvered our way through vehicles and pedestrians to reach the city limits without incident but then had to face road construction. With a rough surface and a nonexistent shoulder, we began a hill climb that introduced me to the reality of California mountains. Don had turned beat red and looked like he might explode by the time we stopped at the roadside diner in the tiny town of Alpine. We had only ridden forty miles and climbed 3,000 feet of elevation. In my attempt to help my husband ascend the remaining hills, I had him attach the trailer to my bike for the afternoon section of the route.

We had to climb another 2,000 feet of elevation to reach Pine Valley where we planned to stay for the night. When the grade of the road pitched above 8 percent, I could barely turn the pedals with the additional weight of the trailer. The hot afternoon sun in combination with the heat radiating off the pavement was overwhelming and sapped what energy I had left. At the top of the hill, I looked over at Don and said, "We have got to lighten the load in the trailer. We are not going to need any cold weather gear so let's ditch the warm clothes and anything else we can do without. I am really struggling to pull all this weight." Don made me change the trailer back to his bike after I had climbed 1,500 feet. We still had several miles to go and 500 more feet to ascend to reach our destination.

Our first day ended with a reality check and an adjustment to our daily mileage goals. We had hoped to cycle nearly a century each day but quickly realized the distance could not be achieved during the heatwave. I laughed as I thought back to our Continental Divide thru-hiking days and decided to modify my old mantra to "cross-country cyclists have to be flexible." Don and I reviewed the contents of our trailer and decided to mail long johns, long sleeve shirts, warm socks, and gloves to my sister. We would visit her at the midpoint of our trip and could reacquire the warmer gear for the last half of the journey if necessary.

HELL CENTRAL

On our second day, we climbed another 2,500 feet of elevation followed by a glorious 6,000-foot descent on Interstate 8 into the small town of El Centro, which we affectionately renamed "Hell Central" because the temperature was 110 degrees. Throughout the long downhill cruise, we could feel ourselves being submerged into a humid layer of hot air that hovered above the flat expanse of highway east of the mountains. Unfortunately, I was not paying attention to how much water I was consuming in the heat and was shocked when I ran out ten miles from our destination. I had learned from hiking the Continental Divide that when in need, beg. I stopped at a roadside business and the nice folks at Taylor Farms allowed me to refill my water carrier using their outdoor faucet.

During that short amount of time, the heat reflecting off the black asphalt combined with the sun and humid air engulfed me like a steam sauna. We had been creating our own breeze while moving on our bikes; when we were standing still, the air became hard to breathe. When we started rolling toward town, I commented, "Please don't get a flat. I think we could die out here trying to fix a tire. I don't remember south Texas or our summers in St. Louis ever feeling this hot." About that same time, we started hearing a strange popping noise coming from our tires. We discovered the tar on the pavement had melted sufficiently to stick to the tread and was creating a sound like riding on a ribbon of bubble wrap.

Glancing out into the landscape, I noticed blue barrels intermittently placed in the desert. Each container was labeled with the word "water" and identified by a flag attached to a twenty-foot wand. "What are those for?" I asked.

"They're barrels of water for the people crossing into the country from Mexico. It's been so hot, the Border Patrol provides water for them because so many were dying in the desert." In that moment, I understood how the desert heat could kill.

The next couple of days provided a few pleasant surprises while riding across the desert terrain. The Imperial Sand Dunes seemed to appear suddenly out of nowhere a few miles before reaching the town of Glamis. The mountains of white sand were a joy to view although they only lasted for a short eight-mile stretch along the highway. Don and I also caught up to a group of five transcontinental cyclists heading east just before the town of Blythe. Our maps had directed us to ride a short distance on Interstate 10 before connecting to more cycling friendly roadways. All of us had concerned looks on our faces when we discovered I-10 was under construction with only one side of the highway available for travel. Approaching the on-ramp, a police officer parked next to the blockade motioned us to his car. The closed lanes of the interstate had been resurfaced and only required line painting before being reopened. The officer surprised us when he directed our group to ride the new pavement for the next twelve miles.

Those dozen miles would remain the best road surface Don and I experienced during our entire transcontinental journey. Enjoying two lanes of new blacktop, the seven of us were able to spread out beside one another and talk as we pedaled. Through our conversations, we discovered two of the guys were from Ohio and were following the same Adventure Cycling itinerary as me and Don. The other three cyclists were from New York and were calling their trip the Coaster to Coaster Tour (San Diego Roller Coaster to the Coney Island Roller Coaster). Their route would diverge in another fifty miles when they turned toward the northeast. We learned that all five had been slowed by the heat and flat tires. The first two hundred miles through California had caused seven flats between the five riders. Don and I were traversing the same roads but traveling with so little weight made us less prone to flats. So far, we had been lucky. I hoped our good fortune would continue throughout our journey.

ARIZONA

We were treated to a couple days of cooler weather and a glorious tailwind allowing us to move swiftly through much of Arizona. The roadways were in good shape with adequate shoulders which made the riding conditions safer and more comfortable. "I feel like Lance Armstrong," I commented early one morning. We were moving at a sustained speed of thirty miles per hour which felt incredibly fast and exhilarating. The experience was exactly what I had hoped for during our ride across the country. Unique to Arizona, the scenery included blooming Saguaro Cactus standing as tall sentinels in the desert landscape. Springtime also provided colorful bouquets of wild-flowers which dotted the terrain and added to the beauty of the countryside.

After riding two days in Arizona aided by a tailwind, we found ourselves halfway across the state. Our maps indicated we would soon begin a short twenty-two-mile section on Highway 70 through the San Carlos Apache Indian Reservation. Having never visited a reservation, I was curious about the Apache lifestyle, and excited to experience this part of the country. We pedaled past signage announcing our arrival onto the reservation. Don was riding behind me on the shoulder of the road as a means of protecting me from traffic and to make sure he was always aware of my status. Within a few miles of entering the native lands, I was glad he was on my rear tire.

An old pickup truck with two men in the cab and another six Native Americans sitting on the edge of the bed drove up beside us and began shrieking at us and then yelling in a language I did not recognize. Don calmly called out to me, "Just keep the same pace and don't stop." The men were quite inebriated at ten o'clock in the morning. Each of them had a beer in their hand and between screams, they would take a drink and then start howling again. I was hopeful the driver was sober and would remain in his lane. With a frozen smile on my face, I kept a steady cadence and hugged the far-right side of the shoulder. When Don and I did not react to their antics, the guys became bored and with one last simultaneous cry, the truck pulled ahead and continued to accelerate until they disappeared from our view.

I was feeling a little shaken by the outward display of hostility as Don pulled up beside me and said, "My Apache's not that good, but roughly trans-lated, I think they said 'Welcome to the Apache Indian Reservation. Have a nice day!'" Don's timing was perfect. I exploded in laughter. Once again, my husband provided a much-needed moment of levity to calm my nerves and put our encounter into perspective. We exited the reservation in less than an hour but not before I noted the extreme level of poverty and the ramshackle buildings and homes within its boundaries. The plight of the Indigenous People is a sad story in our history and modern day. My first exposure to Native Americans was disappointing but left me with a better understanding of their anger and dissatisfaction with the circumstances of their existence. I left the state of Arizona feeling like I had gained a bit of knowledge regarding a different culture. Little did I know, this day was just the beginning of a more extensive education.

NEW MEXICO

By the time we cycled into the state of New Mexico, we had gotten a handle on how to balance the electrolytes in Don's body. Earlier in the week I had looked at my husband and worriedly said, "Oh honey, you look like a salty tomato. Your face is beet red, and you have pretzel size salt chunks in your hair, eyebrows and along the edge of your face."

Don's response alarmed me. "My legs are cramping. I need to stop for a little while."

We were approaching a gas station with a convenience store, so we pulled in to see what type of food they had available. While gazing in the cooler, Don asked, "What do you think about V8 Juice with salt added? My stomach is too upset for straight sugar. Salt sounds best."

"V8 is a good choice. It's loaded with sodium and potassium. If they have a banana, try to eat that too, for more potassium."

After adding several vigorous shakes of salt to the tomato beverage, eating a banana, and drinking an icy cup of water, Don started to feel better, and his skin became a more normal color. Sugary nutrition bars are wonderful for energy, but electrolytes had become much more important with the heatwave and our excessive sweating. Foods high in potassium and sodium, like the V8 Juice, helped the most.

Our primary food source during the day was convenience stores along the highway. Most provided microwave ovens for Grab-N-Go meals. Don could adequately boost his sodium intake with a bowl of salted chicken soup and tomato juice which his stomach readily accepted. His dessert would be pretzels or potato chips with a cold Dr Pepper, all dependent on his current state of nausea. Meanwhile, I found my favorite snack was mini powdered donuts. I laughingly told Don, "I have been powered through two states by Bimbo Donitas."

Our morning meal was most often a traditional breakfast or an egg sandwich, lunch was sweet and salty snack foods high in carbohydrates, and dinner was as nutritious as we could find in the small towns. We tried to add a salad or a vegetable to our supper meal when possible. Following these guidelines, we consumed a diet that served us well throughout the remaining miles of the trip.

DÉJÀ VU

Entry into the state of New Mexico took us down memory lane. Our itinerary intersected the Continental Divide Trail and allowed us to ride many of the same roadways we had hiked two years earlier on the last days of our journey. "Oh look, there is Faywood Hot Springs where we camped!" I said while pointing to the campground on the eastern side of the road. Fifteen miles later, we pulled in for a short bathroom break at the rest area we had visited while walking the Divide. We had already planned to stay in Deming for the evening and had made reservations at the same motel from our previous visit to the area. Thinking about the highlights from our hike, I suggested Mexican food for dinner. After a wonderful day on our bikes, we ended the evening with a lovely meal at Cano's Restaurant, reminiscing about our celebration dinner there after completing the CDT. We toasted our good fortune to have started another adventure and cheered ourselves on to enjoy the rest of the journey traveling across the nation.

We spent another long 120-mile day in the saddle before we rolled into Texas. Late in the afternoon, we experienced one of the highlights of our trip. The twenty-mile section of Highway 28 that connected the small Spanish town of Mesilla to Chamberino was shaded with beautiful overhanging pecan trees. We cycled through a lovely tunnel of green and much cooler temperatures as we bid farewell to New Mexico.

TEXAS

We started our ride across Texas by navigating through the big city of El Paso. Large metropolitan areas slowed our progress because of the time spent off our bikes waiting for lights to turn green. After wasting at least thirty minutes in Tempe, Arizona and El Paso, Texas, we were happy our route generally avoided large cities and restricted our travel to small towns and farm roads. Reviewing our progress thus far, I realized we had ridden 900 miles and crossed three states in the last ten days. With our route in Texas being over 1,000 miles in width and representing a third of our trip, I knew we would spend a considerable amount of time traversing the state's diverse topography. The western half of Texas was sparsely populated and featured a dry, arid landscape. The eastern half was more densely settled, humid and filled with a multitude of trees. As Don and I pedaled along the rolling plains of West Texas, we made a few interesting discoveries regarding Texans and the place they call home.

The best chicken fried steak I have ever eaten was found in the state of Texas. Our first day ended at Fort Hancock where Don and I ate dinner at a little hole-in-the-wall restaurant named Angie's. The chicken fried steak was absolute perfection starting with an extremely tender piece of beef that I could cut with a fork, coated with a crunchy cracker crumb crust, and drowned in rich, cream gravy. The meal was one of the few memorable ones on our transcontinental journey causing us to visit the spot again ten years later during a road trip to south Texas to see my mom. On both occasions, Angie's food was delicious, and the experience was amusing because all the same local patrons were still sitting in the diner, watching Fox News, and talking politics while eating chicken fried steaks. Some things really don't change even after a decade.

In general, Texas had the best road surfaces we experienced during 3,200 miles of cycling. The shoulders were often wide and when rumble strips were present, they left enough room for us to ride safely on the right side of the asphalt divots. Throughout our journey, dealing with rumble strips was a daily challenge and discomfort. A direct hit to a deep divot would cause our tire tubes to pinch and become flat. Our very first flat tire on the trip occurred in this way. The trick was to ride over the divots at an angle and at a very slow speed. Too often, however, we found ourselves surprised by road debris which caused us to swerve and enter the rumble strip unexpectedly, resulting in a flat. Driving over a rumble strip in a car only produces an attention grabbing vibration, but on a bike without shocks, the jarring impact can cause bruising. By the time we exited Texas, our hands and sit bones were discolored from bruises and our shoulders ached from the constant jolting. Rumble strips can also be full of surprises as was the case when Don rolled over a big indention that was filled with a sleeping rattlesnake. Although Don and the snake were unharmed, I am not sure which one was more shocked by the encounter.

Adventure Cycling maps periodically directed us to Interstate 10 for short durations when it was the only eastbound roadway available. Although I was never a fan of traveling on the interstate with high-speed traffic passing by, I was confident with my cycling skills and accepted riding these stretches of highway when needed. The only time I became overwhelmed was the day we got caught in construction on I-10. Comfortably riding on the far-right side of the shoulder's rumble strip, we were surprised when the highway funneled us down to a single lane with cement barriers on both sides of the road. Our ten-mile ride on the interstate became an inescapable trap filled with danger. A never-ending train of semi-trucks barreled past me and Don with zero room for error. We endured the treacherous riding and survived the experience, but as soon as we were able to get off the interstate, I had to pull off the road and sit on the curb to regroup and stop shaking. It was a forced period of lunacy that neither of us were willing to repeat again.

FLAT TIRES

Don and I were fortunate to only have seven flats throughout our transcontinental adventure. Our second flat was somewhat unusual and became a learning experience for us. Climbing up and down the rolling hills of West Texas, I called out to Don who was in front, allowing me to draft, "Honey, I think I have a slow leak in my rear tire. It definitely has less air than it did this morning. It doesn't feel right."

"Pull over up ahead where the pavement is flat so I can check it out," Don yelled over his shoulder. Upon close inspection, Don agreed that the tire had lost a great deal of air. After removing the tire from the wheel, Don inspected the tube and found a small hole. Before inserting a new tube, Don reminded me that we also needed to check the inside of the tire for any type of sharp object that may have caused the flat. Running his finger along the inner rubber surface, Don found a surprise. There was a tiny piece of wire still sticking through the tire tread. "I can feel it's sharp, but I can't grab it with my fingers to pull it out."

"How about using tweezers?" I suggested.

Although Don carried basic bike tools in the trailer, pliers were not part of his repair kit. I grabbed the tweezers from our overnight bag and gave them to Don. With a tight grip, he was able to successfully pull out the wire. Reaching out to take the small piece of metal filament from Don, I asked, "Where did I pick that up?"

"Has to be the tire blowouts along the road. All the black rubber pieces of tread are full of wire. Try not to run over them."

I had never closely observed the remnants of steel belted radial tires. Now that I was traveling the same roadways as the 18-wheeled trucks, I learned this lesson the hard way.

THANK YOU FOR YOUR SERVICE

While rolling along Highway 90, it dawned on me that we were not going to find national forests, wilderness areas, BLM lands, or even state parks on this part of our journey because most of the land in Texas was privately owned. At first glance, the vistas seemed like an endless expanse of rolling hillsides and high plains as far as the eye could see. But upon closer observation, it became apparent that every bit of land was cordoned off and secured with some type of fence line emanating from an elaborate gate. We discovered that although these monstrous entryways could be quite different in construction, design, and materials, a majority were uniformly adorned with a large star. And more often than not, the gate would sport a flagpole flying the stars and stripes and the Texas state flag. Patriotism was proudly on display all along the roadway.

While enjoying lunch at a Mexican restaurant in the little town of Comstock, we noticed a single woman sitting at the bar having a beer. At times, I thought she might be weeping as she slumped forward, eyes staring at the label on the bottle. Then toward the end of our meal, she surprised me by walking by our table and initiating a conversation by asking, "Where are you guys riding?"

"We're cycling across the country from San Diego to Orlando to explore the southern states."

"What kind of bike are you riding? I have never seen one like that." Don's bike had often sparked conversations with the locals because of its unique banana lever design.

"It's called a Softride, and it's new on the market. The bike was created for comfort. That single floating arm where the seat is attached, absorbs all the bumps in the road and feels like a car with great shocks."

The woman smiled at his explanation and then wished us safe travels as she departed. We thanked her for her warm wishes and for saying hello. On his way to our table to clear the plates, our waiter said goodbye to the lady, calling her by name as she left the restaurant. Since our waiter obviously knew the woman, I made the comment to him that it was very nice of her to say hello although she looked really sad, and I hoped she was okay.

With one arm loaded with dishes, the waiter nodded and said, "She is sad because she is grieving. Her son, Sgt. William Harrell, was recently killed in Iraq." He pointed with his free hand to a group of photos on the wall near the entrance to the restaurant. "Those pictures are all the local boys currently fighting in the war and Billy is the one in the center." Don and I had seen similar collages of photos in other small towns we had passed through including Marathon, Sanderson, and Langtry. Comstock was a town of only 300 people but there were seven local young men fighting in conflicts around the world. These small, impoverished towns seemed to pay a disproportionate price in our wars.

HILL COUNTRY

As our route took us closer to the Texas Hill Country, we began to see more trees and noticed the fences were taller in size and made of chain-link metal that housed different types of exotic animals within their enclosures. Ostrich, elk, and African antelope stood within their confines silently staring at us as we rode past. These lands offered private hunting leases and sold big game tags to hunters from all over the world. After passing by the first half dozen, Don looked over at me and said, "One thing about Texans, they like to keep things in or out." No other state flaunted "I own this" quite like the state of Texas.

Our departure from the Texas Hill Country signaled an end to large climbing days on the bike. I had been astonished with each daily journal entry at the elevation gains recorded on my cycling computer. Don and I were consistently climbing close to 3,000 feet just by rolling up and down hills on the highway. Using our ski mountain in Sun Valley for comparison, Bald Mountain's trails climb 3,000 feet from the valley floor to the top of the peak and are considered a hard workout. We were climbing at least that amount daily while pulling a trailer, fighting headwinds, and enduring extreme heat. Total elevation gain for the transcontinental trip was an estimated 71,000 feet. By the time we rolled into the town of Navasota, halfway through the state of Texas, we had climbed 51,290 feet of elevation. With the mountains and hills of California, Arizona, New Mexico, and West Texas providing 75 percent of our climbs, Don and I were looking forward to the eastern half of the country where we hoped to experience more high-speed days on relatively flat terrain.

We took our one and only rest day when we reached Navasota. My sister, Dana, who lived only a hundred miles away, arrived with her truck to shuttle us to her home for a twenty-four-hour respite from the road. As Don was giving the bikes a thorough cleaning and inspection, he noticed his back tire was looking more square across the tread than rounded. The unusual pattern of wear was caused by the additional weight and drag of the trailer. Dana took us to a bike store where we purchased a new tire and a few extra tubes in case we experienced more flats on the eastern roadways. After completing the bike repairs, Don and I spent the day relaxing. We had traveled almost 1,900 miles over the past twenty-two days and my legs were happy for the break in pedaling. That evening, we enjoyed a wonderful meal, a nice visit with my sister, and a good night's sleep. Early the next morning, Dana drove us back to Navasota which allowed us to start at the exact location where she had picked us up the previous day. My legs were a little stiff when we started pedaling, but they felt stronger with a day of rest. Don and I were both ready to tackle the remaining 1,300 miles of our journey.

LOUISIANA

One of the first things I noticed about the state of Louisiana was the humidity. Straddling my bike to begin our early morning ride, I felt like someone had wrapped me in a warm, wet towel. My glasses fogged up forcing me to use my fingers like mini windshield wipers to try to keep them clear while rolling down the road. My arms and legs collected moisture from the air until rivulets of water started running down my shins into my socks and down my upper arms to drip off my elbows. We were soaked within minutes without a drop of rain falling from the sky. It was a cloudy day with a high of eighty-seven degrees. Gone were the dry, sunny days of the west. We had officially entered the dark, gray weather pattern of springtime in the southeast.

Our map had us traveling a three-hundred-mile route through the middle of Louisiana to avoid the heavy traffic of Baton Rouge and New Orleans to the south. We spent our first day in the state riding several miles on levee roads through rice fields. Rice plantations were first established back in the late 1800s and are still there today.

Traveling farther inland, we noticed what looked like small metal boxes in the fields of water. Occasionally, we would also see a little aluminum boat moored to the side of a dike. When Don and I stopped for a quick lunch break, we met a local woman and I asked, "Why are there metal boxes and small boats in the rice fields?"

The woman looked at us in surprise, amazed we were unaware of a major trademark of the state. However, she smiled and patiently explained, "The metal boxes are crawfish cages. The water in the field is only one to two feet deep so the boats are outfitted with special paddles that can maneuver through the mud. The boats are used to collect the crawfish and re-bait the cages." She went on to say, "If you two have never had crawfish, you should try it." Boiled crawfish was served almost everywhere in Louisiana. I had never thought about where they came from or how they were caught. Thanking the lady for her lesson on crawfish farming, I assured her we would try a plate before leaving the state.

There was an abundance of water in Louisiana. The number of lakes, rivers, and bayous we passed was impressive. I was fascinated by how the water filled the land to capacity whether we were riding a levee road just above the water level, or passing a beautiful home where the banks of a river or bayou were overflowing into the yard. Our small backroads took us past sprawling historical homes that reminded me of plantations I had seen in old movies. The grounds were a gorgeously manicured sea of green vegetation. Beyond the homes, the land rapidly transitioned into jungle like forests of ancient oak draped with Spanish moss.

With so many trees, the population of birds increased proportionately providing a symphony of sound. Although we could not identify all the different birds around us, Don decided there were three distinct categories of singing and named the birds accordingly: the R2D2 Warbler, the Telephone Caller, and the Alarm Clock Screecher. Assigning a name to each bird sound became a game and helped us pass the time while cycling down the long stretches of road. Although we never discovered what kind of bird made the Alarm Clock Screecher call, we decided it was the most prevalent in the state of Louisiana.

We met a young college age man riding solo across the country during a convenience store stop shortly after entering the state. He was traveling from east to west following the same Adventure Cycling maps and warned us that Louisiana and Mississippi had an abundance of vicious dogs along the route. He seemed a little flustered. "There is one big black dog about twenty miles from here that almost got a piece of me. He was lying low in a culvert and ambushed me when I rode by. Watch out for him because he doesn't just bark. He really did try to bite me."

Mean dogs had not been a problem thus far on our journey, but as we entered the more heavily populated southeastern states and rode though impoverished sections of small townships, aggressive dogs were on our radar. We found that our best defense against an attacking dog was my own built-in deterrent; a powerful piercing whistle that would stop even the biggest bully in his tracks for a second or two. That couple seconds of confusion and frozen reaction was all Don and I needed to get away. It helped to loudly shout commands at the animal at the same time. So, while I blasted their ear drums with my extremely loud whistle, Don would authoritatively yell at the dog. Using these tactics, Don and I were a formidable team against all our canine adversaries. Although we were chased dozens of times, we were never bitten.

MISSISSIPPI—WHEN IT RAINS, IT POURS

The state of Mississippi introduced us to torrential downpours. A storm blew in from the Gulf of Mexico bringing several inches of rain over a long four-day stretch. One of the biggest challenges on the trip was mentally forcing myself to leave the warm, dry refuge of our hotel room to face a day of soggy shorts and wet clothing on my bike. We had rain proof jackets but found wearing nylon in hot and humid weather made us sweat so much that ultimately, we were just as wet under the coat as on the outside from the rain. Although the temperature of the raindrops and air were warm, we quickly learned how uncomfortable air-conditioning could feel when our bodies and clothing were covered in moisture. We spent four days shivering during mad dashes in and out of convenience stores while purchasing lunch food items. Don took a picture of me outside one of the convenience stores sheltering from a thunderstorm. "The look on your face is priceless. Kind of puts the whole ride today in perspective!" His laughter was infectious and soon, I was chuckling at our situation as well. My husband was the perfect partner because he always offered a much-needed dose of humor during my most difficult moments.

To add insult to injury, during those dreary, wet riding days, we lost all hope in our battle to fight diaper rash and blisters on our buttocks. Throughout the entire trip, we had been managing tender bottoms from spending hours each day in the saddle. Chafing, welting, and heat bumps were all an expected part of the adventure. But with a constant rooster tail of rain flying off our tires and hitting our crotches for hours each day, our skin broke down, producing open sores which had to be cleaned and medicated each night. Fortunately, we did not get any type of infection and our skin scabbed and healed in due time.

ALABAMA—SHORT AND SWEET

Even though we experienced less than seventy-five miles of riding through the state of Alabama, these were some of the most pleasant and memorable roadways on our trip. Our time on the Alabama coastline was short in duration but filled with beautiful beaches, scenic vistas, and unique traveling byways. We entered the state in the southwestern corner through the small town of Grand Bay and within thirty miles we were riding with an ocean view. Quickly arriving at Gordon Persons Bridge, we pedaled across the three-mile causeway to the lovely destination of Dauphin Island. The four-day storm system was still moving out of the area, so our skies were overcast and gray, but that did not mar the panorama of the water crossing. We were surrounded by speed boats, large fishing vessels, seagulls, and whitecaps.

With the weather expected to deteriorate in the late afternoon, Don and I reserved a hotel room with an ocean front view and relaxed for the rest of the day. As I explored Dauphin Island, I learned the land mass was colonized 300 years ago and had been owned by six countries: the United States since 1813. Its location was ideal from a military standpoint but it was also on the main path of gulf coast hurricanes. Walking the pretty streets adorned with colorful flowers and lush vegetation, I had no way of knowing that in two months' time, Hurricane Ivan would cause major damage to the tiny island. The following year, Hurricane Katrina would devastate all that remained.

The only way to travel east from Dauphin Island was by ferry. Don and I caught the 8:45 a.m. boat from the island to the Fort Morgan Historical Site. The day had dawned with clear, blue skies making the ferry ride a fun forty-minute cruise across calm open water. This time our view included large oil rig platforms, shrimp boats as well as pleasure crafts and jet skis. To our surprise, when Don and I rolled our bikes aboard the vessel, we found another set of bicycles that we learned belonged to an older couple also making the transcontinental trip. They had started their journey a couple months before us and were moving more slowly across the nation. We shared stories from our experiences on the road and took each other's photo just before disembarking the ferry. With a wave goodbye, Don and I started our ride on the Fort Morgan Parkway that featured the famous Alabama Gulf Shores.

Our morning ride was outstanding. Having great weather for ocean viewing was delightful especially after enduring four days of rain. The fact that the road had a large shoulder alternating with a bike lane for thirty-five miles made for a nice stress-free ride. All our interactions with the crowds of people walking to the beach or riding the highway alongside us were positive. We seemed to be surrounded by individuals who respected and welcomed cyclists into their playground. For the first time in nearly a month, we no longer stood out or looked different dressed in bike clothing. We were just part of the crowd enjoying the sun, sand, and water.

Don and I decided to have lunch at an ocean front restaurant where we could people watch while we enjoyed our meal. I tried the crawfish patty po-boy sandwich, a local favorite, and found it to be delicious which added to the good vibe of the day. The entire Gulf Shores and Perdido Beach section of our ride was a joy to experience and provided us with some of the best memories of our adventure.

FLORIDA—THE SUNSHINE STATE

Don and I had high hopes that the Sunshine State would provide friendly people, good town stops, and sunny days. Unfortunately, we were wrong on all three accounts. Shortly after crossing the Florida state line, our route left the scenic ocean highway and directed us to travel for almost four hundred miles on backroads through small townships situated a dozen or more miles north or south of Interstate 10. We quickly figured out that the towns we were now visiting were the unfortunate places that had become isolated and poverty-stricken when the construction of the interstate caused millions of tourists, and their dollars, to bypass these locations. We cruised by several old, decaying buildings and billboards all touting defunct tourist services. Most restaurants had gone out of business, leaving only a few second-rate fast-food establishments as replacements. Our diet took a serious turn for the worse, making our breakfast and dinner options on par with our convenience store lunches. On Sunday, even the fast-food choices were unavailable as an older gentleman explained to us, "Quincy is Jesus's town, and no restaurants are open on Sunday."

Nightly accommodation options also became more depressed. After three nights of terrible experiences with dirty, noisy motels, Don and I rode ten miles out of the way, to a fish camp on Lochloosa Lake for our last evening on the road. Aside from the bedspread having the distinct aroma of Old Spice aftershave, our cottage was quaint and clean allowing us to finally get a good night's rest.

Upon entering the state of Florida, we were subjected to multiple encounters with obnoxious people. A group of young men drove by in a car with the windows open and when they got right next to us, they laid on the horn and started yelling at me and Don. We jumped, reacting just as the kids had hoped, making them laugh and yell at us some more. We had two more similar encounters that same day with the last person flipping us the bird to add insult to the car horn. This behavior continued every day we cycled in Florida. In fact, the last day of our journey, a man sporting a mullet style haircut from the 1980s stopped his truck in the middle of the road, left his gun in the vehicle but jumped out to confront us yelling, "Get off the road!" With his truck blocking our ability to continue to ride, we slowed to a stop and Don very calmly put his body between me and the man and tried to reason with the irate individual. After a lengthy bout of yelling, the man got back in his truck and sped away. At that point, we altered our route of travel, making ourselves hard to find just in case he worked himself into a worse state of agitation. There seemed to be a lot of mean, angry people living in the sunshine state and very little sunshine. We had to endure a couple more rainy days in addition to all the unpleasant people we encountered. By the fifth day, we were more than ready to end our adventure and be done with riding in the state of Florida.

I never understood why seeing me and Don pedaling down the road on our bicycles incited such hatred or hostility. Unfortunately, what we were subjected to in Florida was not the first time we had experienced rude, aggressive behavior on our trip. There had been a few previous incidents that had occurred in small towns where signs of religion were on full display. Oddly, it seemed the more churches and religious billboards we saw, the more intolerant the communities were of outsiders and those who were different. And riding down the road in Lycra shorts was definitely deemed different.

I would love to say the last day of our cycling adventure ended in spectacular style, but our story unfolded with a different type of ending. The day was certainly memorable but for all the wrong reasons. My journal entry captured the essence of the last hundred miles ridden in the state of Florida perfectly.

"Wednesday, June 9, 2004"

"Yay, we made it to the beach alive. But not without incident. The day started out with powdered donuts. Don and I both wanted a real breakfast but there was none to be had. We ate hockey pucks (breakfast sandwiches) at the gas station only to find a restaurant a quarter mile away. Our map did not list a food stop. From that disappointment, the day went even further downhill. The roads became more and more crappy with ever increasing volumes of traffic. The traffic was primarily dump trucks alternating with 18-wheeler logging trucks. None of the roads had shoulders. Motorists were not friendly and totally intolerant of our presence. A first, one car stopped in the middle of the road to give us a piece of his mind. We had lunch in the town of Palatka and the server was surly. Don came up with the catch phrase "Palatka was Caca." To make matters worse, we stopped for a snack at a picnic site with tables surrounded by deep sand. The trailer tire got caught in the sand causing Don to fall over and wrench his back and bloody his knee. We were sixteen miles from St. Augustine with another five miles to reach the beach. Our map dumped us into St. Augustine, leaving us find our own way to the ocean. The day was so hot. Bike chains and shoes full of sand now. Good thing it is over because nothing works anymore. All in all, a good day—we are alive!"

Our transcontinental cycling adventure had come to an end. After dipping our fingers in the Atlantic Ocean and taking a few pictures on the St. Augustine Beach to celebrate the occasion, we slowly pedaled five miles back to town and booked a room at a very nice hotel. Washing the sand, sunscreen, and nervous sweat from our bodies after spending the day dodging massive trucks and traffic in extreme heat, felt amazing. We rented a car and dropped off the bikes and trailer at a local bike shop to have them shipped back to Idaho. Finally, it was time to go shopping for all the things we needed for my next bucket list item: a visit to Disney World!

It would be a few weeks before Don and I could stop and digest the enormity of what we had just accomplished. We had spent thirty-six days riding across the United States traveling a total of 3,142 miles. Although we were both happy to have completed our goal, it wasn't exactly the trip we had both been hoping to experience. We enjoyed seeing parts of the nation that we had never had the opportunity to visit previously. However, I think both of us were left wondering if the journey would have been more pleasant by traveling across the northern tier where cyclists were perhaps more welcome.

I decided the point was moot while I enthusiastically reminded Don, "I got to see Mickey Mouse!" And what an incredible time I had at Disney

World. Don and I spent four days and nights at Disney. I rode every roller coaster and thrill ride at least three times in a row until I literally caused Don to become nauseated. My wonderful husband put up with continuous shrieks of laughter, screaming kids having temper tantrums and children in full on melt down mode from too much of Mickey and the gang. He also put up with me on happiness overload as I scrambled from one theme park to another enjoying a full day of fun at each location. I even convinced Don to return to the Magic Kingdom at night so we could see Tinkerbell fly from Cinderella's Castle which was illuminated for the most wonderful visual effect. I was a forty-three-year-old woman going on ten years old. I was thankful that Don was such a trooper and indulged me with my childish whim on what I thought were the four most delightful, carefree days of fun. We had ridden our bikes across the country to see Mickey and ended our adventure with smiles and joy.

RIDE ACROSS AMERICA PHOTOS

1 We started our trip by dipping our fingers into the Pacific Ocean at the marina in San Diego, CA.

2 Imperial Sand Dunes, CA.

3 Barrels of water scattered across the desert on our way to El Centro, CA.

4 Riding past miles of blooming saguaro cactus, AZ.

5 Overhanging pecan trees on Highway 28 between Mesilla and Chamberino, NM.

6 Cycling on Interstate 10 in West Texas.

7 We endured eight rainy days total—four in a row in Mississippi.

8 Atlantic Ocean just outside of St. Augustine, FL.

9 Five fun-filled days with Mickey and the gang at Walt Disney World in Orlando, FL.

THE ITALIAN DREAM

"WELL, DAMN." DON MUMBLED softly while sorting through the mail. Curious as to the source of my husband's frustration, I asked what was wrong. Instead of answering, Don held up a *Welcome to Medicare* booklet he had found within the stack of letters and bills. Clearly annoyed by the discovery, he said, "I always thought Medicare was for old people. I can't believe I've reached the age to qualify."

I couldn't help but laugh. While he sat staring at the booklet, the slight frown on his face transitioned to a much more serious look. "Now what are you in such deep thought about?" I asked.

Looking me in the eyes, Don made a solemn announcement, "I think it's time for us to concentrate on another bucket list item. We always wanted to go to Italy and ride our bikes in the Dolomites. I'm not getting any younger, and that strenuous of a trip needs to happen sooner than later. Let's see if Andy has any openings on one of his tours this summer." Surprised by the suddenness of Don's decision but also realizing the truth of his statement, I found myself nodding in agreement and thinking this was the perfect time for us to experience an Italian adventure.

Andy Hampsten holds a special place in cycling history as the winner of the 1988 Giro d'Italia Bicycle Race and remains the only American to ever finish the event at the top of the podium wearing the Maglia Rosa, pink winner's jersey. Don and I met Andy in 2004 when we were caretaking the Figge estate in Sun Valley, Idaho. Chris Figge, Scott Nichols (founder of Ibis Bicycles) and Andy had spent a long weekend together cycling, wine tasting and cooking elaborate meals at the property. We had been invited to hang out with them one afternoon. It was during our time together that Andy described the vacation packages his company offered and encouraged us to travel to Italy and ride through the beautiful Dolomites with him. Although a dozen years had passed since our conversation, our interest in cycling the Italian Alps had never wavered. Two days after submitting our request online to join Andy's 2016 Dolomite trip, we received an email—*reservation confirmed*. Now I was the one with a very serious look on my face as the full impact of our commitment registered.

This was no ordinary vacation. Andy Hampsten's company is named Cinghiale Tours; cinghiale means wild pig in Italian. Andy rates the difficulty level of each of his tours with an assigned number of pigs: a one-piggy tour, a two-piggy tour, etc. We had signed up for his four-piggy Mighty Dolomite cycling vacation, the most physically challenging trip that he offered. The guidelines recommended that all clients participating in a four-pig tour be physically able to ride a minimum of eighty miles and climb 5,000 feet of elevation daily for nine consecutive days. Those numbers sounded extremely demanding to me and well beyond my current level of fitness. I had just three months to get myself in shape before flying to Italy at the end of August. The reality of the situation was that Don and I were facing a long, physically taxing summer. However, we both felt our goal of seeing the beautiful Dolomites from the unique position of a bicycle seat was worth the effort.

WHERE THERE'S A WILL THERE'S A WAY

Don and I designed an aggressive training program that would allow us to progress in strength, endurance, and speed over the course of the summer. That meant incorporating interval workouts, steep climbs, and long-distance rides into our planned cycling program. It had been fourteen years since we had attempted an interval workout. Enduring the pain of sprint repeats was not something I was looking forward to but knew the effort was necessary to improve overall performance. The county road leading to the local dump had a slight incline over the course of two miles which was the perfect terrain for this type of drill. The refuse collection business was closed on Sundays which greatly reduced traffic in the area and made us feel safer while exercising on the roadway.

There is nothing pleasant about a high intensity training session. We pushed our bodies to a level of intense discomfort to gain cardiovascular fitness. My first interval effort was humbling. During the warm-up ride from our house to our exercise location, I confidently suggested to Don, "Let's go for five repeats today!" Totally overestimating my ability, I was completely exhausted after three sprints up the hill. After making a lackluster effort on the fourth lap, I decided to quit for the day and rode home feeling a bit dejected.

As was often the case in our relationship, Don brought levity and encouragement to the moment with a remark during the easy spin back to our house. "Those intervals hurt, but the effort wasn't as bad as I thought it would be. I bet we can do five repeats by next week!" After seeing how his comment had put a grin on my face, he went on to say, "You, me, and the dump road every Sunday morning is going to be perfect. How awesome is it that we can just focus on feeling pain without having to worry about being hit by a garbage truck!" The absurdity of his comment made me laugh which was the exact response he wanted. Glancing over at me with a smile, Don repeated his favorite saying, "The worst of times are the best of times. These are the memories we'll never forget." He was right, experiencing all aspects of the journey was as important as the destination.

Two days after our interval training, Don and I decided to go for a long road ride. We purposely kept our first outing to a relatively short thirty miles. I was so disappointed by the deep ache that developed in my shoulders and neck during the ride. A couple days later, we increased our distance to forty miles. Now my lower back began to throb along with my neck and shoulders, making me wonder, "Am I ever going to be able to ride eighty miles comfortably?" One of the biggest lessons we learned that summer was how much harder it was to bounce back from a big effort at the age of fifty-five and sixty-four. Persistence ultimately prevailed with the adoption of an exercise schedule that balanced training days with equally important days of recovery.

Although Don and I lived in an area surrounded by mountains, there were no roads that could duplicate the long, sustained climbs in Europe.

We routinely had to travel a few hours from home to find asphalt that was suitable for training. We discovered that the Pomerelle Ski area, located two hours away in Albion, Idaho, had a newly blacktopped road eighteen miles in length that climbed 4,200 feet from the valley floor to the top of Mt. Harrison. With grades of 6 to 12 percent, this was the steepest mountain road we could find. The road climbing up to the Bogus Basin Ski Resort, also two and half hours away in Boise, Idaho, provided climbing grades of 3 to 8 percent over the course of sixteen miles with 3,300 feet of elevation gain. A third training option was our own local ski mountain, Baldy, which offered both an eight- and ten-mile mountain bike trail ascending 3,000 feet to the top. For twelve consecutive weeks, Don and I incorporated one of these routes into our training regimen. By the end of July, we were able to double our climbs on these mountains to finally reach the 5,000-foot elevation gain we expected to experience daily on our vacation.

My summer training program had begun with a great deal of fear of the unknown. Although Don and I had always risen to the task at hand when preparing for our past athletic endeavors, my concerns stemmed from being older, a few pounds heavier, and plagued by migraine headaches. I wasn't fully confident in my ability to get myself into the physical shape our goal demanded. Don, on the other hand, had always maintained an age defying, high-level of physical fitness. Although he felt he needed to get stronger, we both knew I had many more obstacles to overcome for the trip.

A long-distance ride in early August provided the breakthrough moment when we both realized our summer regimen had paid off. Cycling a route through the hilly neighborhood streets of Elkhorn, Trail Creek Summit and along Highway 75 to Prairie Creek and back home allowed us to complete eighty-two miles with 3,500 feet of elevation gain. After spending six hours in the saddle, our necks, lower backs, and elbows only developed a mild ache. We were tired but not wasted and that was the big difference. And for me, there was magic, no headache at the end of the day. Exhaustion can be a trigger for a migraine, but my body was physically able to handle the strain. A distance of eighty miles was no longer worrisome. Self-assured, we now looked forward to the challenges awaiting us on our Cinghiale Tour.

WELCOME TO ITALY

"Hello. I'm Elaine Hampsten, Andy's wife," said the beautiful woman with dark hair and Italian features as she extended her hand toward me.

"I'm Shannon Jackson and this is my husband, Don." I replied, shaking her hand.

"Welcome to Italy. Glad you both could join us on our tour of the Dolomites." After a couple minutes of casual conversation, Elaine introduced Don and me to another member of our group and then excused herself to greet other Cinghiale Tour guests that had arrived. We were gathering in the lobby of a hotel that was located on the mainland very near the floating city of Venice. From here, Andy had arranged a private bus to drive the group to the lakeside Europa Sport Hotel in Alleghe where we would stay for the first half of our trip. Alleghe was a charming village nestled at the base of the imposing Monte Civetta on the southeastern edge of the Dolomite range. We would spend four nights in this location riding epic passes of the Giro d'Italia before cycling to our second destination, Corvara, located in the heart of the Italian Alps.

Our first outing was a short, two-hour bike ride that included a 2,000-foot climb to an overlook with a view of Monte Civetta and our hotel both brilliantly reflected in the blue waters of Lake Alleghe. This was a shakedown ride that allowed Andy to assess our physical abilities and to ensure everyone's bike was in working order. The afternoon spin also provided an opportunity for his guests to get to know each other. There were eighteen people in our party: five women and thirteen men. Ages ranged from thirty to sixty-four years old with Don and a man named Steve sharing the elder statesman title. Seven individuals were returning clients of Cinghiale Tours which was right in line with Andy's claim of a 40 percent repeat business. Later, we discovered that the youngest couple in our group had been on three past trips while Steve was enjoying his twelfth four-piggy excursion. I was a decade older than any other woman in our group. Shelby was forty-five years old and a mountain bike guide in Colorado. Karena and Gaylen were both thirty; one a professional dancer and the other a professional triathlete. The remaining woman was Jennie, a forty-year-old who loved long-distance cycling.

Jennie and I shared a common history having completed the iconic Paris-Brest-Paris Bicycle Race (PBP). For nearly three decades, I had never met another person that had ridden the PBP and was surprised to discover a third person, Karena's husband, Ian, had also participated in the event. Ian's race in 2011 was the most recent, Jennie competed in 2007 and my story occurred in 1987. The first question Ian asked me was, "How long did it take you to finish?" I think he was quite dismayed when I told him my medal was inscribed with eighty-one and a half hours; less time than he had needed to complete the PBP. Jennie, however, finished the 750-mile race in seventy-eight hours—faster than both of us. I had them laughing when I described racing "in the dark ages" with only a paper map, a few stickers placed on street signs to show the way and no means of communication. They both shared how they enjoyed being able to use a GPS to navigate the route and a cell phone to keep them in touch with their support crews. Regardless of the decade in which our races occurred, each of us knew the tenacity and determination it took to sit on a bike for four days. Those collective memories had the three of us revisiting the PBP and sharing highlights of past experiences throughout our Cinghiale Tour.

There were four guides on the trip, two women and two men including Andy and his wife, Elaine. Andy was fifty-four years old but easily demonstrated the cycling prowess and power of someone half his age. Andy rode every mile of the trip with his clients and never seemed to tire, even on the steepest of climbs. Elaine was in her thirties and in great physical shape. The best compliment I could give these two was how personable they were as a couple. Together, Andy and Elaine created the perfect environment for a great cycling vacation.

The other female guide was Kerry Helmuth, an American cyclist I had watched race back in 1994 and 1995 during three stages of the Ore-Ida Women's Challenge held each year in Sun Valley, Idaho. While competing around the world, Kerry had met an Italian man, married, and moved to Italy. Although Kerry was ten years younger than Andy, they both had trained with the same coach who later introduced them to each other. Kerry's professional cycling history and love for Italy made her an awesome guide. She could keep pace with even the fastest rider in the group while enthusiastically sharing information about the towns we were passing through and races that had occurred on the roads we were riding.

Richard Feichter was an Italian bike racer who joined us as our fourth guide just after finishing his competitive season. He was from the Corvara area and was able to share with the group a few rides known only by the locals. All the guides had engaging personalities that added to our overall experience.

NEW EXPERIENCES

Although Don and I had been riding bikes together for more than thirty-four years, we were introduced to two new cycling experiences in Italy. On the second day, our bike route to Passo Duran traveled through a couple of long tunnels; a common feature of mountain roads in Europe. Andy reminded all of us to turn on our taillights and headlights during the approach to the tunnel entrance. When he reached the opening and began to fade into the shadows, he started waving one arm in the air in an exaggerated manner.

"What's he doing?" I asked Don who was pedaling next to me.

"Take off your sunglasses," he replied. "Andy's waving his glasses in the air to remind us."

After quickly removing my sunglasses, my eyes instantly adjusted to the dimly lit interior of the concrete enclosure. "Wow, that made a huge difference! I never even thought about my glasses; totally forgot I was wearing them."

It seems like such a small detail, but the adjustment was dramatic, blinding darkness to visibility within a few seconds. There would be dozens of tunnels throughout the next seven days of cycling. The uneasiness I had felt from being completely blinded that first time made a big enough impact on me that I never forgot to remove my sunglasses upon entering a tunnel again.

Later that same morning while climbing Passo Duran, Elaine Hampsten pedaled up to me and asked, "How are you doing, Shannon?"

"So far, okay." The roadway was steep, allowing me to answer with only a few words.

Launching into a one-sided conversation, Elaine described the area of Italy we were cycling through and then finished by telling me the support van was at the top of the pass with a spread of food for a lunch break. Bringing the conversation to a close, Elaine offered words of encouragement, "You're doing great. Keep pedaling strong and you'll be at the top soon."

Before she could pull away, I quickly asked, "Andy told us this road had a 15 percent grade. Where is that steep section?"

Breaking into a smile, Elaine said, "You just climbed it! We passed a sign showing a 15 percent incline while we were talking."

"I can't believe I didn't see it," I responded in complete surprise. "I've never cycled that steep of a grade before and was worried about having enough gears for the climb. Wish I'd taken a picture of the sign to prove I did it!"

"Don't worry, there will be plenty of opportunities for a photo through-out the rest of the tour," Elaine said with a grin before accelerating to pull ahead of me.

Elaine must have shared our conversation with Andy because the next day, when I approached another sign displaying a 15 percent grade and started to reach into my back pocket for my camera, Andy surprised me with a yell from behind, "Keep riding, Shannon. I'll take your picture next to the sign and give you a copy." That simple, thoughtful gesture was a perfect example of the Hampsten's attentiveness and care for their clients.

I had watched the Tour de France on television for years and always marveled at the beautiful views provided by the helicopter cameras. My goal for our Cinghiale vacation was to witness Europe's magnificent mountain scenery in person. Our third day of cycling brought my dreams to fruition with the famed Sella Ronda which introduced the spectacular granite peaks of the Dolomites. The stunningly gorgeous ride was a seventy-five-mile cir-cuitous route that climbed a total of 8,400 feet over four mountain passes: the

Fedaia, Sella, Gardena and Compolongo. Don and I never stopped smiling throughout the day because every pass provided another awe-inspiring vista that had us grinning in appreciation. The roads we climbed were exactly what I was hoping for on the trip, dozens of switchbacks through healthy forests, green hillsides, and towering walls of rock. Another guest, Don Murtha, took a picture of me, Don, and our guide Richard, on our climb to the top of Passo Sella. The image will always be my favorite from our trip not just because of its grandeur but for the memory of sheer happiness Don and I felt throughout the day. All my Italian Dreams were fulfilled on the spectacular Sella Ronda. I didn't think the trip could get any better than this day. But of course, I was mistaken; there was so much more to come.

PEAKS, PASSES, AND REFUGIOS

The Tour group transferred from Alleghe to Corvara on their bicycles. Andy had a van transport all the luggage while his Cinghiale guests pedaled a scenic sixty-five-mile route over three mountain passes that included the Giau, Falzarego, and Valparola. Since its inception in 1909, Passo Giau has often been a part of the famed Giro d'Italia Bike Race. The renowned climb ascends almost 4,000 feet in six miles with twenty-eight switchbacks. Each bend in the road is chronologically numbered with a concrete marker allowing a rider to easily track their progress and the remaining distance to the summit. Cycling Passo Giau has been touted as one of the most picturesque and stunningly beautiful climbs anywhere in the world. The physical demands of the course are tempered by views of strikingly green hillsides scattered with dolomite rock beneath the reigning spire of Mt. Ra Gusela.

I could tell Don was feeling much stronger than I was when we reached the start of the climb. "You should ride with the stronger riders this morning," I told him. "I'll make it to the top, but I need to ride my own pace. I'll see you on the pass." Throughout most of the trip, Don and I rode together, allowing us to share our new experiences and to encourage one another during the most demanding sections. Only on a few occasions did we separate. However, with wonderful weather and spectacular scenery, Don felt inspired to challenge himself by riding at a faster tempo with Andy and a few of the younger men. Don would later tell me he really enjoyed his effort and the entertaining commentary that Andy provided during the ride. Just three months earlier, Passo Giau had been included in the Giro d'Italia. Cheers and words of encouragement for individual racers could still be seen written on the pavement throughout the climb. Andy provided highlights of the race while he and his small entourage charged their way to the top. As was often the case, after Don and the men reached the summit, Andy rode back down to check the progress of the other clients. On his return trip, he slowed his pace to ride alongside me which allowed us a few minutes for conversation. After a short chat, Andy pedaled uphill to the next client and repeated the effort all the way to the top of the pass.

Climbing the Passo Giau was challenging but the feeling of accomplishment made the effort worthwhile. Lingering over a mocha from the coffee shop on the summit, we enjoyed our final moments on the pass before donning our jackets and checking our brakes one final time in anticipation of the long descent to the valley floor.

An exhilarating downhill spin on a winding, narrow road led us to Cortina d'Ampezzo, host to the 1956 Olympics and the 1932 World Ski Championships. We then traversed to an area of the Dolomites called the Cinque Torri (Five Towers) where Andy had a surprise awaiting us. The pavement maintained a gentle uphill gradient through a tunnel of trees. We were climbing but could not see our destination. Two miles before reaching Passo Falzarego, Andy led us off the asphalt onto a dirt road leading to a large parking area where a chairlift was located. Leaving the bikes at the support van with our mechanic, we took the cable car up Mt. Lagazuoi to a restaurant located on the summit. High above tree line, the panorama of the Cinque Torri area was stunning. Five dolostone towers dominated the landscape creating 360 degrees of incredible views. Rock climbers could be seen at various heights scaling the sheer walls of the spires. Hiking trails connecting the Giau, Falzarego, and other passes crisscrossed the terrain. As far as the eye could see, there were mountains visible in every direction. The setting was magnificent.

If not for the gondola ride, we would have remained totally unaware of the beauty that surrounded us high above the forested valley floor.

Andy's surprise was lunch at the Rifugio il Scoiattoli Ristorante which allowed us to experience their fabulous Italian cuisine while taking in the view. It was welcoming and cozy while the food was plentiful and delicious. We were served multiple courses during our leisurely lunch that included wine and, of course, coffee with our dessert. Italian coffee was wonderful everywhere we visited, and I made sure to include a cup at the end of a meal as often as possible. Following lunch, we took Andy's advice and went for a walk to see the sights and allow our food to settle before getting back on our bikes to ride to Corvara.

The Mt. Lagazuoi—Cinque Torri area offered a walking tour of an open-air war museum. This special location bore the indelible marks of the First World War, and in particular, the bloody battles fought in the Alps between the Italians and Austro-Hungarians. The grounds surrounding Rifugio il Scoiattoli featured life-sized mannequins simulating the operation of heavy artillery and posing in restored trenches, bomb shelters, and the original huts that had sheltered the enlisted men. Don and I were able to walk in the trenches and peer out of the gunports at the surrounding landscape. "These mountains are so pretty. I'm finding it hard to envision this area as a combat zone," I commented to Don. "It's difficult to comprehend what it would have been like to witness such incredible beauty and violence at the same time." I was glad to see the land had endured despite the destructiveness of war.

The late afternoon bike ride to Corvara started by climbing the remaining two miles to the top of Passo Falzerago. The summit was relatively unremarkable; a false flat that featured a handful of restaurants and cafés at the intersection of three roadways. Heading west, we ascended the even higher Passo Valparola and were delighted by its unique landscape of huge boulders and rock. The road over the mountain top twisted and turned as it wound its way through walls of dolomite before descending through dark green forests and pristine pastureland leading to Corvara. After cycling sixty-five miles with 8,000 feet of climbing, we arrived at the Gran Ander Hotel tired but extremely pleased with the experiences of the day. Before falling asleep that night, I whispered to Don, "I am really enjoying this vacation. I love the physical challenges of the climbs, the beautiful scenery, the food, coffee, and unique side trips. Every day has been amazing." Still smiling, I drifted off to sleep thinking, "I can't wait for tomorrow."

LEAVE THE HUSTLE AND BUSTLE AT HOME

We cycled fast and hard each day, but once off the bikes, our vacation revolved around appreciating the slower pace of the Italian lifestyle. Corvara, and specifically the Gran Ander Hotel, exemplified this way of living. Our accommodations were described as a family-owned culinary hotel where the husband was the head chef and the wife, the sommelier. The couple took pride in the relaxed atmosphere and creative menus they shared with their guests. The food was not only delicious but always homemade and beautifully presented. Painted plates and exquisite garnishes were the standard during the multiple courses each evening. Our leisurely dinners felt more like extravagant daily celebrations where we toasted the wonderful riding experience of the day.

The origin of the food was just as important to the owners as the dishes they served. Our first night in Corvara, Don and I slept with our windows open allowing a cool, late-summer breeze to circulate through the room. Waking early in the morning, I was drawn to the window by the softly humming motor of a small open bed truck. Fresh milk was being delivered directly from a local dairy farm in stainless steel cylinders along with an actual basket of eggs. Beyond the vehicle, a small garden was thriving in the backyard of the hotel. Red ripe tomatoes could be seen hanging on the vine along with cultivated rows of herbs and greens. During a conversation with the chef, I would later learn that the family used only homegrown organic produce in all the dishes they served either harvested from their own garden or a neighboring small farm. The time and effort required to grow vegetables was a natural part of their lives.

Coffee was a drink to be savored. I never saw a to-go cup in any establishment while we were in Italy. A shot of espresso might have been sipped quickly but the ambience in the coffeehouses was focused on taking pleasure in the moment while consuming the revered beverage. Don and I visited many Italian coffee shops and were always aware of the attention to detail when making our drinks and the soothing atmosphere inside. Fortunately for us, Andy also had a love for Italian coffee and routinely stopped at a mountain top rifugio or other special location to treat everyone to a coffee during our daily rides.

Taking a gelato break quickly became an everyday event. Italian gelato differed from American ice cream in its smoother texture and more intense flavor. Don's choice was always cioccolato fondente, a rich, dark chocolate gelato. I tried a few varieties but found tiramisu and stracciatella, a classic vanilla swirled with chocolate pieces, to be my favorites. After a long day on the bike, taking time out to sit at a roadside café to enjoy a gelato was a feature of the Italian culture that Don and I readily embraced.

HIGHLIGHTS

Climbing Passo Pordoi was one of the highlights of the trip. The Pordoi is one of the most famous passes in the world of cycling and has been a part of the Giro d'Italia an incredible thirty-nine times. The road over the pass is considered something of an engineering marvel. Built in 1904, it has thirty-three hairpin turns and is the highest paved road in the Dolomites at a height of 6,717 feet. More impressive than its numbers, the scenery from the small alpine town of Arabba to the top of the Pordoi is simply beautiful.

Passo Pordoi was one of the six passes on Stage 14 of the 2016 Giro d'Italia. While ascending the mountain, Don and I discovered a large portion of the roadway surface was still covered with graffiti and words of encouragement for members of the Giro's peloton. The climb up the Pordoi and back to our hotel was only thirty-six miles with 4,700 feet of elevation gain making this cycling excursion the shortest and easiest ride of our entire trip. The moderate physical effort combined with great weather and lovely views made the day seem extra special. When Don and I reached the Passo Pordoi sign on the summit, we found another Cinghiale guest, Karena, standing next to it with her bike. I offered to take Karena's photo and then asked if she would take ours. "No one would ever know this is Pordoi Pass if we didn't tell them." I commented. "The sign is completely covered with stickers!" All the signage on the passes had stickers applied to them, but the Pordoi's lettering was entirely obliterated. However, the surrounding landscape was so iconic, the pass was unmistakable making the signage irrelevant.

My favorite evening of the trip was our gathering for "Beer and Race Stories" on the deck of our hotel in Alleghe. With blue skies overhead and the warm, fading rays of the sun shimmering across a calm Lake Alleghe, Andy delighted us with tales about his 1988 Giro d'Italia win and how he broke away during his ascent of Passo Gavia in a raging snowstorm. While describing his experience during the race, Andy said he had never been so cold in his life and has never been that cold since that day. Fortunately for him, his team director had seen the weather forecast and quickly scoured the local shops purchasing all the warm gloves, hats, and neck gators he could find for the team to wear. A famous poster of Andy shows him summiting the Gavia covered in snow and wearing a bulky pair of ski gloves. We loved his enthusiasm and the humorous anecdotes he incorporated into his stories while sharing unique insights into the world of professional cycling. Andy also talked about the various teams he raced for and, his 7-Eleven teammate Bob Roll, whom he credited for providing great lead outs during their racing career together. The lively discussion and the opportunity to spend time with Andy within the relaxed, comfortable setting made for a perfect evening.

In addition to the famous Italian locations and mountain passes, Andy also shared with his guests lesser-known places like the Serrai di Sottoguda; a little park that could only be visited on foot or bike. The Sottoguda was accessed by an ancient path, one and a quarter mile in length, that wound through an extremely narrow river gorge with rock walls 150 feet high. The tiny road was paved during the First World War, at the time of the construction of twelve bridges, two ammunition depots and a chapel that remains standing today. The park is a delightful sanctuary filled with lush green ferns, grasses, and trees growing alongside a bubbling stream with cascading waterfalls. Our visit took place on a warm summer day in late August.

"I can't believe how much cooler the temperature feels," I commented upon entering the park.

After glancing up at the sheer walls of rock, Don responded, "This area only gets heat when the sun is directly overhead. The steep rock walls block most of the sunshine during the day, so it never gets hot in here."

The shade and pleasant temperature were a welcome relief while cycling through the gorge. The tiny road was barely more than a mile long and maintained a very steep grade forcing us to climb 625 feet before reaching the exit gate. Although surprised by the steepness, we didn't mind the slower pace because it allowed us to more fully appreciate and enjoy all the natural features of the Sottoguda; a little jewel in the Veneto Alps.

CODA

Don and I were the only guests on the trip without electronic gadgets recording every mile, percent gradient and total feet of elevation gained each day. Everyone happily shared riding information allowing me to compile their data into a grand total of cycling statistics at the end of our vacation. The group rode eight of nine scheduled days; taking a rest day on a rainy afternoon. Our bike routes covered a little over 500 miles with 50,000 feet of climbing. In addition to the outing where Andy took a photo of me cycling past the 15 percent grade sign on the highway, Don and I also encountered gradients of 18 percent including one very memorable and challenging section of forested roadway that was nearly a mile in length. The numbers reinforced that our summer of training had been necessary and allowed us to endure the physical demands of the trip. However, regarding our lasting impressions of Italy, the data is unimportant. Our memories are more focused on the winding narrow Italian roads that led us through dense forests, flourishing farmlands, and over mountain passes featuring towering monoliths of dolostone. Recalling the tiny villages adorned with colorful flowers, inviting fountains, coffee and gelato shops always brings a smile to my face. These are the remembrances of our Italian dream that we hold dear.

During our private bus ride back to Venice, I kept thinking, "We have to come back again next year!" Andy held a tour in the Dolomites annually but alternated the starting point between Bormio or Alleghe. Bormio, located on the northwestern side of the country, allowed access to the famous Passes Stelvio and Gavia. Fortunately, Don felt the same desire to vacation in Europe again. Shortly after returning to the states, we made reservations to join Andy's 2017 Mighty Dolomite Cinghiale Tour.

Cycling Stelvio Pass the following year was exceptional and by far the most dramatic climb of all the passes we encountered during our two Italian vacations. An amazing forty-eight switchbacks define the route on the eastern side of the pass; surrounded by the incredibly majestic Italian and Swiss Alps. The British motoring magazine, *TopGear,* defines Italy's Passo Stelvio as "One of the world's greatest roads to drive." The statement can also be applied to experiencing the pass while sitting on a bicycle seat. On the day we climbed the Stelvio, there were many tourists gathered at the top watching the cars, motorcycles, bicycles, and buses ascending the tight hairpin turns. When Don and I finally made it to the summit, dozens of people started clapping and cheering our success in reaching the top without motorized assistance. I couldn't help but smile. For a few short seconds, I was racing the Giro with the crowd encouraging me over the pass. I felt the same joy and elation climbing Passo Gavia with Andy the next day. His story of breaking away from the peloton during the 1988 Giro d'Italia became a tangible thing; our own physical effort providing a better understanding of his achievement than his mere words could ever convey.

Don and I thoroughly enjoyed our time cycling in Italy. We still find ourselves reliving the magic during conversations about our Cinghiale Tours or when a familiar scene is shown on television. With both trips surpassing our expectations, we feel we lived our Italian dream.

ITALY PHOTOS (1 OF 2)

1 Mighty Dolomite Cinghiale Tour guests—Andy center, Don front row, second from left, Shannon behind him.

2 Midway on Passo Fedaia— Andy captured 15% grade.

3 Passo Sella—Don in white, Shannon in yellow.

4 Gardena Pass—Part of the Sella Ronda.

5 Don at Cinque Torri—Dozens of rock climbers could be seen scaling the five dolostone towers.

6 Lunch views at the Cinque Torri.

Italy 2016

ITALY PHOTOS (2 OF 2)

7   Don and Shannon climbing Valparola Pass.

8   The grades were as high as 18% but the lush green farmlands and quaint villages adorned with flowers are what we remember most.

9   Stelvio Pass.

10   Cycling Through the Serrai di Sottoguda.

11   Don and Shannon on the summit of Passo Gavia.

12   Andy sitting in front of his iconic poster—cycling a snowy Passo Gavia to win the 1988 Giro d'Italia.

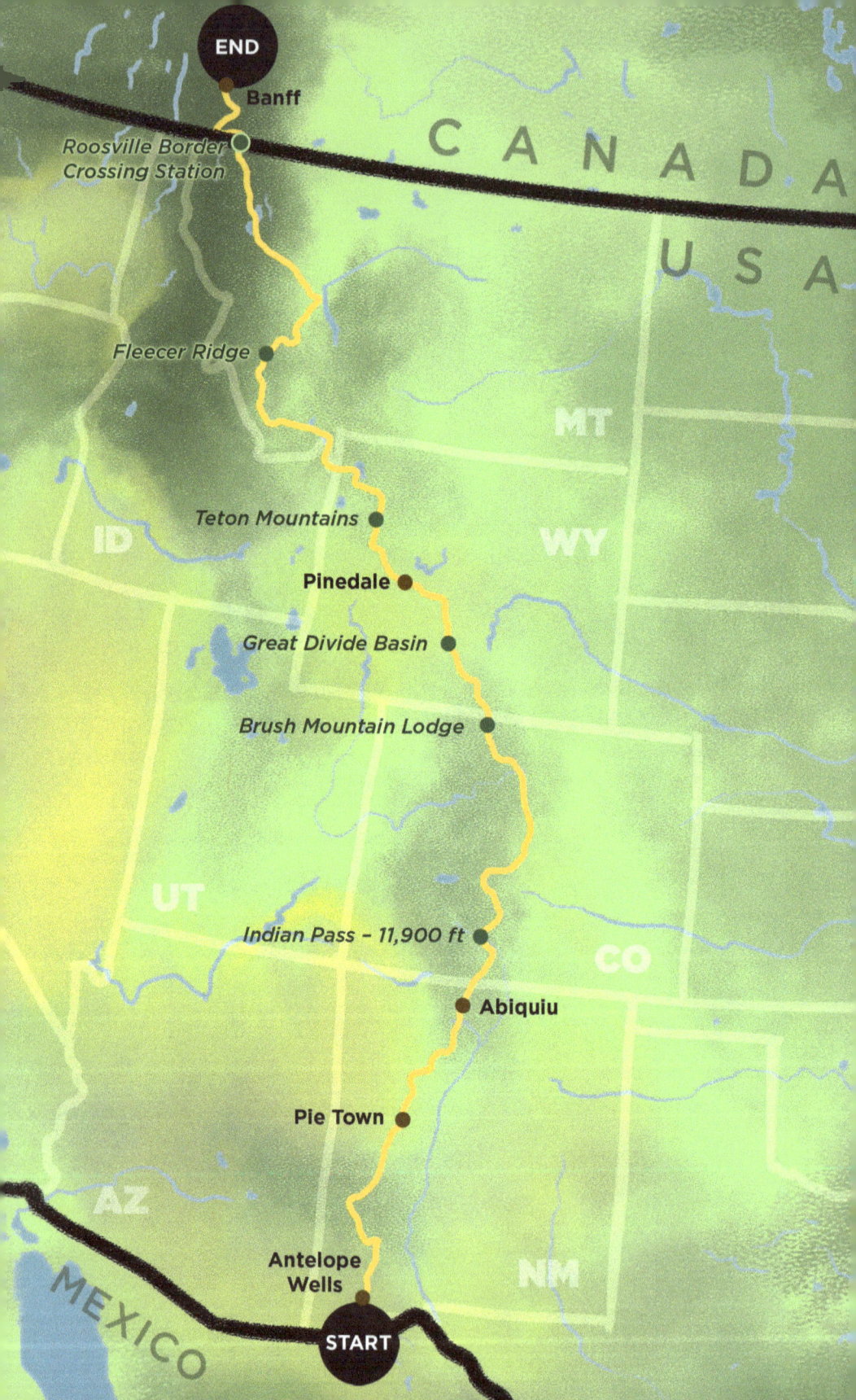

CANADA

USA

END

Banff

Roosville Border
Crossing Station

Fleecer Ridge

MT

Teton Mountains

WY

Pinedale

Great Divide Basin

Brush Mountain Lodge

ID

UT

Indian Pass – 11,900 ft

CO

Abiquiu

Pie Town

AZ

Antelope
Wells

NM

MEXICO

START

THE GREAT DIVIDE MOUNTAIN BIKE ROUTE

FOUR OF US WERE gathered around a table at Java, Don's favorite coffee-house, when our friend, Mike, made the announcement, "I think we should call this trip 'The Search for a Great Donut Shop.'"

Don agreed. "Maybe we'll find another Sweet Coloradough like Shannon and I did when we were traveling across the country two years ago. That place had amazing donuts!"

After laughing at the guys' excitement over discovering the perfect sugary treat, I summarized the new plan, "It's settled then. Our goal for this adventure is to pedal 2,700 miles from the Mexican border to Banff, taste-testing donuts along the way to determine the best donut shop on the Great Divide Mountain Bike Route."

Mike's wife, Jeanne, quickly added, "Sounds fun to me. I can't wait to leave."

We were sitting in the sunshine enjoying a hot cup of coffee after a chilly bike ride over Trail Creek Summit. Cold, wet, windy weather had been the norm throughout the entire spring season in the Wood River Valley. Although May had provided a couple of warm seventy-degree days, more often than not, we had been forced to cycle in cool, blustery conditions often combined with raindrops or snowflakes. Everyone was looking forward to the warmth awaiting us in New Mexico where we would begin our journey on June 16, 2022.

The weather and environment in the southwestern United States was in complete contrast to Idaho. New Mexico had suffered a spring season of intense heat and drought that was a catalyst for multiple wildfires now causing widespread destruction of public land. In a surprise move, the Forest Service shut down five New Mexico national forests two weeks before the start of our trip. The ban blocked travel on four hundred miles of our cycling route's gravel roads and left only dangerous highway alternatives for pedaling around the closures. With safety being paramount, the group made the decision to change the start of our journey from the Mexican border to Abiquiu, New Mexico, which would allow us to bypass the wildfire restrictions and the hazardous roadways. During the initial discussion of our options, memories of hiking the Continental Divide Trail twenty years earlier and the mantra "Thru-hikers have to be flexible," came to mind. Once again, Don and I were being forced to adjust our journey because of Mother Nature, but this time our previous experience made the choice much easier. "We can always go back and cycle the rest of New Mexico next year if we want to complete the entire trail," I commented to Don. Just as we had returned to hike an aborted section of the CDT, we vowed to experience the full New Mexico section of the Great Divide Mountain Bike Route (GDMBR) the following spring.

The idea of tackling the longest off-pavement cycling route in the world was initiated by Don following the celebration of his 70th birthday on November 25, 2021. We had crossed paths with GDMBR cyclists during our CDT hike across Wyoming's Great Desert Basin twenty years earlier and had always thought cycling the Continental Divide would be a wonderful adventure for us at some point in our lives. Don's monumental birthday prompted a serious discussion of the topic while his heartfelt comments cemented my commitment to the goal. "I've always wanted to ride the Divide and I'm not getting any younger. Let's celebrate our fortieth anniversary by cycling the GDMBR this summer." His excitement for the journey was all I needed to get onboard with the plan. Once the decision was made, we extended an invitation to our friends Mike and Jeanne, and were thrilled when they agreed to join us.

Adventure Cycling Association provided maps and downloadable GPS data files for the entire GDMBR. A review of their maps showed the 2,700-

mile route was primarily composed of remote Forest Service, BLM, and Canadian provincial dirt roads. There was also sixty miles of single-track, fifty miles of paved bike paths and nearly nine-hundred miles of pavement included in the total mileage. The trail crisscrossed the Continental Divide thirty-two times, ultimately climbing over eighteen major passes and 200,000 feet of elevation. Although the route often passed through tiny towns and small cities, sections with a few hundred miles of uninhabited roadway still occurred. Our preference was to end each riding day at a hotel where we could enjoy the comforts of a bed, shower, and air-conditioning. The remoteness of the trail, however, would force us to camp for fifteen nights—about a third of the trip.

The first step in our planning process was to create an itinerary that outlined each day's targeted mileage and resulting destination. Our daily goal of riding seventy-five miles could be lengthened or shortened for us to reach a town with supplies or a suitable campsite with water. We purchased bike packs that could accommodate two changes of clothing, camping gear, toiletries, electronics, bike tools, spare parts, a tire repair kit, forty-eight hours of food and thirteen liters of water. As backup, we took foldable backpacks to carry an additional day of food for those rare occasions when the terrain would necessitate camping for multiple nights. My lightweight mountain bike quickly blossomed from a mere twenty pounds to nearly fifty pounds when fully loaded. If I was going to be able to ride this beast of a machine, I knew I had to vastly improve my level of physical fitness.

Don and I own a stationary bike which allowed us to cycle indoors throughout the winter. Spinning our legs kept our muscles toned and our bottoms conditioned for sitting on a bike seat, but the effort couldn't duplicate the physical demands of long days in the saddle riding rough roads in inclement weather. Living in a ski resort town with snow on the ground nearly six months out of the year, the earliest we could begin to safely cycle outdoors in 2022 was the last week in March. Our spring training started with a short twenty-mile ride on our road bikes. We quickly progressed to riding for a couple hours on our mountain bikes when the local gravel roads were dry. Unrelenting spring snowstorms and rain would delay us from reaching our goal of riding seventy-five miles in a single day until the latter part of May. We were able to duplicate the effort a few times during the first part of June making us confident that we were adequately fit and ready to start our adventure.

AN ARDUOUS INTRODUCTION TO NEW MEXICO

"My bike computer is reading 118 degrees right now," Mike announced to the group.

"I believe it," I responded. Sweat was tricking down the sides of my face and the shins of my legs. The weather had been forecasted to be sunny and warm with a high of one hundred degrees. We all realized that Mike's bike computer was probably impacted by the black bag hanging from the handlebars directly behind the device, but regardless of accuracy, the day felt dangerously hot. We were cycling on a newly laid road surface of black asphalt and the heat reflected off the ground was stifling. Our goal was to travel from Abiquiu to Chama, New Mexico; a total of fifty-eight miles with a surprising 3,400 feet of elevation gain. What we thought would be an easy day riding on pavement became a brutal challenge. Excessive heat, lack of shade and continuous rolling hills made the day much tougher than expected and our time in the sun much longer than anticipated. Fortunately, we all were wearing white solar arm coverings and large goofy looking helmet visors that protected our faces and shoulders from direct sunlight. Those items, along with multiple stops at convenient stores for cold drinks and access to air-conditioning, likely saved us from heatstroke on the very first day of our adventure.

Flat tires are expected by everyone cycling the GDMBR because of the harsh road conditions and the immense distance. Don picked up a treble fishing hook with several feet of monofilament line a few miles south of Chama. Prior to the trip, we had debated back and forth on bringing our heavy Leatherman tool and were fortunate to have it with us because pulling the hook out of the tire would not have been possible without the pliers. Our tires were tubeless and relied on a liquid sealant inside to plug holes and stop air from leaking out. The product repaired the puncture and kept the tire inflated for the rest of the trip. As the miles passed, our tires developed many micro cuts to the tread and sidewalls but continued to maintain pressure, displaying only a freckle of oozing sealant each morning from the nicks. Remarkably, the four of us never had to fix a flat tire throughout the entire adventure.

More surprises were awaiting us at our first destination. The small town of Chama, New Mexico discovered a break in their main water line and as a result, a boil water order had been issued for the community. We arrived in town exhausted, overheated and focused on finding an icy cold beverage to drink. Unfortunately, our hotel had been forced to empty their ice bins and could only provide a couple bottles of room temperature water for drinking. While shopping for supplies, we discovered the locals had already purchased all the bags of ice and just about all the bottled water at the grocery and convenience stores, leaving the shelves empty until the next day's delivery. There were a few gallon-jugs of distilled water still available for purchase which we used for brushing our teeth, rehydrating throughout the evening, and refilling our bottles for the next day's ride. Although initially disappointed by the lack of ice, we made the best of the situation and celebrated our first day with dinner at a nearby restaurant.

Our clear, blue-sky day had not been kind to me. My legs and thighs were completely covered with huge heat welts from the intense sunlight and my body's inability to cool itself. My skin's reaction to the sun was a complication that I would battle throughout the journey; a little uncomfortable but not incapacitating. I fell asleep focused on the positive aspects of the day: the air conditioner worked well, the wet compresses covering my legs felt wonderful, the pizza at dinner had been great, the colorful mountain scenery of New Mexico had been beautiful, the four of us had laughed throughout the day and together we had triumphed over all the challenges along the way. All in all, it was a good beginning to our journey.

THE RYTHM OF THE ROAD

Daily life evolves into a rhythmic sequence of activities when participating in an endurance type adventure. Our days were filled cycling endless miles of challenging terrain only interrupted by snack stops, bathroom breaks, and picture taking. Whether camping or staying in a motel, time off the bike continued to be physically taxing because of the numerous responsibilities we had to complete each evening in preparation for the next day's travel. About halfway through Colorado, Jeanne expressed her growing concerns about our demanding schedule during town stops. "I feel like there is barely enough time to get everything done. We only have a few hours to shower, eat, wash clothes and shop for supplies after we arrive." She was right. At the end of the day when our bodies were totally spent and we just wanted to lay down and rest, that's when we had to find an inner strength to complete all the necessary chores.

Over time, we developed a routine that allowed us to become more efficient during the fifteen nights of camping and twenty-six overnight town stops. However, the routine was completely abandoned when we treated ourselves to a rest day off the bike; affectionately called a "zero day" by the long-distance cycling community. These layover days provided precious hours of "normalcy" where we spent a lengthy amount of time savoring drinks and treats at a new coffeehouse, shopping, perusing the internet, exploring new cities, and talking to family and friends. Only a couple of these extended stops were scheduled in advance; most occurred when our bodies needed time off the bike. One unplanned rest day was especially memorable.

BRUSH MOUNTAIN LODGE

Sometimes a special place or person can touch you in ways that defy reasoning. Such was our experience at Brush Mountain Lodge; a small family ranch in the middle of nowhere Colorado that quickly became more important to each of us than just a convenient place to stop on our journey. Though the time spent with the owner was brief, Kirstin's unique style of hospitality had a powerful impact on us and provided unforgettable memories of this location.

We saw the sign that read GDMBR Cyclists Welcome, and quickly realized the large ranch house and adjoining cabins were all part of the renowned Brush Mountain Lodge. After slowing to a stop, we heard Kirstin shout hello followed by a request to place our bikes under a small pavilion to keep them dry. Storm clouds were on the horizon and rain was imminent. Kirstin greeted each of us with a warm embrace and then introduced herself and her friends that were visiting. "Can I get you a beer, soda, or coffee?" she asked as we made ourselves comfortable within the large seating area on her covered deck. After taking our beverage requests, Kirstin headed toward the kitchen. "The door is unlocked. Feel free to use the bathroom, take a shower or just relax inside if you want. I'll be cooking snack pizzas in about an hour if you are hungry. There's plenty for everyone." In a matter of minutes, we were fully a part of the Brush Mountain Lodge experience.

Kirstin is a very laid-back, unassuming individual who spends her summers taking care of GDMBR racers and riders. She tracks the individuals competing on the GDMBR, officially called The Tour Divide, via the internet and knows when racers are close to the ranch. Kirstin serves them meals, shares her shower facilities, and washes their clothes while they sleep. In this manner, she contributes to their well-being and keeps them going. While her primary focus is seeing to each competitor's needs, she also provides great care to folks like us touring the GDMBR.

After settling in, we joined the gathering on her deck for conversations about riding the GDMBR as well as what it was like living and ranching within the Routt National Forest. While we were all telling stories and eating pizza, additional riders pulled into the compound and were welcomed in the same manner that we had been greeted earlier in the day. Kirstin told all of us that we were welcome to stay overnight, but the one bedroom in the lodge was reserved for Andrew, a racer that was expected to arrive between nine and eleven o'clock that night. Kirstin followed Andrew's progress on her computer and did not go bed until she had fed him, washed his clothes, and set him up in a bedroom for sleeping. There were eleven of us spread out on the floor and on the large sectional couch where Don and I laid our sleeping bags. Andrew arrived per schedule but only slept a few hours before packing up and heading out in the pouring rain at two o'clock in the morning. A group of three riders left a couple hours later with the remaining four cyclists pedaling away at 6:00 a.m. under dark skies and a sprinkling of raindrops.

Kirstin had offered to make Jeanne, Mike, Don, and me breakfast at seven o'clock. The weather forecast predicted continuous rain for the next twenty-four hours, so a hot breakfast of blueberry pancakes, sausage, and eggs sounded very appealing. Although Kirstin did not have a culinary background, she prepared the meal with ease. After offering seconds and ensuring everyone was full, Kirstin made herself a plate. She joined us at the large dining room table and entertained us with stories of Tour Divide racers who had recently stayed at the lodge. We were enjoying our final cup of coffee when the lights flickered once and then went out completely. Without missing a beat, Kirstin retrieved a couple of deer antler candelabras and placed them on the table, creating a cozy ambience of light within the gloomy, early morning darkness. Before excusing herself to make phone calls regarding the outage, Kirstin offered, "You guys are all welcome to take a zero day here at the lodge. It's supposed to rain all day. Why be miserable out cycling when you can stay and just chill?" Her gracious invitation seemed to indicate she was interested in our company. Together, the four of us made the decision to stay at the lodge for another night. I'm so glad we did because the following twelve hours developed into an emotional journey that would become one of my most treasured experiences of the entire adventure.

While Kirstin was outside in the rain, standing at the one spot on the hillside where she could receive cell service, the four of us started clearing the table. My walk through the kitchen and into the dish room made for an eye-opening moment. I had heard Kirstin tell her friends the previous evening that she was running on empty trying to take care of all the people arriving at the lodge, but it wasn't until I got a good look at the kitchen and laundry room that I fully understood her situation. The dish room was full of dirty dishes while piles of soiled sheets and towels covered the laundry room floor. We had seen Kirstin in action. The evening before, she had entertained friends, handled all eleven riders, Andrew the racer, and took care of the guests staying in her three cabins. She was managing all the work on the compound by herself, without a complaint and all for free. Brush Mountain Lodge is known by everyone cycling the GDMBR as an oasis along the trail. The internet had an incredible number of posts by cyclists raving about their visit. Looking around, I began to realize the personal sacrifice this lone woman was making just to keep the establishment running and to be able to offer such generous services. I decided that while I was lazing around for the day, I would donate a few hours to help organize the place once the power was restored.

Don and I rested on the couch until the lights blinked on brightly. With the electrical line repaired, I found the vacuum and cleaned the rugs while Don dusted the furniture. Mike began to sweep the floors at the same time Jeanne headed into the laundry room to start a new load of wash and to fold the clean towels that were in the dryer. Once Don, Mike, and Jeanne had completed their chores and moved on to surfing the web via their phones, I helped Kirstin in the kitchen by loading and unloading the dishwasher.

Working side by side provided an opportunity to learn more about our host. After thanking me for helping, Kirstin told me she had been running the lodge for more than a decade, but this was the first summer she had seriously contemplated not opening. She went on to say she had recently lost her best friend to Covid and that her cat had died at the same time. Kirstin had endured an extremely difficult year. As tactfully as possible, I maneuvered the conversation to what I hoped was a more pleasant topic by asking Kirstin what her life was like when she wasn't living in Colorado and managing the lodge during the summer. She told me about adopting her new rescue puppy and that she was writing a book about her experiences with the GDMBR Racers; both were positive influences on her life. She in turn, asked about me and Don. I provided the Cliff Notes version of our story: Don and I were celebrating our 40th wedding anniversary, the GDMBR was the latest of a dozen grand adventures Don and I had enjoyed throughout our marriage and that I was capturing our experiences in a book as well. In that moment, Kirstin turned to face me and said, "I feel like we just scratched the surface and there is so much more to your story. I'd like to spend more time together. You and Don should come back and visit sometime."

I thanked her for the invitation and said, "We've really enjoyed our stay and appreciate your generosity. You have a way about you that is very welcoming and warm."

"It's not me, Shannon, it's more about the location," she replied. "By the time racers and riders reach my door they are fragile. A small act of kindness feels like so much more when you are cold, hungry, and exhausted." I let her know I recognized the truth in her statement but also stressed that she was, unquestionably, what made the place so special.

At four o'clock, Kirstin fired up the wood burning stove and cooked more pizzas for the five of us while the cold, rainy weather continued to hammer the compound. We were happy to have stayed indoors and out of the elements for the day. Sharing the warmth of the fireplace, a hot meal and good conversation made for a great evening. After everyone was fed, Kirstin asked me for a favor. "I'm so tired right now, I'd like to go up to my cabin and sleep. There are no racers scheduled to arrive tonight. Would you greet any riders who show up at the door and then text me to come take care of them this evening?" I told her I would handle any unexpected cyclists and to go get some rest. After exchanging phone numbers, Kirstin retired to her cabin and entrusted us with her property.

Mike, Jeanne, Don, and I had our run of the place for the evening. No one showed up at the door until the next morning. Mike and Jeanne slept in the single bedroom while Don and I remained on the couches for the night. In addition to providing lodging and meals, Kirstin offered a variety of snacks, nutrition bars, chamois creams, skin ointments, and discarded bear spray canisters for free. Donations were accepted but very few people seemed to contribute to the collection jar. Eleven cyclists had been in the house overnight and ten people the previous evening; yet we found the donation container taped shut and almost empty. Although we never figured out how Kirstin could financially run the place with so little offerings, we saw first-hand how hard she worked to keep the operation going. Out of respect for her, we added money to the jar and continued to donate our time by finishing the ninth load of laundry just before going to bed.

The four of us rose early and made our own breakfast of scrambled eggs, toasted English muffins, and coffee. After tidying up the kitchen, we began packing our gear for an early departure. Kirstin arrived a little before 7:00 a.m. When she glanced in the laundry room on her way in from the back-door, she was surprised by what she saw. The floor that had been covered with piles of soiled laundry was completely clean and, on the counters, sat towering stacks of neatly folded towels and sheets. Again, Kirstin dispensed warm hugs all around while conveying her sincere appreciation of our efforts. "You guys are the best! Thanks so much for helping me." There was a brightness in her eyes and a real smile on her face that hadn't been there the previous day. I would like to think the reciprocal care shown by the four of us had lifted her spirits.

Like clockwork, early morning brought cyclists knocking at the lodge door looking for food and shelter. Once the new arrivals were shown where the coffee pot and supplies were located, Kirstin came outside to bid us farewell. After a few photos and another hug goodbye, we left Brush Mountain Lodge and cycled north toward the nearby state line of Wyoming and onward to the town of Rawlins. I was bursting with emotions as we pedaled away. Just as Kirstin had described, I had arrived at the lodge a bit worn and weary, however, it wasn't just the warm food and surroundings that had provided contentment. Impacting another's wellbeing through my own act of kindness had made me happy. The visit to Brush Mountain Lodge left an indelible impression on all of us.

TRAIL ANGELS ON THE GDMBR

When Don and I were hiking the Continental Divide Trail in 2002, we were amazed by the number of people we met who were interested in our adventure and wanted to support our effort. Thru-hikers call these folks trail angels. Twenty years later, we found the concept was even more prevalent in the long-distance cycling community. Caring individuals providing random acts of kindness were found all along the GDMBR. Kirstin at Brush Mountain Lodge was just one example of the many trail angels that offered their help.

On the fourth day of the trip, we experienced both our first night of camping and our initial encounter with trail angels. We had left the small town of Del Norte, Colorado with the intention of cycling eighty miles to a guaranteed water source at Dome Reservoir. Exhausted after nine hours in the saddle, climbing 6,200 feet, and riding seventy-two miles, we decided to make camp early at Luder's Campground near Cochetopa Pass, elevation 10,067 feet. Darkness was approaching and at such a high altitude, a rapid drop in temperature would soon follow. A cyclist we had met two days earlier told us there was a hidden spring at the back of the campground: the only water available for miles on either side of the pass. A family of four was camping at the primitive campground and I asked the father if they had found the secret water source. "We brought our own water jugs, but I think there is a trail just off the road up ahead that may lead to a spring." I thanked him for the directions and set out with our filter and bottles hoping to find water. A small spring was flowing in a thickly vegetated area just outside the fenced boundary of the campground. After filling all our water containers, Don and I walked back to our tent site, stopping for a short conversation with the family about our cycling adventure and the goal to reach Banff.

As a group, we had decided not to carry a stove because of weight and space limitations. Although the stove, fuel and cooking pot may not have been too heavy to manage, finding room in our bags to pack the equipment would have been nearly impossible. Freezing overnight temperatures on June 20th were the coldest we would experience throughout the entire adventure. Donning my down jacket, rain pants, and heavy gloves for warmth, I was seriously wishing I had access to a hot meal and a warm drink. Cold peanut butter and jelly on a tortilla was not sounding very appealing. As I was contemplating dinner, the daughter walked over from her family's campsite with an overflowing plate of deep-dish cherry pie. "My parents wanted to share my mom's homemade pie with you guys. The cherries are from the tree in our backyard. It's a family favorite and we hope you like it." We were thrilled with the cherry pie. After dinner, I visited the family to thank them for their generosity. The pie may not have been a hot meal, but the unexpected gift warmed my soul just the same.

The kindness of strangers never ceased to amaze me. We were repeatedly shown both small and large offerings of support throughout the trip. When a husband and wife stopped to chat with us and learned we had run out of mosquito repellant during a two-day camping stretch, they gave us one of two cans they had in their truck so that we would be protected until we reached our next town stop. One stormy evening, a couple offered their rustic cabin for a place to sleep out of the rain because the tiny township we were passing through did not have a campground or motel. While riding a fifty-mile waterless stretch of road, a sheriff's deputy pulled us over to offer us Gatorade. Several people stopped and offered water when the days became warm or the miles between towns were dry and desolate. On a grand scale, the Lost Llama Ranch offered cabins for sleeping, outside showers, cold drinks, and food for all GDMBR cyclists. Their only request: pay it forward. And a friend of a friend offered us her luxury condo in Steamboat because there were no hotel rooms available on the weekend when we arrived in the busy resort town. The generosity of trail angels added many wonderful moments to our journey.

ALL YOU CAN EAT—PLUS A LITTLE MORE

Convenience stores are a lifeline for GDMBR cyclists. Like a string of pearls, finding these gems along the route can save the day. A cold drink on a hot afternoon with a bag of chips or just an ice cream treat could lift our spirits, put a smile on our faces, and provide enough energy to get us back out on the road. Most store owners had learned the preferences of bikepackers and stocked foods for them in addition to the more traditional gas station fare. Peanut butter and jelly on a tortilla was the primary food item eaten on the road. Tortillas were easier to pack than bread, making them a true staple for everyone cycling the GDMBR.

After our first night's cold PB&J tortilla sandwich, we tried canned chicken with green chilies and cheese on a tortilla. The unpleasant taste, texture, and cat food appearance of the meat made the meal almost impossible to consume; a true one-and-done. Our third camp supper was refried beans on a tortilla with corn chips as a side dish. Although flavorful, the combination was still lacking. During the next trip to a convenience store, I perfected the menu by selecting Fritos Scoops, Fritos Bean Dip, Snickers Bars, and a Dr Pepper. This meal hit the sweet spot on the satisfaction and happiness scale. I grew up eating corn chips and bean dip as a kid in Texas but hadn't had the combination for forty years. Fortunately, Don liked the meal as much as I did, and every gas station stocked our new dinner favorites. Twice, we alternated the meal with Dinty Moore beef stew. Even without heating, we could choke down a can for some much-needed protein and calories. There is a truism that states "everything tastes better when camping in the woods." It's a fact. Although Don and I were content with our meals, I would never think about eating these foods for dinner back home.

One of the highlights of the trip included the surprising number of great restaurants we found along the GDMBR. When asked what our favorite meal was, Don and I quickly reply, "Amish breakfast was the best ever!" The tiny unincorporated community of La Garita, Colorado was a few miles off the official trail, but the food they served was well worth the extra mileage. A large sign on the dining room wall provided an explanation for why the food was so outstanding, "Our food is locally grown. We hand cut our potatoes and fry them in lard. Each meal is made to order and with care." The bacon, eggs, hash browns, and toasted Amish bread was by far the tastiest breakfast on the Divide. In regard to dinner, all four of us agreed that Amicas restaurant in Salida served the best lasagna any of us had ever eaten, and the restaurant at Crooked Creek Lodge, also in Colorado, made the most wonderful pulled pork sandwich. Jeanne, who rarely eats meat, surprised us all by ordering the sandwich for lunch and then again for dinner later that evening. It was that outstanding. The ice cream we had in Ovando, Montana as well as Boulton Creek Campground in Canada are tied for both best flavor and the largest double scoops we had ever been served. Being hungry cyclists, the generous portions did not go unnoticed by the gang.

After two weeks of traveling, Don, Jeanne, Mike, and I had cycled a distance of seven hundred miles and crossed the state line into Wyoming. The enormous mountains of Colorado were behind us. Having climbed nine major passes and hundreds of rolling hills for a total of 53,000 feet of elevation gain, we were feeling much stronger on our bikes. We also began to feel something else, a constant sensation of hunger. A nutrition bar that normally provided a couple hours of satiety now relieved our hunger for no more than thirty minutes. Stopping every hour for a snack became a new routine. Snickers were our favorite candy and the one item Don, and I never tired of despite eating five or more bars a day. Each couple was spending fifty dollars on snacks every time we visited a convenience store because our metabolism demanded we eat more. Although the four of us consumed massive amounts of food during town stops, we were still unable to ingest enough calories to balance the amount burned while riding. We all lost weight. By the end of the trip, Mike and I had lost the most: eight pounds each. Don and Jeanne, who were both very lean at the start of our journey, also shed a few pounds despite their best efforts to maintain their body weight. Knowing we were in a losing battle, we gave ourselves free rein to eat foods with concentrated calories like ice cream and donuts as often as we desired.

"Wow. This is a really good chocolate Long John. I can't believe my favorite donut is going to be from the City Market in Rawlins, Wyoming!" Don said before starting in on his second pastry.

"Hold on there. We're only halfway through the trip. There could still be a great donut shop somewhere on the trail ahead," Mike offered.

"I still think Powder Donuts could have won our contest for best donut shop on the GDMBR," I added. "The Powder Donuts we ate at the Marriott kiosk in the Grand Hotel were outstanding."

"I'm still disappointed their bakery was closed!" Jeanne commented. "I can't believe we were standing outside the door at six o'clock in the morning reading a 'sorry we're closed today- short staffed' sign. I really wanted to try more of their donuts."

A feeling of disappointment resonated with all of us over the Steamboat Springs donut shop closure. We had left the resort town dispirited and unfulfilled after patronizing a coffee shop that offered only marginal pastries for breakfast. A week later, the four of us were standing outside the Rawlins grocery store eating donuts after picking at the lackluster continental breakfast provided by our hotel. We were about to head into the Great Divide Basin and knew we needed to stock up on calories to fuel us through the desert. Donuts seemed to be the best choice to meet our needs and improve our morale. To quote Mike, "All donuts are good, some are just better than others."

THE DESERT REVISITED

The Great Divide Basin in Wyoming was the most anticipated section of the GDMBR for Don and me to visit because of our history hiking this same area on the CDT twenty years earlier. Back then, extreme heat and drought made our six-day trek through the desert dangerous and unforgettable. We both had a desire to once again face the elements and unique challenges found within this 138-mile stretch of barren land. The GDMBR merges with the CDT for the first twenty miles out of Rawlins which allowed us to retrace our actual steps before venturing into new territory. Our plan was to complete the desert segment in two days with only one night of camping. We expected the miles to be difficult and the conditions brutal, and once again, the Basin did not disappoint.

"You could land a 747 on this road. It's so flat and goes on forever!" Mike commented before laying down on the warm tarmac to take a short nap. We had stopped for a snack break on Mineral-X Road, the same stretch of roadway Don and I had hiked on the CDT. Much to our surprise, the seven-mile-long dirt road had been paved which made our initial segment of cycling in the desert much easier. A heat wave was crossing the United States and above normal temperatures were expected throughout the Great Divide Basin. By two o'clock in the afternoon, our thermometer read 102 degrees. There were no trees or buildings to provide any protection from the intense rays of the sun. We were heading to A & M Reservoir, the first of only two water sources on our route. I could feel my skin burning through the white solar sleeves, knee coverings and white reflective shorts I was wearing making me wonder how much heat all of us were going to have to endure before the day ended. My plan was to find water and then rig some sort of shelter using our tent's ground cloth strung between our bikes to provide a break from the harsh sunlight. I just had to pace myself on the bike so that I could get there without experiencing heat exhaustion.

"We are so lucky those clouds rolled in," I said to the group. We were at A & M Reservoir watching storm clouds move at a very fast pace across the horizon and more importantly, block the sun from our view. An immediate drop in temperature provided me a sense of relief. I had been sitting on the bank of the reservoir with a nauseated stomach from a pounding migraine, trying to ignore the heat welts that had developed on my skin and all the while wondering if I was going to survive the desert this time around. I knew there was no choice but to push onward and make the most of the situation. We were fortunate to have the dark clouds overhead but with them came high winds out of the west, the direction we were traveling. After filling our bottles and a large collapsible container with enough water to sustain us for the next twenty-four hours, we began pedaling again, this time into a direct headwind.

Travel was slow but we continued to make progress and ultimately completed seventy-six miles, over halfway, before stopping to make camp. The Great Basin is a vast desert filled with rolling hills, sagebrush, and cactus. It is home to wild horses, antelope and cattle that roam freely across the land. There were some private areas with barbed wire fences, however, most of the desert was unrestricted and available for camping. Our two-person bikepacking tent had a relatively small footprint but finding a flat area free of prickly pear and scrub brush to accommodate the tiny shelter was surprisingly difficult. We found success a short distance from the main road, next to a fence line and behind a small bluff that provided a little bit of privacy within the open landscape. While setting up the tent, I paused briefly to appreciate an incredibly beautiful moment. The evening clouds that remained on the western horizon not only kept the temperature from soaring but also created a spectacularly colorful sunset to end our day.

I awoke the next morning to the sound of a few raindrops lightly hitting the nylon of our tent. The dark, cloudy skies were a nice surprise, but I was anxious about the possibility of a hard rain. The sandy soil in the Great Basin turns into what cyclists call "peanut butter mud" when mixed with rainwater. The sticky concoction has been known to completely clog the drivetrain and wheels of a bike bringing all forward progress to a halt. Climbing out of my tent to look around, I noticed several things that restored my calm. A beautiful rainbow had formed while the sun was rising, and open patches of blue could be found within the dark clouds, leading me to believe we might get a few raindrops but probably not a big storm. I was delighted to discover wild mustangs roaming the hillside on the other side of the fence. We had seen numerous antelope running across the landscape, but the untamed horses had eluded us. I felt a special kinship with the mustangs from our interactions with them twenty years ago and was happy to know they were still thriving. Cattle were also scattered all around our camp. One particularly vocal cow began to head toward our tent bellowing what I humorously interpreted as, "Wake up and get moving. This is my home. Time for you to go!" My first twenty-four hours in the Basin had not been easy. Another big day full of challenges lay ahead of us. It was time to kick into gear, pack up and get started.

The headwind we experienced the previous afternoon was nothing compared to the twenty-five to thirty mile per hour sustained winds we endured the entire way to Atlantic City, Wyoming. We formed an echelon to draft one another, however, the terrain wasn't always conducive to this strategy. Most people think a desert is flat, but the Great Basin was filled with rolling hills and offered an impressive 6,700 feet of total elevation gain. During our second day of riding, we climbed over 4,000 feet of elevation while butting a headwind for sixty miles. We found it almost impossible to form a pace line with our bikes while riding uphill, downhill, through pockets of deep sand and being buffeted by winds that were constantly changing on a winding road. In addition to the normal challenges of the desert, the arrival of a scary, black mushroom cloud in the early afternoon had all of us concerned. The enormous, menacing looking formation was a constant threat slowly moving in an easterly direction across the Basin. I had read about cloud bursts and had seen footage of the dangerous downpours on the internet. We could see a huge curtain of rain falling out of the cloud and knew we would suffer severe consequences if we met the storm. Fortunately, our direction of travel kept us just out of harm's way, allowing us to arrive in Atlantic City after seven hours of arduous riding.

Cycling and hiking through the Great Divide Basin were totally different experiences. Moving more quickly on the bike allowed for easier access to water and limited our time in the desert. The terrain itself, however, remained one of the most striking, harsh, and remote environments Don and I have ever encountered. We found great satisfaction in having crossed the desert twice.

NO EASY DAYS

Predicting how hard a day in the saddle was going to be could never be based on just mileage alone. Wind and road surfaces made a huge impact on each day's effort. One of the shortest sections we cycled was thirty-seven miles and the exhaustion we felt at the end of the day was the same as our longest distance of ninety-one miles. Our ride out of Atlantic City, Wyoming will always stand out as one of the most challenging days we faced on the GDMBR. Forty mile per hour headwinds with gusts well over fifty miles per hour blew us sideways across the road and periodically brought us to a stop with an invisible wall of air. We were climbing incredibly steep pitches across a rolling landscape the entire day. Completely beat-up and worn out after six hours in the saddle, 4,200 feet of crazy ups and downs and battling gale force wind, we had to stop. It was only eighty-six miles from Atlantic City to Pinedale, Wyoming but we were too tired to reach the small town. Fortunately, a trail angel named Gary, pulled to the side of the dirt road to talk with us and at the end of the conversation, offered his land for camping. His ranch was only a mile up the road and had a stream running the length of the property, allowing us access to water. This was not the first time, nor would it be the last, that rough terrain and the wrath of Mother Nature would impact our total mileage for a given day.

Our maps provided distance information and general elevation changes for planning purposes. More than once, however, what we thought was going to be an easy day became more challenging because of a surprise washboard road. We all have vivid memories of the slow, painful forty miles we endured to reach the little township of Hartsel, Colorado. As Don so accurately stated, "That was the most hand numbing, butt bruising, spine crushing section of washboard road I've ever ridden." Unfortunately, when we left the little community the next morning, we discovered the road heading out of town was just as bumpy, requiring us to face the same discomfort for another forty miles. Rough roads were a frequent feature of the GDMBR.

There were only sixty miles of single-track on the entire GDMBR, but the experience on each trail section was intense and quite memorable. Our first exposure to single-track occurred at Thompson Park just south of Butte, Montana. All four of us had raced mountain bikes in our past and possessed strong bike handling abilities for riding over roots, rocks, and logs. Therefore, it was a bit of a shock to feel how differently a fully loaded fifty-pound mountain bike behaved on technical terrain. Shifting weight within the packs constantly changed the bike's center of gravity and demanded quick adjustments on the fly. The extra pounds required additional force to clear trail obstacles and climb steep pitches which added stress on my knees. The three heavy bags hanging off the handlebars affected steering making maneuverability around tight corners and switchbacks more difficult and sometimes impossible. I quickly concluded that riding a heavily loaded mountain bike on a single-track trail added a level of unnecessary risk, made for very slow traveling, and in general, lowered the fun factor. On a couple occasions, however, we did find bikepacking on single-track to be thrilling.

Wyoming, Montana, and Canada are considered grizzly country and sightings had been reported by all the southbound GDMBR cyclists we spoke to and on posts we read. Many roads were heavily forested and on those sections of travel we became more vigilant in our watch for a possible bear encounter. The feeling of vulnerability increased significantly when cycling on single-track through densely wooded terrain where visibility was limited to only a few feet in any direction making it impossible to detect an animal next to the trail.

The most exhilarating five miles of single-track occurred in Montana north of Seeley Lake. Late in the day with the sun low on the horizon, our GPS directed us off the gravel road we had been traveling onto a dark, deeply forested path. We had been trying to find an acceptable location to wild camp for the last several miles but the thick vegetation along the roadway had not been suitable for pitching a tent. Now we faced entering what looked like a dimly lit tunnel of green trees, shrubs, and high grasses—perfect bear country. We had no choice but to continue riding. We were losing daylight and needed to find a campsite quickly. Although the scenery was pretty, my attention was laser focused on detecting any movement or inappropriate color pattern within the surrounding landscape. The berry laden scat we saw periodically along the trail had my adrenaline pumping a little harder with each mile pedaled. I was leading the four of us and knew if a bear was on the pathway ahead, there would only be seconds to react. My voice became hoarse from the strain of singing and yelling so loudly. Finally, our tiny single-track trail that connected one side of the mountain to the other, ended at a major trailhead. I felt an immediate sense of relief when I realized that we had safely made it through the woods by making a lot of noise—a strategy we would use repeatedly. Don had always hoped to see a bear at some point on our trip. Much to his dismay, our vocal deterrent was a total success because bears remained out of sight throughout the entire adventure.

BE PREPARED—HOPE FOR THE BEST—GRIN AND BEAR IT

Before leaving Idaho, Don created a tool pouch filled with wrenches, bike parts, and products that would allow him to fix a wide assortment of mechanical issues. All four of us were riding Specialized mountain bikes, but each bike differed in age and model. A derailleur hanger is specific to each bike frame and would not be something a small-town bike shop would stock, so we carried a spare for each bike. Don also carried a derailleur cable that could be used on any of our bikes as well as spare bolts, screws, zip ties, and a length of duct tape wrapped around our pump because in an emergency, duct tape can fix almost anything. Having the skill and knowledge to repair a mechanical problem was never a concern. Don is a certified bike mechanic and has serviced our bikes for the last forty years. Mike was a sponsored, professional BMX bike racer as a young teenager and continued to race and maintain his bikes through adulthood. I felt confident these two could keep us rolling no matter what disaster we encountered. Perhaps it was luck or because the guys had the bikes running perfectly from the start, we never suffered a mechanical problem on the entire GDMBR ride.

I truly believe luck was with us when it came to avoiding rain. Frequently we could see storm clouds in the distance, often with a curtain of rain falling and yet, somehow, we stayed in a donut hole and remained dry. The rain pants and jacket that we carried were worn intermittently on two different days while in Colorado. We cycled for fifteen miles through a horrendous downpour to reach the Wyoming state line and the town of Rawlins. The rain was falling in sheets and blowing sideways with gusting winds that made hydroplaning a great concern. Kudos to the Fairfield Marriott for letting us roll our dripping bikes into our room when we arrived completely soaked. Although I am not sure any rain gear could have kept us dry in such a violent rainstorm, I was happy to never have to test the gear again on the trip.

Our luck ran out when we arrived in Pinedale, Wyoming. After cycling almost halfway through our journey, my biggest concern came to fruition. Heading out of town the morning of July 6th, we were attacked by a swarm of mosquitoes when we stopped for a bathroom break. Don and I carried a travel size bottle of mosquito spray and immediately doused ourselves. Mike and Jeanne preferred not to use anything containing Deet, so they carried a small bottle of herbal repellant. Although their product had worked for them in the past, these were no ordinary mosquitoes. Eucalyptus, citronella, and essential oils were not going to deter these insects from biting. Mike's back became a landing zone for the voracious mosquitoes. I rode next to him and swatted the bugs away several times only to have them repeatedly return. We could see the little, winged bloodsuckers hovering all around us even while moving. We were pedaling an average of twelve miles per hour or coasting as fast as twenty-five miles per hour on the downhills and could not escape them. Don and I had head nets buried in our packs with our sleeping bags ready to use while camping. I seriously considered wearing my head net over my helmet while cycling but worried my vision might be too restricted. There was no resting during snack breaks. We found ourselves being forced to eat while walking around because sitting or standing still was not an option. Constant slapping helped during bathroom breaks, however, a glimpse of Jeanne's red and white polka-dot butt confirmed that her battle with the bugs had been lost that day.

We continued to contend with a high concentration of mosquitoes throughout the rest of our journey. Jeanne and Mike reluctantly began to use insect repellant containing Deet. "Welcome to the dark side!" I humorously commented. "Using Deet is the only way to remain sane." Pinedale, Wyoming is considered a pivotal point on the GDMBR because the terrain heading north enters grizzly country. We had purchased canisters of bear spray before leaving town and made sure they were easily assessable in the cockpit area of our handlebars. I held my can of mosquito spray in the same high regard and always kept it close.

THE UPS AND DOWNS OF THE GDMBR: FLEECER RIDGE

Major mountain passes and steeply pitched rolling hills were a part of nearly every mile traveled on the GDMBR. Flat stretches of road rarely occurred along the flanks of the Continental Divide. Our days were filled with continuous ups and downs that totaled a remarkable 143,583 feet of elevation gain by the end of our adventure. The time we spent climbing the multitude of passes and foothills created many special moments, none however, more memorable than our experience on Fleecer Ridge.

Located between Wise River and Butte, Montana, Fleecer Ridge is an iconic part of the GDMBR. During conversations with Divide racers and riders, internet blogs we read, and videos we reviewed, the cyclist's experience on Fleecer Ridge was a popular topic of discussion. For south bounders, the route was a gentle ten-mile ascent to the top of the mountain with an extremely steep downhill to negotiate. For cyclists traveling north, like us, the approach included technically challenging terrain with a final climb that required both physical strength and emotional fortitude to conquer.

We left the tiny town of Wise River in late afternoon after enjoying a wonderful salad, sandwich, and ice cream cone at the local saloon. Joy, our server, offered some advice before saying goodbye, "Be careful on Fleecer Ridge. Twelve people had to be rescued this year. Don't underestimate the mountain!" The combination of high altitude and Fleecer's fame for being ridiculously steep provided the basis for Joy's warning. There was always a heightened concern for weather deterioration when traveling over passes. Storm clouds were on the horizon; however, they were flowing in a south-eastern direction and did not appear threatening. I wasn't feeling worried, just excitement when the four of us headed out of town. The renowned Fleecer Ridge was close by, and I was ready to go see the mountain for myself.

Our first eight miles of pedaling were uneventful; a few miles of scenic highway followed by a forested dirt road. When the roadway transitioned to a rocky jeep trail through the woods, the gradient noticeably changed to a more challenging 4 to 7 percent incline. The route quickly became a technical mountain bike trail with features that were difficult but still rideable. A couple miles later, we came around a corner and met a wall. The last mile to the top of Fleecer Ridge went uphill at a 40 percent grade. Pedaling was no longer an option.

The effort it took to push our loaded bikes up the slope was shocking. We began by thrusting our mountain bikes a foot or two forward with our arms, squeezing the brakes to keep the bike from rolling backward, taking two steps uphill and then stopping to gasp for air from the effort. Repeating this process allowed us to advance very slowly. Experienced cyclists had warned us that completing this uphill section could take three to four hours. I had not believed the stories, but during those first few hundred yards the reality of the challenge became clear. Everyone was struggling. Less than halfway up the hill, Mike burst out laughing. His laughter was infectious, making the rest of us chuckle as well. With sweat dripping down our faces and holding a tight grip on the brakes to prevent gravity from dragging us back down the hill, we all stood there giggling like kids, fully aware of the absurdity of the situation. We were in a battle against the mountain, gravity, and our own physical limitations. With renewed vigor, we attacked the uphill terrain again.

I was sweating profusely, and my arms had begun to shake when I heard Jeanne yell, "Hey Mike, I need help. Let's work together. I'll push on the seat from behind while you steer and push on the handlebars. Maybe with two of us, my bike will be easier to get uphill." Their renewed effort resulted in immediate progress on the challenging slope encouraging me and Don to follow suit. With both of us straining, we successfully pushed my bike steadily upward until the ground leveled out enough to lay it down. We then turned around to hike back down the hill to retrieve Don's bike. The view of the valley caused us to pause to appreciate how beautiful the surrounding mountains looked illuminated by the fading sunlight. With a great deal of caution, we started our way down the treacherous landscape, carefully stepping over loose rolling rocks to keep ourselves from falling on our way to the bike left behind. Repeating the process over and over again allowed us to advance up the mountain much more quickly than would have been possible with an individual effort.

The last hundred yards was an overgrown trail with an incline of only 9 percent allowing us to remount our bikes and ride them to the summit. The clouds and setting sun created a spectacular 360-degree view from the top—a stunning gift for all our effort. Conquering the mountain produced intense feelings of accomplishment and contentment. We had climbed Fleecer Ridge in an hour and a half, much faster than others had warned it would take us. Our goal had been achieved through sheer tenacity, determination, and teamwork. Perhaps laughter at a critical moment had helped as well. The four of us now had our own Fleecer Ridge story to tell; an achievement filled with triumphant memories.

A SIGN OF THE TIMES: THE COVID IMPACT

"Seriously? Lima has only one restaurant serving dinner and it's closed tonight?" I asked while shaking my head in disbelief. Don had just read aloud the notice taped on the door of the local steak house.

"Covid strikes again," Jeanne said in exasperation.

Business closures happened with alarming frequency. Nearly every town we visited along the divide had been affected by staffing shortages forcing food establishments to reduce the number of days or hours they were open each week. Numerous times our arrival in a town coincided with these scheduling constraints leaving us disappointed and hungry. Once again, we would be perusing the isles at a convenience store searching for something to eat for dinner.

A young girl was working the register at the gas station when we arrived. Knowing how much kids love pizza, Jeanne asked her, "Is there a pizza place nearby? Where do you guys get pizza?"

Surprising all of us, the girl replied, "Here. We have a pizza oven. I can heat up a frozen pizza if you want."

There wasn't any signage on the walls about pizza being available and the oven was out of sight buried under papers and a purse. If Jeanne hadn't asked the question, we would have missed out on a hot meal that night. Two southbound GDMBR riders arrived at the convenience store while our pies were cooking. The delicious aroma wafting through the building encouraged them to order pizza for dinner as well. The six of us ate our meal together sitting at a shaded picnic table in front of the gas pumps while sharing stories about cycling the Divide. It wasn't the evening we had envisioned but it turned out to be an enjoyable one after all.

"OH CANADA"

"Just one at a time. The rest of you stay back until it is your turn," shouted the Border Services Officer (BSO). The agent had leaned out of his window to inform us that approaching the customs office together was unacceptable.

We had reached the Canadian border, a major milestone on our trip, and had just taken a photo in front of the *CANADA UNITED STATES BOUNDARY* sign at the Roosville Border Crossing Station. The port of entry isn't really designed for travelers on bikes, which made us unsure of how we were supposed to proceed. It appeared each of us would be treated as if we were in an automobile. Don rolled his bike up to the window to be interviewed first.

"May I see your passport?" Asked the BSO. Don handed the officer his passport and then began answering questions.

"What is your purpose for traveling to Canada?"

"Vacation," Don answered.

"How long do you plan to stay in Canada?"

"A week."

"What is your destination, Mr. Jackson?"

"Banff"

"Where are you staying in Banff?"

At this point, answering the interview questions became more difficult. "I don't know where I will be staying."

"Do you have a reservation?"

"No, I am not able to make a reservation because I do not know how many days it will take me to cycle to Banff."

"Where are you staying tonight?"

"I plan to camp."

"Do you have a reservation at a campground?"

"No, we plan to cycle until we are tired and then wild camp."

"May I see your proof of vaccination?" Don handed the officer his vaccination card showing his original shots and boosters over the past two years. "Are you healthy, Mr. Jackson?"

"Yes, I am well."

"Do you have any ammunition, firearms, or fireworks with you?"

"No, I do not."

After pausing for a few seconds, the BSO rolled his eyes and handed Don his documents and said, "Pull forward and wait in the holding area until I have interviewed the rest of your group."

My interview closely resembled Don's. I was also asked if I was carrying more than ten thousand dollars. I almost laughed until I realized the officer was serious and quickly answered, "No." He then asked if I was carrying any fruits or vegetables and again, I answered, "No."

Mike's line of questioning was an abbreviated version of Don's. By the time Jeanne pulled up to the window, the officer looked at her documents, asked her two questions and ushered her through with a short, "Welcome to Canada."

The officer was clearly frustrated by our lack of itinerary which I found surprising. I expected the customs agents to have interviewed many northbound GDMBR riders and to be aware of the accommodation difficulties we faced on the route. When I returned home, I searched the internet and was unable to find the percentage of GDMBR riders who travel northbound versus southbound. We encountered only four other northbound cyclists throughout our journey and the southbound riders we met never mentioned any northbound riders traveling ahead of us. Although this is just a guess, I suspect over 90 percent of the GDMBR cyclists ride the route North to South, following the racers each year.

We saw our first racer, Sofiane Sehili, sixty miles north of Del Norte, Colorado. He flew by us heading south and would ultimately win the Tour Divide Race in a total of fourteen days, sixteen hours, and thirty-six minutes. When he passed us, Mike said, "Man, that guy is red!" Although we didn't know who he was at the time, we cheered and yelled encouragement only later realizing that Sofiane was the sunburned man moving so quickly past us. Sofiane would be the first of hundreds of GDMBR cyclists we would encounter throughout our journey. We were like salmon moving upstream in contrast to the dozens of combined racers and riders that passed us daily heading south, especially in Colorado. As we made our way north through the other states and into Canada, we saw fewer cyclists each day, but the trend continued until we arrived in Banff.

We were only sixty miles from completing our journey when we met our last southbound rider. The young man was in his early twenties and clearly impressed that the four of us had nearly completed the GDMBR. He asked,

"How was your trip? Was it great?" So many thoughts went through my mind regarding all that awaited this young man; the highs, lows, challenges, triumphs, trail angels, spectacular scenery, and wonderful places to visit.

There wasn't an easy answer that could describe the magnitude of our experiences during the last forty-seven days, so I simply said, "The trip was amazing and something you will remember for the rest of your life." The young rider was smiling as he pedaled away; clearly thrilled to be at the start of his journey while the four of us were as delighted to be at the end of ours.

Canada provided a fitting end to our grand adventure. The Canadian section of our trip was 256 miles in length and offered some of the most spectacular scenery found along the route. Several southbound riders had told us, "Wait until you see the mountains in Canada! They are incredible."

Wanting to know more, I pressed one man and asked, "How are they different from those in the United States?"

His answer, "The mountains are just bigger."

It wasn't until we were cycling along the western flank of the Elk Range, a sixteen-mile-long section of the Great Divide which serves as a border between the provinces of Alberta and British Columbia, that I finally understood. I wouldn't say the mountains were bigger, but they were certainly closer. This unique section of road is sandwiched between the spine of the Divide on the east and a cluster of enormous mountains within the Elk Lakes Provincial Park to the west. The mountains are not off in the distance; they are right next to both sides of the road. The granite cliff walls give an impression of being so close that you could reach out and touch them. These magnificent mountains made for a very impressive day of riding in British Columbia.

The Adventure Cycling Association established the GDMBR along the United States Continental Divide twenty-five years ago. The Canadian section was added recently in 2018. We never had any problems navigating the GDMBR with the American GPS data files and found them to be completely accurate. In Canada, we found ourselves led astray at least a half dozen times which added confusion and frustration to our days.

A majority of the Canadian GDMBR followed abandoned mining and logging roads to avoid the busy highways. Although these roads were safer for bikes, they were often in disrepair because the extractive industries were not currently active and contributing to their maintenance. Canada had suffered severe winter storms during the past year that felled trees, created major ruts, washouts and in two cases, eliminated sections of a dirt road. We were forced to climb up and down ravines and push our loaded bikes across steep mountainsides to stay on course.

Although Canada offered several sections of mountain biking trails, the best eleven miles of single-track was the High Rockies/Spray River Trail which also served as the final miles of our adventure. We spent most of our last afternoon pedaling on a remote, heavily forested path through the beautiful woodlands of Banff National Park.

Our journey ended at the Spray River West Trailhead which delivered us onto the paved parking lot of a castle, the magnificent Fairmont Banff Springs Hotel. We had spent the last four nights either camping or sleeping in a small-town motel so our arrival in a thriving metropolis with throngs of international tourists was a little disorienting. While cycling into the center of the city, Don made the comment, "I thought Breckenridge was crowded but this place is like Breckenridge on steroids!" Our original plan had been to stay in Banff for a few extra days to see Lake Louise and other prominent attractions near the resort town, but the deteriorating weather forecast, and the unexpected hordes of people made us quickly change our minds about vacationing in the area.

Banff is home to less than 8,000 people, however, four million people visit the city each year. This stunningly beautiful community could easily have eleven thousand extra bodies walking the streets on any given day. Our arrival on August 2nd was during the height of the tourist season making it a good bet that we had been surrounded by at least that many folks each day while we were there.

The four of us would spend two nights in Banff making arrangements to have our bikes sent home, packing our bike bags, mailing our gear, arranging a shuttle to Calgary, and confirming airline reservations for traveling back to Idaho. We spent our free time walking the city, enjoying meals at restaurants, sampling new drinks and pastries at coffeehouses, eating a few ice cream cones, and all the while continuing to search for a great donut shop. Re-entry into the real world would take far longer than just a couple days, but the time spent in Banff was a good start toward making the physical and emotional adjustments necessary to bring the journey to a close.

THE MAJESTIC CONTINENTAL DIVIDE

There are too many beautiful places along the route of the GDMBR to list them all, however, a few remarkable locations deserve to be highlighted. The transition from New Mexico's red rock desert to the tiny, forested community of Platoro, Colorado occurred within a ninety-mile section of cycling. The change in scenery was dramatic and made the mountains surrounding Indiana Pass, the highest point on the entire GDMBR at 11,900 feet elevation, seem even more magnificent.

Climbing up Togwatee Pass and seeing the Tetons come into view was a breathtaking sight. These grand snowcapped mountains stood like sentinels against a backdrop of crystal blue sky, as imposing as they were pleasing to the eye. We were close to our home in Idaho and halfway through our journey. The familiarity of the Tetons brought a feeling of calm while cycling the roads of northern Wyoming.

The Canadian Rockies will be remembered as the most stunning of all the impressive scenery viewed throughout the Divide. Our route passed by massive peaks that dominated the skyline along both sides of the road. These colossal hulks of granite were captivating; making me want to capture their beauty in a photograph. The wildness and grandeur of the area left a strong impression on me and a longing to return one day to explore the mountains more fully.

The majestic beauty of the Continental Divide is only one facet that encourages a person to ride the GDMBR. The desire to test oneself against the elements and experience the physical demands of long-distance cycling can be very enticing. For me and Don it was all those things and the excitement of the unknown. Not knowing what is over the next hill or around the next corner is thrilling and discovering new places is something we have always enjoyed together.

Sharing the adventure with friends added a new layer of fun to the trip. An abundance of laughter permeates all my memories. There was always one person that was quick with a joke or a quip to make light of any difficult situation we were exposed to on the journey. We started our trip filled with a sense of happiness and a desire to experience the GDMBR. We returned home feeling a great deal of satisfaction with the completion of our goal. We became stronger physically and mentally and cemented our bond of friendship throughout our journey. Our only disappointment was not being able to find a great donut shop despite testing as many samples as we could find along the GDMBR. The pandemic impacted the available selection by forcing the closure of so many bakeries. The suggestion I made to the group was to hold off on declaring a winner and to continue our search on another adventure. Everyone agreed it was an excellent plan.

GREAT DIVIDE MOUNTAIN BIKE ROUTE PHOTOS (1 OF 3)

1   Beginning of our journey. Abiquiu, NM.

2   One of the convenience stores that saved us on our first day cycling to Chama, NM. Courtesy of Mike Lynch.

3   Cycling up to Marshall Pass twenty-five miles south of Salida, CO. Courtesy of Mike Lynch.

4   Heading to Platoro, CO.

5   Departing Brush Mountain Lodge, CO.

6   The Tetons Mountains, WY.

GREAT DIVIDE MOUNTAIN BIKE ROUTE PHOTOS (2 OF 3)

7 Mushroom cloud moving across the desert. Courtesy of Mike Lynch.

8 Early morning rainbow in the Great Divide Basin, WY.

9 Don cycling on a forested road in Montana.

10 Shannon's tire displaying freckles of sealant each morning but no flats.

11 Roosville Border Crossing Station.

12 Canadian Rockies. Courtesy of Mike Lynch.

GREAT DIVIDE MOUNTAIN BIKE ROUTE PHOTOS (3 OF 3)

13   World's largest truck. Sparwood, British Columbia.

14   Mike, Shannon, and Jeanne negotiating a damaged section of Canadian Road.

15   Don entering dust cloud on the Smith-Dorrien / Spray Lakes Road in Canada.

16   Don cycling on the GDMBR near Banff.

17   Shannon, Don, Jeanne, and Mike. Spray River Trailhead. End of Journey—Banff, Canada.

EPILOGUE

IN 2023, DON AND I successfully completed the 571-mile New Mexico section of the Great Divide Mountain Bike Route (GDMBR) we missed the previous year because of forest fires. Once again, Jeanne and Mike joined us for the adventure and together we enjoyed ten days of riding on timbered roadways through the Gila and Santa Fe National Forests alternating with desert byways filled with blooming cactus and colorful rock. Although the diverse terrain provided some of the most challenging riding conditions of the entire GDMBR, the camaraderie of being together again and the views we experienced from our bike saddles made every pedal stroke worth the effort.

A highlight of our journey was finally eating pie in Pie Town, New Mexico. Pie town was three hundred miles from Antelope Wells, our starting point on the Mexican Border. The CDT and GDMBR trails intersected at the location and both hikers and cyclists consider Pie Town a "not to be missed" oasis in a desolate section of desert.

When Don and I hiked the Continental Divide Trail in 2002, our trek took us through the tiny community. Unfortunately, our arrival occurred on a day when the famous Pie-O-Neer restaurant was closed, leaving us very disappointed not being able to try their renowned pastries. We scheduled a stop at Pie Town as part of our itinerary during the previous year's ride on the GDMBR but had to abort the plan when the New Mexico wildfires and national forest closures caused us to reroute our trip.

During the first few miles of our journey, I said, "Third time's a charm, you know. This is the year we'll finally experience a pie in Pie Town."

Smiling, Don looked over at me and replied, "After twenty years and two attempts, I hope you're right."

We cycled into Pie Town at noon the following week and were delighted to discover two restaurants serving pie. After enjoying a slice of pie at the Pie-O-Neer with our lunch, we had dinner at the 'Ohana' Café where we enjoyed a second serving of pie and each of us were given a free piece to enjoy for breakfast the next morning. Three meals, three flavors of pie and all of them were delicious. Don and I agreed: Pie Town had been worth the wait!

A FORTY-YEAR LOVE STORY

Completing the GDMBR was a wonderful trip and a great addition to the many exciting adventures we have experienced throughout the years. In retrospect, the stories are important in that they provide some insight into our long and happy marriage; every journey reinforced our belief that we are *better and happier together*. The fact that Don and I share the same memories has strengthened and enriched our relationship. It only takes one of us to describe a moment in our past and immediately we travel back in time to a location that brought us joy, laughter, or satisfaction in overcoming a difficult situation with each other's support. We are often asked what the secret is to our marriage. I believe the answer is simple: develop common interests, set goals, and pursue your dreams together.

While I wanted this book to reflect our first forty years of marriage, Don was concerned there would be even greater adventures on the horizon and our story would be incomplete. Despite our ages of seventy-one and sixty-two, we have not stopped dreaming of new challenges and places to visit. As long as we remain healthy, our plan is to stay active and to explore the world together. Who knows, maybe there will be a Better and Happier Together—Part II.

EPILOGUE PHOTOS

1. Started at Antelope Wells, NM on the Mexican border.

2. Blooming cactus along the scenic desert roadway.

3. Cycling through the San Pedro Parks Wilderness in the Santa Fe National Forest.

4. Finally enjoyed pie in Pie Town.

5. Colorful rock of the El Malpais National Monument near Grants.

6. Great last day—Cuba to Abiquiu, NM. 78 miles with 7,300 feet of climbing and a 12-mile technical descent.

Yucca plant

1

2

3

4

5

6

ABOUT THE AUTHOR

Shannon Jackson is a retired registered dietitian and sports nutritionist. She lives in the mountains of Idaho and is an avid Nordic skier, mountain biker, and hiker. She and her husband, Don, recently celebrated their fortieth wedding anniversary. This is her first book.

BETTER *and happier* TOGETHER

Stories of Epic Adventures During Our
First Forty Years of Marriage

SHANNON A. JACKSON

LEAVE A REVIEW!

For a self-published author like myself, reviews mean the world! So, please, leave a review on the platform from which you purchased this book. I read every one!

www.ingramcontent.com/pod-product-compliance
Lightning Source LLC
Chambersburg PA
CBHW051506120626
46551CB00012B/804